The STORY

of

The WEST FLORIDA
REBELLION

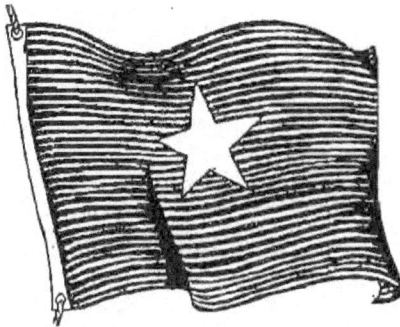

BY
STANLEY CLISBY ARTHUR

The following pages preserve in type form a series of articles published in the "Pictures of the Past" section of the Saint Francisville (La.) Democrat.

Originally published 1935

Reprinted 1975
by
Claitor's Publishing Division
PO BOX 261333
Baton Rouge, LA 70826

0-87511-148-3

TABLE OF CONTENTS

The Story of the West Florida Rebellion v

Introduction 2

Part One 25

Part Two 53

Part Three 99

Part Four 122

Part Five 149

Notes 175

Index 181

THE STORY OF
THE WEST FLORIDA REBELLION

By *Stanley Clisby Arthur*

That section of Louisiana east of the Mississippi river, south of the Mississippi state line, north of lakes Pontchartrain and Maurepas, extending to the Pearl River, which includes the parishes of West Feliciana, East Feliciana, East Baton Rouge, St. Helena, Livingston, Tangipahoa, Washington, and St. Tammany—a territory once called the "County of Feliciana," is known today by many as the "Florida Parishes."

It was the westernmost section of a land that was known for nearly half a century (1763-1810) as "West Florida" and over it flags of two European kingdoms flew, the Union Jack of England for 16 years, and the banner of Spain for 31 years. On the soil of this fruitful southern land was enacted one of the most spectacular events in Louisiana's colorful history. For the space of 74 days this part of the present state was a free and independent nation, with its own governing officials, its own army, its own navy, its own flag, its own declaration of independence. To secure this daring, if short-lived freedom, liberty-loving Anglo-Saxon inhabitants, many British to the backbone, literally fashioned their plowshares into swords and, at the point of these weapons, captured a fort by force and beat down the defenders, to throw off the shackles of a hated European despotism.

It is a pulse-stirring story—one that every Louisianian should know in its intimate detail for, although the event is mentioned in our standard histories, full justice has never been done either the tale or the men who wrote the tale in blood and courage.

This manly move for freedom, which resulted in annexation to the United States in 1810—seven years after the Louisiana Purchase—had its inception in the minds and courage of those living in that pleasant section of West Florida upon which Spanish masters had bestowed the pleasing name of Feliciana. Therefore, it seems only fit that these details should be chronicled in a newspaper published in the very territory where lived and died the men who were not only the instigators but the very brains of this liberty-winning event.

To this end, Mr. Elrie Robinson has volunteered to preserve by type in the "Pictures of the Past" section of the Saint Francisville Democrat the mass of documentary material I have gathered from here and from there during the past seven or eight years that I have been seeking "more light" on the story of the West Florida Rebellion, so that what has been unearthed from the files of the past may be made available to present and future historians.

Files of old newsprints have been searched; letters, in faded ink and crumbling paper, have been placed at my disposal by descendants of those who wrested this land from the haughty Dons; museums and libraries, private, state, and national, as well as other institutions, even the archives of Spain, have placed their treasures at my disposal so that the picture can be made complete in its every detail.

To understand and correctly picture this event of past years, it appears necessary that a backward glance be given the land and its people before detailing the taking of the fort at Baton Rouge, or the unfurling of the first "Lone Star Flag," the signing of the "Floridian Declaration of Independence," the forming of the Tom Thumb Republic, the selection of Saint Francisville as its capital, and then the inclusion of the tiny independent territory as a section of the young United States by making it a part of Louisiana.

So we will consider first—the place and its people, the flags of domination that waved over its hills, productive acres, and beautiful forests and streams, something of the names bestowed upon it by French, English, and Spanish masters.

THE FIRST FLAG

The ancient banner of Castile and Leon, the same red and white ensign Columbus flew on the Santa Maria, was the first bit of white man's bunting to flaunt its folds over Feliciana. The flag was quartered red and, white with two golden castles and a pair of rampant red lions.

vi

THE PROPOSED BRITISH SEAT OF GOVERNMENT IN WEST FLORIDA.

As proved by this map, England selected the Feliciana country for its twin town and fortification. The legend reads: "A Plan Shewing the Situation and Construction for a Seat of Government on the Mississippi." The insert plan reading: "This shews the construction on the side of each gate." This reproduction is from an original manuscript map, 17½x27½ inches, found in the collection of Lord George Germaine, minister of state under George III, and the man who influenced the policy of Britain in the American Revolution. The proposed seat was to be located on *Les Ecores au de Laid*, or "Milk White Cliffs," near the mouth of Thompson's Creek, known now as Port Hudson. (See details page 155.)

1

Athanase de Mézièrs erected his concession further north. In Cabildo records we find that on November 9, 1720 the ship *"La Loire"* had on it "186 persons for Ste. Reine under the direction of MM. Sicard and Tibain," but whether they were bound for the properties near New Orleans or the concession in the Tunicas is not proved.

Another map of Louisiana, drawn by N. Bellin, *Ingenieur de la Marine*, which carries the date of 1764, specifically locates "Concession de St. Reine" at the same place where Saint Francisville now stands. Below it we find he names "Thompson's Creek," which is evidently the first time this name so appears on a chart. The stream now called Bayou Sara, on the Bellin map, is properly located but the engineer names it *"Rivière des Tonicas"* and on the north side of this Bayou he locates the Tonica village.

The map of the province, drawn 32 years previously by Saint d'Anville, is not only one of the best but the earliest maps of the Mississippi river and the settlements along its banks. This Frenchman was a noted engineer and acknowledged one of the best sent to the colony. His full name was Jean Baptiste Bourguion d'Anville and he was born in Paris in 1687, where he died in 1782.

Unquestionably the French were the first Europeans to settle in the Feliciana country. One of the first pioneers, if not the very first, to erect a habitation in this "Happyland" was a certain Frenchman named Le Jeune. His plantation lay on "the eastern bank of the Bayou Sarah about 10 miles from where it emptied into the Mississippi." This would place his habitation quite near the dividing line of the present Ventress and John M. Parker properties, and today, on this spot, a grove of age-old live oak trees, "the Le Jeune Oaks," still defy the relentless and ruthless march of time.

M. le Jeune, in addition to his farming enterprise had a store or *"magazine"* as it was then termed, as well as a tavern at this ford or crossing of the bayou, for the main trail to Fort Rosalie at Natchez passed this way.

HOUMAS THE FIRST INDIANS

However, other documents examined point to an earlier occupancy of this territory. It was originally the land of the Houmas (Oumas) Indians. They occupied the land that extended from the high ground in the extreme southern part of what is now Wilkinson County, Mississippi, to the bluffs at Baton Rouge where, as is well known to all readers of Louisiana history, a red pole, called by the French *baton rouge* (red stick) marked the boundary line between the Houmas and the Bayou Goula tribes.

4

The Houmas had two landing places on the Mississippi river. This mighty stream in the early days made a wide sweep to the westward in front of the bluffs to meet the mouth of the Red River. The first village, and the principal one, was located above the bend and their smaller village below it.

In 1682, La Salle on his historic voyage down the Mississippi to its diverging mouths, when he claimed the entire wilderness drained by this stream for Louis of France, did not visit this tribe although the hardy Frenchman knew of the existence of the villages. Four years later, Tonti of the "Iron Hand" (on his ascent of the Mississippi following his failure to join forces with La Salle at the mouths of the river) did land at the Houmas village and from his journal we learn he considered them "the bravest savages on the river."

Therefore, to Henri Tonti goes the honor of being the first white man to set foot on the soil of Feliciana.

In March of 1699, Pierre Le Moyne, the Sieur d'Iberville, together with his brother Jean Baptiste, the Sieur de Bienville, and another Frenchman who deserves to have his name written large in the pages of Louisiana's history—Sauvol de Villantary, who became the first governor of Louisiana (Sauvol was not a Le Moyne, in spite of statements in our early histories that he was a brother to Iberville and Bienville—he was not even related to them!) visited the "Ouma" Indians, for so Iberville spelled the tribe's name in his journal, and the three white men learned much about the savages occupying the highlands of Feliciana. Sauvol in his able narrative, "The Journal of the Frigate *Le Marin*," has preserved for present day readers many interesting details of Iberville's visit to the chiefs and something about the habits of these original inhabitants of the Bayou Sara region.

A study of ancient maps indicate that the upper village was close to the present upper or northern boundry of West Feliciana parish, and that the second village, the one just above the "big bend," must have been on the bluffs on which Saint Francisville is now located. There is, of course, a possibility that it was further north, where Bayou Tunica empties into the Mississippi, but Saint d'Anville's splendid map of 1732 indicates that the high ground just above the "big bend" (which later became Pointe Coupée) is the site of Ste. Reyne.

Father Gravier, whose journal of his memorable journey down the Mississippi in 1700 is a valuable source book for those delving into Louisiana's early history, arrived at the village of the Houmas in late November of that year. He records: "I counted 70 cabins in the village, which I visited with Father de Limoges, who chose to give me the first fruits of his mission in the baptism that I administered to a

5

child three days old. I gave him the name of Saint Francis Xavier, the patron of the mission."

A strange coincidence, is it not, that the first child to be baptised in this territory by the white men's rites should have been given the same name now borne by the present seat of government of the parish?

The Houmas papoose thus christened by the good Jesuit did not live to bear the name of the patron saint for, as Father Gravier piously adds to his account, "God took him to paradise a few days afterwards, there to labor for the conversion of his parents and of his countrymen."

THE TUNICAS

Although the Houmas were the original inhabitants of Feliciana popular belief is that the Tunicas were the aboriginals found there. The Tunicas originally inhabited the country in the neighborhood of the mouth of the Yazoo river. They abandoned that location in 1706 (or 1709, there is a conflict of dates), migrated down river, and were hospitably received by the Houmas. Shortly thereafter the Tunicas fell upon their hosts and massacred most of them. The remnant of the tribe, those few who escaped the arrows, knives, and clubs of the perfidious Tunicas, fled to the south and a Houmas colony settled first on the banks of Bayou Saint Jean back of New Orleans and then moved up the river to what is now Ascension parish and settled along Bayou Lafourche.

It was this usurpation of the Houmas' territory by the stronger Tunicas that caused the name of the victorious but treacherous tribe to be fastened upon the Tunica Hills, the Tunica Bayou, and the tiny village that nestles in the hills that guide a pleasant little stream to its union with the mighty Mississippi. As Miss Louise Butler has so neatly put it: "Of the name of Houmas, not an echo remains in the parish, while that of the betraying Tunicas is perpetuated in hill and stream and town."

The Houmas belonged to what has been described as the Muskhogean tribes; their name meant in their tongue "red" and their totem or war emblem was the crawfish. The French found them a peaceable people and Iberville said that the main village was about three leagues from the landing place on the Mississippi. It was composed of from six to seven hundred persons, according to Sauvol, who claimed they were much more civilized and honest than their southern neighbors the Bayou Goulas. They put their dead on posts and when anyone fell ill two men of the community were chosen "to sing, so as to chase away the evil spirits" that caused the illness.

6

Iberville described a formal entertainment the head man gave in honor of the French adventures. It was held in the center of the square and music was furnished by "drums and chychycouchy, which are gourds in which there are dry seeds, and sticks for holding them; they make a little noise and serve to mark the time for the dancers." Could the "chychycouchy" been the forerunner to the celebrated "hoochy-couchy" of the first Chicago World's Fair?

The Houmas' dance was performed by "twenty young people of from 20 to 30 years old, and fifteen of the prettiest young girls magnificently adorned after their manner, entirely naked, having only their breech-cloths on, which they wore above a kind of belt a foot broad, made of feathers and skin or hair painted red, yellow, and white, the face and body daubed or painted with different colors, bearing feathers in their hands, which served them as fans to keep time." Not unlike Sally Rand's fan dance, eh? The young men participating in the dance, continues Iberville, were also naked, "having only a belt like the girls, which concealed them in part, they being well daubed with paint and their hair well provided with bunches of feathers. Many had pieces of copper in the form of flattened plates, two and three together fastened to their belts, and hanging as far down as the knee, which made a noise and assisted in marking time."

The young Houmas danced for three hours in a very active and spritely manner, Iberville goes on to say, and when night fell the white visitors supped with the chief and the meal consisted of a hominy made of Indian corn. After the feast, the Indians armed themselves with bows and arrows, war clubs, and other warlike instruments, and danced until midnight.

Iberville described the village being about 2½ leagues from the river towards the north, the woods being open, a mixture of all kinds of oaks; the entire country being of quite good black earth with no rocks; situated on a hill, in a double row of cabins, in a circle, there being about 140 cabins which housed about 350 men, in addition to many squaws and children. The cornfields were in the valleys, although some of the stalks grew on the sides of the hills. "They have not cultivated anything else," said Iberville, "except melons and have sowed tobacco."

The Houmas had a sacred fire, which was kept alive by an old man charged with the duty of never letting it become extinguished, in front of a temple situated at one side of the main square. The square was the main gathering place and in it the youngsters played their games. The young men of the tribe exercised themselves by "running after a flat stone, which they throw in the air from one end of the square to the other, and try and make it fall on two cylinders, which they roll wherever they think the stone will fall."

7

Father Gravier, the first Jesuit to descend the Mississippi, was impressed with the docility of the Houmas. "The women and girls are more modest than those of neighboring tribes," he related. "May God be pleased to convert them and make the road to their village impracticable for certain French libertines."

When the men sallied forth to hunt, the women wept over them, as though they were going to their death, and when they returned unscathed, they wept again—for joy. While the Houmas had a reputation for bravery and were feared as warriors, they were not cruel and did not put to death those of neighboring tribes they captured, but made slaves of them and treated them like their own children, and, still according to Father Gravier, there were few villages in France where there were more hens and cocks than in the Houmas' villages, "because they never kill any and will not even eat any of those that their dogs quite often kill. When one wishes to obtain chickens from them he must not say that he intends to kill or eat them."

The Houmas women were described as wearing fringed skirts, which covered them from the waist to below the knees, and when they went out of their cabins they threw over their shoulders a robe made either of muskrat skins or turkey feathers. They tattooed their faces with figures, plaited their hair, and blackened their teeth as aids to beauty and masculine allure.

After the coming of the white men the Houmas became lazy, diseased, and debased with the Frenchmen's "fire water." The Tunicas, who succeeded the Houmas in Feliciana, were in name and fact "the people," for that is what Tunica meant in the Indian tongue, and they continued as such until the white men ousted them from the pleasant hills of their "Happyland."

FIRST WHITE SETTLERS

The domination of the white men over this section of Louisiana is divided into five epochs:

French............................1717 to 1763.
British............................1763 to 1779.
Spanish............................1779 to 1810.
Independent......................1810 74 days, Sept. 10 to Dec. 7.
United States....................1810.

The first white settlements in the district included the concessions granted Diron d'Artaguette, who settled at Baton Rouge, the one given de Mézière, just above the Red Stick, and the settlement of Sainte Reyne. These and others inhabited by Frenchmen were taken over about 1717. The erection of a habitation by M. le Jeune on the Bayou Sara has already been recounted.

8

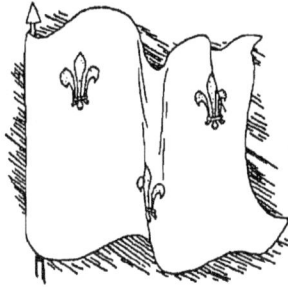

THE SECOND FLAG

The fleur-de-lis banner of Saint Louis which waved over Feliciana and Louisiana from 1682, when La Salle claimed most of the continent for his king, until 1763, when France ceded most of Louisiana to Spain, and Feliciana and West Florida to England. This banner of Bourbon France was white with three golden lilies and not blue with trois fleur-de-lis as sometimes shown.

On the authority of a number of maps, near to the spot where the Bayou Sara empties into the Mississippi a fort was erected and later abandoned, and its name was Fort Ste. Reyne. Whether it was close to the river's edge or on the heights where now sets Saint Francisville is not clear, although the natural presumption is that the elevated spot would have been selected for the practical purposes of a fortification. The date of the establishment of Fort Ste. Reyne, or "Queen's Fort," as it can be translated, or when it was abandoned and allowed to fall into decay, has not yet been ascertained.

It is known however, that Jean Joseph Delfau de Pontalba (grand-father of the Baron Pontalba who married the daughter of Don Andres Almonester) was at one time in command of the Ste. Reine fort. Delfau de Pontalba, at the age of 19, came to the colony in 1732 as an *enseigne en second* of the Louisiana troops. He was first sent to Fort Rosalie (Natchez) where he served under Captain de Bénac, before being trans-ferred to Ste. Reine. Etienne de Périer de Cenier, governor of Louisiana from 1726 to 1733, evidently erected the fort at Ste. Reine as a protective measure following the Fort Rosalie massacre when the French com-mandant, Sieur d'Etchéparre (his name has been erroneously spelled Chopart, Chépart, de Chepare, etc., in Louisiana histories), all of his soldiers, and most of the planters in the Natchez concession, about 300 all told, were put to death by the Choctaws. This Indian uprising oc-curing in December of 1729.

When Governor Périer was recalled to France and Bienville, after seven years absence in France, again ruled over Louisiana, one of his first moves was to place Lieutenant de Pontalba, June 1733, in command of the "fort at the Tonicas." Here he remained until the early part of 1736 when he, with his whole command, was ordered to join Bienville at New Orleans to participate in the governor's disastrous campaign against the Chickasaw Indians. In 1740 de Pontalba was placed in charge of Fort St. Joseph at Pointe Coupée and he served here, in the Illinois country, and at other posts in the colony with distinction, was raised in rank to captain and was made a chevalier of the Order of Saint Louis. He married Marguerite Madeleine Broutin, the widow of Francois Philippe de Marigny de Mandeville, in 1743. His only son was Joseph Xavier Delfau de Pontalba, in turn the father of Celestine de Pontalba who married Almonester's daughter and it was she who erected the celebrated Pontalba buildings that flank Jackson Square in New Orleans.

It appears most probable, while not proved, that "Fort Ste. Reine" after being established in the early part of 1730, was abandoned when Lieutenant de Pontalba marched his troops away from it in April of 1736.

THE BRITISH DOMINATION

In 1763, following the end of the seven-year struggle in America known as the French and Indian War, France lost Canada and her other North American colonial possessions. Canada and that part of Louisiana lying east of the Mississippi river were relinquished to the triumphant British and the Union Jack, bearing only the two crosses of Saint George and Saint Andrew, flew over the former French territory. The rest of her colonial property France ceded to her late ally Spain—this included the territory west of the Mississippi river as well as "the island of Orleans," and the red and white pavilion of Castile and Leon waved over the city Bienville founded and the wilderness that stretched out towards the setting sun. The golden lilies of Saint Louis disappeared forever.

In 1765, when England began plans for taking possession of her newly acquired property along the Mexican Gulf, Lieutenant Ross, a British engineer attached to the 34th Regiment, was instructed to chart the course of the Mississippi from its mouths to Fort Chartres in the Illinois country. This he did, basing many of his surveys on former French works, and on this first English chart we find names of many of the villages and streams emptying into the big river not only correctly positioned but their names correctly spelled. While St. d'Anville

10

in 1732 located *le Baton Rouge, Isle Iberville* (Profit's Island), *les Ecors blanc* (Port Hudson)' and *Ste. Reyne* on his map, when Lieutenant Ross came along 33 years later he designated the site as "Fort Ste. Reine, abandoned."

The location of the lower Pointe Coupèe village on the opposite shore, the indication of the Port Hudson bluffs; the course of Thompson's Creek and the Bayou Sara proves that Ste. Reine occupied the present site of Saint Francisville.

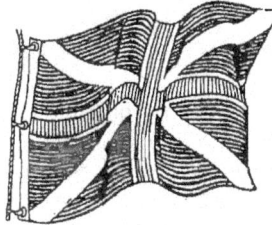

THE THIRD FLAG

For sixteen years, 1763 to 1779, the Union Jack of Great Britain waved over the two Floridas and Feliciana. At that time it displayed two crosses only—St. Andrew's cross, white on a blue field, and superimposed upon it the red cross of St. George. The cross of St. Patrick was not added to England's famed Jack until 1801. In this and the other reproductions of flags in black-and-white the colors of each are indicated, viz: horizontal lines, "blue;" vertical, "red;" dotted areas, "yellow;" blank, "white."

UNDER THE UNION JACK

For sixteen years the criss-crossed banner of England waved over the Feliciana country, taking the place of the white banner bearing the three golden *fleur de lis* of Bourbon, France. When good King George's government wrested New France (Canada) and Louisiana from Louis XIV covetous English eyes were turned on the possessions that Spain owned in America.

After witnessing five years of conflict between St. George and St. Denis, and observing that France was losing on sea and on land, Spain, in 1761, allied herself with France and pledged her resources and forces in the famous "Family Compact" to treat the enemies of France as her own. England promptly declared war against the kingdom of Castile and Leon and her far-flung possession in the New World. Havana was captured in the very beginning of 1762 and, panic-stricken over the possibility of further disasters, Spain sued for peace. France, completely

11

exhausted and having lost Quebec—the long-considered impregnable Gibraltar of America—also bent the knee and asked for the price of peace. The price was high for both France and Spain—but each paid what was asked after but little haggling. We know what France had to relinquish—everything she owned in North America.

What price did the Dons have to pay for attempting to thwart the purpose of Albion? England, to Spain's great dismay, demanded Florida because the ownership of the peninsular was necessary to insure the peace and prosperity of the English colonies of Georgia and the Carolinas. France, it is true, tried to spare Spain the humiliation of being stripped of this prized possession and even offered to surrender to the English all French Louisiana lying west of the Mississippi but the offer was refused—the British not only wanted Florida but other lands along the Gulf of Mexico.

In such a fashion, as Professor Chambers pointed out in his excellent (and the best) history of Louisiana, did Louisiana become a pawn in the great game of diplomacy-chess that the European masters of the world played in those far-off days. Beg as did both Spain and France, England refused to be moved by tears and stubbornly demanded Florida—and the land of flowers, in which Ponce de Leon sought the fountain of youth in vain, was ceded to the victorious British.

As it then devolved upon France to make some sort of reparation to her late ally for what she lost in making common cause with her against England, all of Louisiana lying west of the Mississippi river, and the island of Orleans on the east bank from the Iberville (Manchac or Ascantia) river to the mouths of the Mississippi were given Spain as balm to her hurts.

In such fashion came the British to Feliciana—it was not thus named, of course, for it was indeed an unnamed wilderness, a *terra incognita*, which even France at that time considered of insignificant value. It was in February of 1763 that the terms of peace were signed at Paris and before the ink was dry on the parchment England became the possessor of Canada, Nova Scotia, Cape Breton, and all land in North America, east of the Mississippi river, with the single exception of the island of Orleans. Spain was given back her island of Cuba as a concession for relinquishing Florida. In such a fashion was the banner of Bourbon France, the white banner sprinkled with three golden fleur-de-lis, furled in Louisiana in general and in the Feliciana country in particular.

In October of 1763, eight months after the treaty of peace and parceling of territory was signed in Paris, George Rex, the third of that name, and in the third year of his reign, issued a lengthy proclamation from his court of St. James, and in it for the first time the name of "West Florida" was penned.

12

Said his Britannic Majesty, after penning a number of whereases a firstly and a secondly, "The government of East Florida, bounded to the Westward by the Gulf of Mexico and the Apalachicola river; to the Northward, by a line drawn from that part of the said river where the Catahouchee and Flint Rivers meet, to the source of St. Mary's river, and by the course of the said river to the Atlantic Ocean, and to the East and South by the Atlantic Ocean, and the Gulf of Florida, including all islands within six leagues of the sea coast."

And so we had East Florida. But listen to the crow-quilling of his rotund, gouty majesty as he dipped afresh into the ink:

"Thirdly, The government of West Florida, bounded to the Southward by the Gulf of Mexico, including all islands within six leagues of the coast from the river Apalachicola to lake Pontchartrain; to the Westward by the said lake, the lake Maurepas, and the river Mississippi; to the Northward, by a line drawn due East from that part of the river Mississippi which lies in 31 degrees North latitude, to the river Apalachicola, or Catahouchee; and to the Eastward by the said river."

In such fashion was West Florida, on the seventh day of October, 1763, formed and baptised. Pensacola was made its capital, and the Gentleman's Magazine of London, soon after the royal proclamaton was issued, predicted: "The immense gain which this trade produces will probably soon make West Florida be numbered among our most flourishing colonies."

The first British governor of West Florida was a Scot, George Johnstone, who ruled from 1763 to 1766; he was followed by Governor John Elliott, who was a suicide; in 1770 Peter Chester took charge and was the eye and the instrument of the British crown until West Florida was wrested from England by force in 1779-1780.

Governor Johnstone when he took possession of the former French and Spanish territories changed many of the old-time names. Especially so was this true of the forts, the one at Pensacola was rebaptised Fort George, the fort at Natchez became Fort Panmure instead of Rosalie, and a new fort was set up at Manchac on the Mississippi and named Fort Bute. Baton Rouge was renamed "New Richmond," and a stockade was erected on Thompson's Creek.

Settlers were invited to this fertile land nestling along the course of the Mississippi river and Governor Johnstone was authorized to make free grants of land to retired British officers and soldiers who had participated in the war just ended against France and Spain. A field officer was entitled to 5,000 acres; a captain to 3,000 acres, while a private's portion was 300 acres. Thus Feliciana and Baton Rouge received many of their early inhabitants—men of quality, enterprise, and intelligence—and so was implanted a sturdy stock in this heretofore Latin-infested territory.

For years all went well. Then, on the eastern seaboard the colonists began rebelling against King George. A declaration of independence was signed, a long war was begun, and soon, as a result of this rebellion, many loyalists ("damned Tories" to those enlisting under George Washington's banners) decided to immigrate to a land where the Union Jack fluttered in every breeze without being tainted with the poison of the rebellious. And in such fashion came many others of the English tongue to the lands of West Florida in general and the Feliciana district in particular.

All went well, the settlers in this new Southern Utopia resisted every inducement proffered to make them become the "Fourteenth Colony," and every night the plantation owners, those who spoke English, of course, nightly petitioned the Almighty with their "God Save the King." And he certainly needed their prayers!

Into this new British possession came many settlers—all bearing sturdy Anglo-Saxon names. Many were, of course, British, some canny Scots, and others turbulent Irishers. They were mostly Loyalists fleeing the war-wracked provinces along the Atlantic seaboard. With these settlers came such names as Barrow, Baker, Brown, Campbell, Carson, Cox, Clark, Collins, Cooper, Devall, Ellis, Green, Herries, Hicky, Johnson, Jones, Kemper, Kennedy, Lilley, Norwood, McDermott, Mather, Mills, O'Fallon, O'Connor, Percy, Pollock, Randolph, Stirling, Thomas, Moore, and many were named Smith—which is not surprising.

They worshipped God through the kindly offices of the Church of England, raised huge cotton crops with the aid of negro slaves imported from Jamaica, and large families by their own unaided efforts.

SPANISH DOMINATION

For the sixteen years that England exercised sway over the East and West Floridas, Spain had waited a chance to get even, to regain what she had been forced to yield at the point of the bayonet, and to teach the perfidious Albions a lesson in Spanish hate.

The American colonists had struggled on alone against the master England until 1777 in the attempt to gain independence. In that year France espoused the cause of the Americans. Two years later, in 1779, Spain scenting a possibility of regaining the lost American possessions, stripped from her in 1763, and also winning back the coveted fortress of Gibraltar, allied herself with the struggling colonists.

Word was sent to the stripling acting governor of Louisiana at New Orleans, Don Bernardo de Galvez, to take up arms and drive the hated British from West Florida. How well young Galvez did this, how he re-

14

took not only West Florida but planted the banner of Castile and Leon along the Mississippi as far north as Natchez is history that here needs no repeating. Suffice it to say he overwhelmed Fort Bute at Manchac at the point of the bayonet, took "New Richmond" by cannonade, restored its original name of Baton Rouge, and later invested Pensacola.

From that time on the sun set at eventide across the wide twisting course of the Mississippi without its yellow rays shining on the criss-crossed banner of Old England and gave lie to Britain's proudest boast.

For the many true-hearted British who had taken up lands there were two courses open—they could move out bag and baggage and leave behind their productive acres, or they could remain with their British grants recognized—providing they renounce their allegiance to the British crown, swear fealty to his Catholic Majesty, Carlos of Spain, and embrace the tenets of his church. This latter proviso a bitter, bitter pill for the Church of England men to swallow. In spite of this nauseous dose, practically all the leading Britishers owning rich lands decided to stay and, in spite of their oaths, signatures, and protestations of fealty, there slumbered in each Britisher's heart a flickering hope for a return of England's sovereignty—as soon as His Britannic Majesty had thoroughly chastised George Washington and his ragged band of rebels on the Atlantic coast.

When the red and white banner of Castile and Leon was raised over this happy land there was, apparently, no settlement at either Bayou Sara or Saint Francisville, but the countryside, especially that along the Tunica Hills, was known as "Distrito de Bayou Sara" and a census taken by the Spanish in 1792 lists twelve names as inhabitants. This census, in all likelihood incomplete, did not refer to a village of the same name—as a matter of fact it is difficult to determine just what constituted the district of Bayou Sara which was, in turn, attached to the "Distrito de Natchez." Those named in the census were:

Guillermo Brown.	Juan Green.	Abram Horton.
Francisco Pausset.	Roberto Stark.	Juan Wall.
Reuben Dunman.	Andres Here.	Juan O'Connor.
Davis Ross.	Jaime Ryan.	Juan Welton.

Land office records show dates upon which a number of the earlier settlers made their purchases of land, and frequently footnotes to the records carry interesting information. For instance we learn that John H. Mills purchased from William Wikoff certain lands on January 12, 1789, and that Bayou Tunica was settled by Patrick McDermot in 1795. Other settlers and the dates of their acquisition of lands follows:

15

David Waugh, 1770.

J. B. O. Coin, 1786.

Claudio Bougard, 1787.

Felix Bernard, 1790.

Juan Barclay, 1792.

Juan Allen, 1795.

Franca Ashton Watts, 1796.

Patrick Holland, 1796.

Alexander McCoy, 1796.

Juan Raffray, 1797.

Nathan Lytle, 1797.

John Eldergill, 1798.

Matthew Hughes, 1798.

John O'Connor, 1802.

George Freeland, 1802.

James Foster, 1803.

John Higgins, 1804.

Cornelius Seeley, 1804.

James Clark, 1804.

James Kavenagh, 1806.

W. Aairs, 1806.

Henry Flower, 1806.

There were, naturally, many others whose names at this late day are not easily procurable but the foregoing indicates the class and nationality of those who took up lands here under the Spanish rule.

These English-speaking inhabitants led a care-free and prosperous life on their plantations and their hospitality was a tradition—listen to what one visitor wrote:

"These Feliciana planters live profusely—they also drink profusely costly port, madiera, sherry, after the English fashion, and are exceed-ingly hospitable. Your coffee in the morning before sunrise; little stews and sudorifices [something which causes sweats] at night, warm footbaths if you have a cold; boquets of fresh flowers and mint juleps sent to your room; a horse and saddle at your disposal—everything free and easy and cheerful and cordial."

There were places along the twisting roads where the traveler could purchase a "coonbox" to slack his thirst or to satisfy a certain yearning of the stomach, for, be it known, a "coonbox" proved to be Jamaica rum sold in an egg shell! Illegally sold at that! To a flip [a flip was a mixed drink usually sweetened, spiced, and heated generally by the immersion of a hot iron in the concoction] generally one loaded egg was used. "Coonboxes" were not costly—two rum laden eggs shells cost the wayfarer one bit, and the taverns and wayside houses did a thriving business in supplying the demand in those happy Hispanic days. The eggs were deftly blown of their albumen and yolk contents through one hole in the end, the contents as deftly replaced with the fiery product of sugar cane molasses, and then again deftly sealed to await the com-ing of a traveler who needed a little rum, tax free, for his stomach's sake.

Those *were* the happy days.

BAYOU SARAH VILLAGE FOUNDED

The present village of Bayou Sarah was founded in 1790 by John H. Mills. He settled first in the Natchez district, near Second Creek, where he formed a partnership with Isaac Johnson, an Englishman from

Liverpool, and the two erected a sawmill there. When the profitable mill was swept away by a spring freshet, Mills prevailed upon Johnson to move to the Bayou Sarah region. Johnson established himself upon a plantation near the Mississippi river, which he named "Troy," and there with his wife (she had been Mary Routh, a Virginia girl), reared a large family, and a grandson who bore his name became a governor of the state of Louisiana in 1846.

John Mills, after leaving the Natchez district, entered into a partnership with Christopher Strong Stewart, set up a trading post on the river batture to care for the growing Mississippi flatboat trade. In a short time the settlement at the mouth of Bayou Sarah became the most important flatboat stop between Natchez and New Orleans, and the village that sprang up about the Mills' trading post took its name from the nearby bayou.

In 1809 Christopher Stewart moved to Mobile where he died. Even when steam-propelled boats began their conquest of the Mississippi river, the little village founded by John Mills retained its importance in the river trade.

"The settlement at Bayou Sarah, or St. Francisville, only commenced about 1790 when John Mills established at this place," wrote Dr. William Marbury Carpenter in De Bow's Review (vol. iii, 1846), and his statement agrees with the records of the Johnson family which shows that Ann Waugh Johnson, eldest daughter of Isaac Johnson, married Gilbert Mills, a son of the founder of Bayou Sarah. A daughter, Mary Mills, became the second wife of Stephen Minor of Natchez.

Doctor Carpenter was one of Feliciana's distinguished sons but few today seem to be aware of that fact. William Marbury Carpenter, son of James Carpenter, was born on his father's Feliciana plantation June 25, 1811, and before he died in 1848 had attained prominence as a botanist, physician, and general scientist. As a lad he became interested in natural history and at the time his three sisters, Mary, Anne, and Louise, were pupils of Mrs. Audubon when she taught at the William Garret Johnson plantation, the boy collected specimens for John James Audubon, then in London publishing his monumental "The Birds of America."

In his mature years botany and the study of the Indians of Louisiana became Doctor Carpenter's hobby and medicine his life work. He was a careful student of folk lore and one of his works was a translation of Martin Duralde's account of Chitimacha Indian mythology, one of the earliest works of its kind, now in the collection of the United States Museum of American Ethnology.

17

Doctor Carpenter's grandfather was Richard Carpenter, who settled in Louisiana in 1771. Richard Carpenter's brother Caleb, who had first settled at Pensacola, wrote a journal of a trip he made up the Mississippi in 1776 and it proves to be a very interesting and valuable historical document as it describes the many settlements and plantations between New Orleans and Natchez but strange to relate, he said nothing about a settlement at Bayou Sarah, not even mentioning that Ste. Reine had been established there.

THE SAINT FRANCIS VILLAGE

The original naming of Saint Francisville, too, seems shrouded in mystery. A settlement on the very backbone of a mile-long ridge overlooking the tawny Mississippi river appears to have been a logical place for a village more so than the batture which John Mills selected as a site for his town, and in all probability houses were erected there when the Bayou Sarah town was begun.

The name of this ridge, when the French were in possession, unquestionably was "Sainte Reine," as proved by the several French maps already mentioned. But between the days of the coming of the first Frenchmen and 1790 when John Mills established there, the ridge appears to have been only a burial place for the dead, mostly those ferried across the wide river from the Pointe Coupée side. About the time New Orleans was founded, the French built a fort on the low lands on the opposite side of the river and named it Fort Saint Joseph. It was quadrangular in shape with four bastions, storehouses were erected. as well as a prison, so documents tell us, and the place was guarded by a considerable garrison.

In 1736, when Father Raphael, a Capuchin from Luxenburg and superior of the Capuchin missions in Louisiana, visited the Pointe Coupée fort he was horrified to find the place without a church and expressed fear for the souls of the members of the garrison. It was not until 1738, however, that Father Anselm de Langres was authorized to build a chapel at Pointe Coupée under the patronage of the patron saint of the Caupchins—Saint Francis of Assissi.

Thereafter, when deaths occurred on the lowlands, the bodies were boated across the river to the highlands on the east and interred in consecrated ground. And, so tradition further has it, the name of Saint Francis was likewise ferried across the muddy waters and the name of the patron given the village that later arose there.

When the British took possession of this land in 1765 it would seem probable that there was a settlement of some kind on this ridge that marked the extreme western boundary of the new British territory, but the maps of that period do not designate one.

About 1785, after Spain's banner succeeded the British ensign, Spanish Capuchins supplanted their French brethern of the cowl and crucifix, a grant of land was acquired from the Spanish king and a church and rectory erected, only to be destroyed by fire shortly thereafter. The grant fixes the church property on the lands now occupied by the cemetery of the Catholic church and also included the ground where the present Episcopal church now stands. One of the first priests stationed there was the Reverend Michael O'Reilly, educated for the priesthood in Spain, who came to Louisiana to administer religion to the English-speaking inhabitants in 1787.

When a village grew up around the church the name Saint Francis became attached to it. The Britishers, Scots, Irish, and Americans who had set up nearby plantations usually referred to the settlement as the "Village of Saint Francis," but, according to documents handed down in the Routh and Johnson families, when John Mills founded Bayou Sarah and Saint Francisville the latter "was named for an old Catholic priest, Father Francis, a wandering missionary, who baptised and married the people with impunity."

This Father Francis was, undoubtedly, Francois Lennan, not a Capuchin but a secular priest attached to the diocese of Bishop Penalvert y Cardenas, and who had been stationed at a number of places along the river, including Natchez and Pointe Coupée, as noted by Mr. Roger Baudin, who is presently writing a comprehensive history of the Catholic Church in Louisiana, which promises to be a notable and sadly needed work. Father Francis, or "Don Francisco," as he was termed by the Spanish, was located at Saint Francisville in 1810 when the Spanish were expelled by the Feliciana patriots when they rebelled, captured the fort at Baton Rouge, and established their own spectacular although short-lived republic.

In the testimony given by Spanish soldiers relating to the taking of the fort at Baton Rouge, one of the soldiers stationed at Bayou Sara spoke of the place as *"El pueblo de San Francisco."*

Letters written by English-speaking planters in the early part of 1800 show that many of these landowners mention the settlement on the ridge as "the village of Saint Francis"—the "ville" being, evidently, a later Anglo-American addition. An abomination not confined to this place—as witness the many "villes" and "burgs" throughout Louisiana and other sections of our country.

Whether named in honor of the Indian papoose Father Galvez baptised with the name of Saint Francis Xavier, for the patron saint of the Franciscan order, Saint Francis of Assissi, or for the wandering *cura* Francisco Lennan—Saint Francisville is Saint Francisville. And that's that.

Saint Francisville was never called *Neuvo Valencia* by the Spanish, as has sometimes been stated. This naming refers to an entirely different village, one that was projected early in 1800 as a possible rival settlement to Bayou Sara.

Nor was the place named for Valencia, the Spanish seaport on the Mediterranean, but was christened by a patriotic Irishman for his birthplace in County Kerry—the tiny island of Valentia on the west coast of the Emerald Isle, the same port that today is the westernmost harbor of the British Isles where transatlantic cables are brought to shore.

New Valentia (which became Latinized and written frequently "Valencia") was intended as a rival of Mills' Bayou Sarah, and high hopes were expressed by its originators that it would become the most important settlement in Feliciana. It was to be situated on the Bayou Sarah, just a little above the town laid out by John Mills, and its sponsor was the notorious Senator John Smith of Ohio, the same Baptist clergyman who came to grips with the formidable Kemper brothers, as detailed in my "The Story of the Kemper Brothers," published in the St. Francisville Democrat July 8, 15, 22, 29, 1933.

Senator Smith purchased the land from Armand Duplantier in 1804 and evidently planned the new town then but his troubles with the Kempers, particularly Reuben Kemper, put a temporary stop to his ambitious plan. In 1807 the land was deeded to one Ambrose D. Smith (his relationship, if any, to Senator Smith is not clear at this writing) who launched what was in those days a strenuous advertising campaign to induce investors to purchase town lots.

Why the establishment of this new port on the Mississippi was not a success, and whether or not wharves, piers, and warehouses were ever started or completed is not known, but Ambrose Smith's advertisement in the Louisiana Courier (New Orleans) of Friday, March 25, 1808, is in existence, and as it tells its own story it is worth reprinting here.

THE TOWN OF NEW VALENCIA

The tract of land at the mouth of Bayou Sarah having been legally transferred to the undersigned Ambrose D. Smith, he hereby offers at private sale, after the thirty-first of March next, a number of lots which form the town of New Valencia; the lots containing sixty feet in front, and from 120 to 150 feet in depth, and of other sizes, of French measure; a formal sale of each lot will be made to the respective purchasers, and the title guaranteed; the lots to remain mortgaged for the security of the payment. The proprietor reserves to himself the exclusive right

20

to erect wharves or piers for the preservation of the banks and general utility and to erect warehouses thereon, whether on the shore of the river or bayou; as also the rights to all the lands on the two bayous not laid out in Lots or Streets, and every benefit resulting therefrom, either by a ferry or otherwise.

As a number of reports have been circulated, tending to prejudice the interests of the proprietor, respecting the validity of his title, the following documents may serve to elucidate that point:

Don Charles de Grand Pré, Colonel of the Royal Armies, Governor Civil and Military of the Place and Jurisdiction of Baton Rouge in West Florida, etc. . . . .

I do hereby certify that in consequence of the final settlement of accounts between Mr. John Smith and Reuben Kemper, the said John Smith is the sole and only legitimate proprietor of the land which they formerly bought from Mr. Armand Duplantier, as appears by the records kept in the archives of this jurisdiction, and besides of one hundred and twenty acres which the said John Smith bought afterwards of the said Duplantier, the whole consisting of 750 acres, according to the figurative plan of the Surveyor General, and the original grant of the government. In testimony whereof I have delivered the present certificates under my hand and seal at the request of those concerned, in Baton Rouge, this 29th day of August, in the year of our Lord one thousand eight hundred and seven.

CHARLES DE GRAND PRE.

I certify that the present has been well and truly translated, to the best of my knowledge, *date ut supra.*

PEDRO LUIS MOREL, *Interpreter per interim.*

The naturally advantageous position of New Valenica, which by uniting all the public roads through a large extent of the richest highlands on the river, and the excellence of the landing are such, as must forever render it the depot of all the produce of the finest country on the Mississippi, as well as the center of business; a further description of it is deemed unnecessary.

A Plan of the Lots may be seen at the Coffee-House in New Orleans, Mr. Byrnes Hotel at Natchez, and with Mr. John Murdock, the attorney of the proprietor, who will make known the terms of sale on application. Baton Rouge, 26th February, 1808.

AMBROSE D. SMITH.

21

"FELICIANA"

For a long, long time, in this search for information regarding the early days of the West Florida section of Louisiana, much time and energy has been given over to what appeared to be a fruitless endeavor to discover the genesis of the name "Feliciana" and why it was bestowed upon this land.

Truly Spanish, and meaning in that graceful and poetic language "happyland," the name does not appear on either the early French or English maps nor is it so mentioned in any of the early documents concerning the historic periods of occupation by Frenchmen or the English.

"Feliciana!"—was ever a beautiful region more appropriately named? But who named it so? And why? And when?

The name apparently first appears on maps designating the course of Thompson's Creek, a stream for which I have not as yet been successful in finding an Indian or French designation. During the British occupation a man named Thompson was given the privilege of operating a ferry from the lower Pointe Coupée village on the west side to the eastern bank of the Mississippi. His landing on the east side of the river was just inside this creek where was situated "Port Jackson" where Cochrane & Rhea conducted a store. It would seem that the creek was given the ferryman's name.

After Galvez and his Spanish soldiers took possession of West Florida, the creek's name was changed to *"Rio Feliciana,"* for it is so designated on a number of Pintado's survey maps, and as it ran through the very heart of the district the Dons had designated Feliciana, the naming of the stream was not inappropriate.

A beautiful land named for a beautiful woman.

Who was she?

None other than a fair daughter of Louisiana. A very beautiful Creole whose charms of body, face, and mind so captivated two manly hearts that they married her. A charming beauty who became not only a governor's wife, but in turn a Comtesse, and then Vice-reine of Mexico.

Let me then introduce Mlle. Félicité de Saint Maxent, wife of Don Bernardo de Galvez, governor of Spanish Louisiana who wrested West Florida from the British.

As she was godmother of Feliciana we should know more of her. She was the daughter of Gilbert Antoine de Saint Maxent and Elisabeth Maroché, both of distinguished French families. The Saint Maxents had six children—(1) Gilbert Antoine de Saint Maxent, Jr., the first to enter the fort at Manchac when Galvez took it from the British at the point of the bayonet, who married a daughter of the house of Forstall; (2) Francois Maxmillian de Saint Maxent, who later became a Spanish governor of West Florida; (3) Josephine de Saint Maxent, who became the wife of Governor Louis de Unzaga y Amezaga; (4) Félicité de Saint Maxent, the godmother of Feliciana; (5) Pupon de Saint Maxent, a girl who married into the d'Estréhan family; (6) Celestino de Saint Maxent, who became a captain in the Third Louisiana Regiment, and was one cf the Spanish defenders of the fort at Baton Rouge in 1810.

Félicité de Saint Maxent was first married to Jean Baptisté Honoré d'Estréhan, member of a prominent Louisiana French family. After her husband's death, which occurred October 20, 1773, shortly after he led the accomplished Creole girl to the altar, Félicité was wooed by Colonel Bernardo de Galvez, at that time commander of the Louisiana Regiment, and second in rank only to Governor Unzaga.

Galvez, only 21 at the time of his arrival in Louisiana, came from a distinguished Spanish family. He was a son of Don Mathias de Galvez, the Viceroy of Mexico, a nephew of Don José de Galvez, the president of the Council of the Indes, and, as the ranking officer of this council, Don José was, next to the king, the most powerful official in Spain.

In marrying Félicité, Bernardo de Galvez merely followed the example of Governor Unzaga who had chosen from among the many fair Creole damsels of New Orleans for his wife, Josephine, another daughter of the Sieur de Saint Maxent. In 1776, after he had ruled Louisiana for six years, Governor Unzaga was promoted to the rank of brigadier general and sent to rule at Caracas in Venezuela, and his brother-in-law and brother in arms was made acting governor. In such fashion did Félicité take her sister's place in the governor's mansion.

With the triumph of Spanish arms over British valor, and the land that George the Third had named West Florida occupied by the Dons, the territory was called officially *"Florida Occidental Jurisdiccion de Baton Rouge."* This regained territory was further divided into districts, viz: *Distrito de Baton Rouge, Distrito de Sainte Helena, Distrito de Chifoncté,* and *Distrito de la Feliciana,* and the sturdy Anglo-Saxon plantation owners in the district named for Senora de Galvez began their 30-year term as faithful vassals of His Catholic Majesty Carlos the Fourth of Spain.

And so was named Félicité's land—Feliciana. In 1785 she followed her husband to Havana, where he was raised to the peerage with the title of Count and appointed Captain General of Cuba, the Province of Louisiana and the two Floridas. Upon the death of his father, Count de Galvez succeeded him as Viceroy of Mexico and Félicité became Vice-reine. She was, so one writer claimed, "of surprising loveliness, as charitable, gracious and intelligent as she was beautiful. She was literally adored by the Spaniards and Mexicans, and she greatly contributed to her husband's popularity."

Galvez died in Mexico in 1794 at the age of 38 years. His only child, Guadalupe, like her mother, gave her name to a portion of that land—a section of Northern Mexico that carries the child's name today.

Feliciana was well named—it is indeed a beautiful happyland.

All of the foregoing, long as it has turned out to be, is at that only a sketchy history of the region that became the scene of the most romantic and adventurous series of events that led up to the determined action on the part of Feliciana planters to throw off the yoke of Spain and strike a telling blow of freedom and independence.

Not only did these Feliciana planters burst asunder the chains that bound them to an Old World power, but they declared this land free and independent, and established a lusty Tom Thumb Republic that lived for seventy-four hectic days—a short life but a merry one.

Now that the stage has been set, let us look to the actors and the parts they played in the stirring drama that ensued.

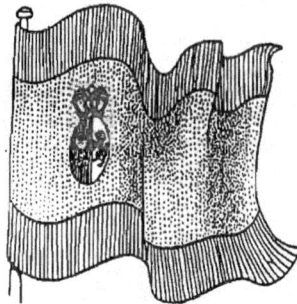

THE FOURTH FLAG

Soon after wresting West Florida from England, Spain's national emblem was changed from the banner of Castile and Leon to the "Bars of Aragon," adopted in 1787. It had three horizontal stripes—the top and bottom ones red, each a quarter of the whole breadth, while the middle stripe of yellow, constituting one-half of the banner, carried the royal arms.

24

PART ONE

The Purchase

It is still a prevalent impression that when President Thomas Jefferson consummated his famous "Louisiana Purchase", when he paid Napoleon and France $15,000,000 for a great pie-shaped slice of land out of the very heart of the North American continent, at the rate of four cents an acre, that *all* the territory which today comprises the present State of Louisiana was included in the domain that passed to the United States on December 20, 1803, the day William C. C. Claiborne raised the stars and stripes in the ancient *Place d'Armes* in New Orleans. Such was not the case; the Spanish flag continued to fly over West Florida, Baton Rouge, Ste. Helena, Feliciana, and Spanish governors and their soldiers and alcaldes continued to rule.

With the exception of "the island of Orleans," all the territory south of the 31o line and east of the Mississippi river remained a province of Spain. For seven long years after the banner of fifteen stars and fifteen stripes was unfurled over Louisiana, this strip along the Gulf of Mexico was doggedly held by the Dons who maintained that the "Purchase" had not included this area. This brought on an argument, for the United States claimed that this particular piece of property was included in the sale by France. In this, as in many other like cases, possession proved nine points in a ten-point debate. In consequence Governor Claiborne's jurisdiction on the east bank of the Mississippi extended north only to the junction of the big river with the stream called the Iberville, at Manchac, to the great and outspoken disgust and disappointment of many in this Spanish-ruled territory, for they had expected to become citizens of the United States coincident with the Purchase.

The majority of those populating this western section of West Florida, as has already been pointed out, were of the English-speaking races. But all were not British; many and many a settler came from that independent, pioneer, and turbulent western section, Kentucky. "Kaintucks" they were called. There were many from Georgia. "Crackers" these latter were designated; still others came from the Carolinas, and, while a considerable number were Loyalists, still there were those there who were proud of the fact that they had been patriots and not "damned Tories" during the war of the Revolution.

25

Practically all of these English-speaking planters and settlers in Spanish West Florida openly resented the fact that this land had not been included in the Purchase, and it was with impatience that they watched the seven-year period of bickering between the diplomats who argued the case, with the shirt-sleeved Yankee diplomats getting the worst of the duel of words with the more experienced and limber-tongued representatives of Castile and Leon.

The Twin-starred Kemper Brothers' Flag.

That section of West Florida which had for its seat of government the fort at Baton Rouge was ruled by Colonel Don Carlos de Grand-Pré, Frenchman by birth, who had won fame and promotion for himself when he commanded French troops in the colony during the time the Bourbon flag waved over Louisiana. When the province was ceded to Spain in 1763, like many another French officer, Colonel de Grande-Pré offered his sword to Spain. When he was placed in charge of the Baton Rouge sector his troubles began, especially during the Kemper rebellion in 1804 when Reuben, Nathan and Sam Kemper, exasperated by the fact that the United States had not taken West Florida as part of the land it had purchased from Napoleon, courageously raised their own flag of seven white and blue stripes and twin stars on a red union and started their own move for freedom which, (as related in "The Story of the Kemper Brothers" q. v. "Saint Francisville Democrat", July 8, 15, 22, 29, 1933) came to an untimely end.

However, dissatisfaction among the inhabitants continued and the feeling of unrest under the continuing rule of Spanish officials grew and threatened to burst all bonds. What else could be expected when the nationality of these "Spanish" citizens is considered?

No better picture of these people has been given than that by Henry Skipwith of Clinton who, in his pen portraits of these pioneers in his little known and exceedingly scarce "East Feliciana, Past and Present," wrote in 1889:

"Vast schemes of colonization were generated in the older settlements when Mr. Jefferson made proclamation, in October, 1803, that a boundless fertile unpopulated empire had been transferred the previous April by France to the United States. That famous state paper found eager readers among our immediate ancestors.

"Still hunting our genealogical source which is common with the population of each of the eight wards without groping in the dark, we can inquire a step farther back for the origin of the sturdy mountaineers who colonized East Feliciana. We can go back to a settlement on the shores of Albemarle Sound by the Cavaliers, fleeing from the cruelties and oppression of Cromwell, back to the settlement along the South Carolina sea coast by the persecuted Huguenots who, after the siege of Rochelle, sought an asylum in the new world for the freedom of conscience denied them by Cardinal Richelieu and the Pope of Rome.

"When the sea coast hives of the Cavaliers of North Carolina and the Huguenots in South Carolina became overpopulated, they spread out in search of homes, the two lines of homeseekers crossed and commingled among the mountain ranges of the Carolinas. From the comminglings of these two lines sprang the great Marion, Sumter, Laurens and Pickens, and many of the great southern chiefs of the Revolutionary War; and from the commingling of these two historical lines, we claim lineal descent.

"If here amid the cane-breaks and vine clad forests of these southern wilds, we have constructed a civilization characterized by all the virtues of both lines of our haughty aristocratic forefathers, we arrogate to ourselves with pardonable pride some little credit.

"If under the enervating influence of southern heats, our progress and development has been slow, when contrasted with the more populous, faster moving northern societies still we claim to be the better, happier, purer civilization, because we have maintained uncontaminated and undefiled the moral and social characteristics of our patriotic high strung ancestors, and because no new fangled 'ism', foreign or native, has ever taken root in our societies which we have always jealously guarded against the poisonous preachings of visionary enthusiasts who come from abroad to teach them to be freer, who know and feel that they are already free as they ought to be—as free as they want to be.

"By these cautionary acts of vigilance we have maintained our civilization, socially and politically free from the turbulent teachings of Irish saloonists and free from the socialistic heresies of the beer guzzling Germans. Happy would it be for our own country if the older and more trumpeted colonies of Jamestown, Plymouth Rock, and Manhattan Island had preserved the civilization entrusted to them by ancestors as jealously as we have guarded ours.

"A population clinging to the sides of the mountain ranges of the Carolinas and Southwestern Virginia, cultivating the narrow valleys of the Clinch and Holston, rugged as the crags; impetuous as the torrents of their native mountains, still full of the military spirit inspired by the camp fires and on the battlefields of the Revolutionary War, still rehearsing by the light of their pine torches, the shame of Camden and Guilford Courthouse and the glory of Saratoga, King's Mountain and Yorktown, still burning with patriotic fires which lighted Sumter, Pickens, Laurens and all the heroic chiefs of cavalier and Huguenot strain the path of glory, and many a Tory minion of King George the way to dusky death.

"On such a population, restless and ill at ease, environed by the dull monotonies of peace, paying willing homage to the authority of the law, relying more on their own valor and trusty rifles for the protection rarely extended by the laws in those early days to segregated and remote communities. On such a population, the stirring announcement that a boundless and fertile empire, larger than the thirteen original states, for which they had risked their lives and freely shed their blood, lay to the south of them waiting to be peopled; and the promise of homes in the genial southland dazzled their imaginations, as did the spoils of England, the restless imaginations of the feudal chieftains who rallied to the standard of William Duke of Normandy.

"Tradition, corroborated by vestiges of a decayed Fort, Mission House, Cemetery and Store House, tell of a small center of population settled between Murdock's Ford on Thompson's Creek, and the great river and along the public thoroughfare leading from Baton Rouge, the metropolis of the political and ecclesiastical power of Spain, in West Florida to St. Francisville, and the Church of St. Francis. An old blotter or day book, of Cochran & Rhea, an adventurous firm doing business in September, 1802, in the old store house now decayed, informs us from day to day until the close of 1803, who were the clients of that earliest commercial venture within the borders of our parish, and likewise discloses the names of many of the old pioneers who first awakened the primeval forests of East Feliciana with the echoing thuds of the woodsman's axe.

[This list of names of the clients of the Cochran & Rhea store was published in the St. Francisville Democrat, May 20, 1933, under the caption "Early Feliciana Residents." S. C. A.]

"Inasmuch as the junior partner of the old store on Thompson's Creek, by his marriage with one of old Dr. Raoul's (a French Emigré) lovely daughters, founded a

28

family which has played a prominent part in the material and social development of Ward One, and has moreover fastened his name and deeds conspicuously on the pages of history, I will devote a short paragraph, to keep green the memory of old John Rhea, who in 1802 was merchant, planter and alcalde for Feliciana (an officer about the equivalent of parish judge in our system). The King of Spain's jurisdiction, as it was administered by his mild and benevolent old Anglo-Saxon alcalde, was doubtless equitable and paternal, and the people of that day lived contentedly under it. When, however, a few years later, the country began to fill up with the fiery Huguenot and Cavalier immigrants from the Carolinas, and loud protests against monarchial government began to stir the hearts of the Anglo-American communities, I am afraid the King of Spain's old Anglo-Saxon alcalde, blinded by that love of liberty characteristic of his race, forgot his royal master at Madrid, and in 1810 the alcalde figures prominently as member and president of the convention which founded and governed the free and sovereign State of West Florida."

These were the folk who were restive under the Spanish yoke. The clever Dons, suave, polished, and courteous, maintained that West Florida was theirs, because France could not sell that which did not belong to her. And so the situation dragged along for seven long years.

When Madison, he who had suggested the Louisiana Purchase, followed Thomas Jefferson into the presidential chair the Kingdom of Spain, then under the domination of the acknowledged "master of the world," was compelled to accept the Little Corporal's brother, Joseph Bonaparte, as their king, for Carlos IV had abdicated and fled from Madrid to Rome and his son, Ferdinand VII, had thrown himself on Napoleon's mercy—and Napoleon had thrown the young King of Spain in jail!

West Florida, then nominally under the Spanish domination, was pro-United States at heart; at least nine-tenths of the population wanted to join the newly formed collection of states. But neither West Florida, nor even the Feliciana district, was unanimous in wanting annexation to the infant republic. There was an active pro-French party among these citizens. There was a strong pro-British party among the planters. Also a pro-Spanish aggregation of land owners, and, worse, a turbulent, uncontrollable anti-Spanish and pro-nothing band of men in the district who had no use for laws of any land nor use for those who made them. Most of these "citizens" had been forced to flee American law to find harbor in this Spanish land, consequently their abhorrence for law, in any form, can be understood for many of this rag-tag and bob-tail collection were deserters from the United States Army.

Don Carlos de Grande-Pré, who did have the confidence of many of the more responsible planter folk in the jurisdiction over which he ruled as governor in 1809, was accused of pro-French sympathies, removed, and died in Havana of a broken heart before being tried. He was replaced by another French-born Spanish executive and then trouble began in earnest. The new governor was bland and easy-going. He was so vacillating in his policies that a number of historians have jumped to the conclusion that his character was weak. This is an error, for he had won his many commissions in the Spanish army and service by bravery and ability in other sections of Spanish Louisiana in his dual capacities as military and civil commander. He was unquestionably unfortunate in his selection of subordinates and they, particularly his secretary, were responsible for what happened in 1810 when the planter folk arose in rebellion.

DON CARLOS de HAULT de LASSUS

As he played such an important role in the events to be later described it is necessary I properly introduce Charles de Hault de Lassus de Luzière, to give him his full name. He was the eldest son of Chevalier Pierre de Lassus de Luzière, holder of the knight grand-cross of the royal order of Saint Michael, of an ancient noble family established in the town of Bouchaine, in Hainault, French Flanders, who had married Domitille Joséphe Dumont Danzin de Beaufort, of Beauchamp, bishopric of Arras. The chevalier was probably the same "Delousiere" mentioned by Michaux, the botanist, as having been exiled from France for having been concerned in a plot to deliver Havre to the combined English fleets. At any rate he fled from France during the Revolution, went to Spain, and then removed to Louisiana, arriving in New Orleans in 1793.

Charles de Lassus (or Don Carlos, as he becomes better identified in Louisiana history) was born in France in April of 1764, and entered the Spanish service at the age of 18 as a cadet in the Royal Regiment of which the king was colonel, known as the *Cuerpo de gardias Walonas* or the Waloon Infantry. He became a second lieutenant of the Grenadiers of the Fifth Battalion, and when 29 was brevetted Lieutenant Colonel in recognition of his bravery in leading a successful assault upon and capturing Fort Saint Elmo in the Pyrenees in 1793. A year later he was again promoted and placed in charge of the king's body-guard in Madrid. Shortly thereafter he requested his transfer to the Louisiana regiment so that he could follow his father, sister and brothers to the New World colony.

Upon his arrival in New Orleans, Governor the Baron de Carondelet, upon receipt of orders from the Spanish court, made Don Carlos commandant at New Madrid, a post on the Mississippi river, and at the same time gave his father the command of the post of New Bourbon.

In 1799 Don Carlos was made Lieutenant Governor of Upper Louisiana and stationed at Saint Louis where he ruled until 1804, when he turned over that portion of Louisiana to Captain Amos Stoddard of the United States Army under the terms of the Louisiana Purchase. It was while he was lieutenant governor of Upper Louisiana in 1802, that he was promoted to the full rank of colonel in the Spanish armies.

When he was at the New Madrid post Don Carlos had for his secretary an interpreter, Pierre d'Herbigny (he later changed the spelling of his name to Derbigny and became in 1828 a governor of the state of Louisiana) who married Félicité Odile de Hault de Lassus de Luzière, sister of the commandant. Two of his brothers were also in the Spanish service in Louisiana, Jacques Marcelin Céran de Hault de Lassus de Saint Varin, who had served in the French navy before the Revolution, in Louisiana commanded the *galliot* or war galley *"La Flecha"* (The Arrow); while Camille de Hault de Lassus de Luzière was interpreter and adjutant of the New Bourbon post.

In the spring of 1807 Don Carlos de Lassus was placed in charge of the Baton Rouge fort where he was immediately plunged into hot water, raised to the boiling point by the corruption of the officials under him and the lax methods by which they handled crimes. Spain, and the immediate superiors of de Lassus at Pensacola and Havana, being so far away and engrossed with other affairs, it was nigh to impossible for the complaining planters in Feliciana to refer any of their grievances to other than local officials, and these gentlemen, naturally, were prejudiced against any and all complaints lodged against their own actions and activities.

In the midst of this general discontent a trustworthy rumor was spread throughout the district that Napoleon Bonaparte had decided to regain the territory he had sold to the United States and that this occupation of West Florida would be merely his opening wedge in a campaign to retake all Louisiana. Many of the planter folk of Feliciana, although they preferred the jurisdiction of the United States, were tolerant of Spanish rule as long as they were justly treated, but the very thought of being ruled by the Corsican threw them into a state of apprehension. Something must be done to stave off the coming of the French. Consequently they, those of the better element, met secretly and decided upon a bold action to end uncertainty.

The Feliciana planters decided what they needed was a more effective, a well organized local government; but how could they accomplish this and at the same time maintain an attitude of loyalty? Admittedly this was a big problem but one, so they believed, they could solve. These planters sensibly realized that they were about to engage in a ticklish proposition and that any move they would make might be construed as treasonable; that the rope, or incarceration in Morro Castle at Havana, would result if their plans were made public or went astray.

"ON THE SQUARE"

Absolute secrecy was essential to success and the planters, British, Irish, Scottish and American, realized that there was only one bond that could keep these several nationals together—their membership in an old, a very old, secret society. In consequence all their meetings were held "on the square," and on the "five points of fellowship," in spite of the fact that in the Feliciana district, as elsewhere in Spanish West Florida, such fraternal gatherings were strictly taboo.

The months of May and June, 1810, in the Feliciana country were hectic ones. There were many imputations of graft leveled against the governor's secretary, one Don Raphael Croker (there seems to be evidence he was called "Croquer" at different times) and a captain in the Louisiana regiment. Governor de Lassus objected to the general tone of the complaints against his confidential assistant and demanded specific charges; he even objected to the form of remonstrances made by Captain Croker's fellow-officers stationed at the Baton Rouge fort.

El Capitán Croker airly characterized all the charges of bribery made against him as the "pretext of embryo insurgents to justify the revolution they were formenting", claimed that "American officials in Mississippi and in New Orleans were inspiring the unrest", and charged that the movement then getting underway in the Feliciana countryside was "due to the machinations of a group of physicians who were meeting secretly with some of the wealthy planters in the neighborhood of Bayou Sarah and Saint Francisville."

The commandant of the Feliciana district was one Tomaso Estevan, who, before being placed in charge of the Bayou Sara post, had been the head Spanish officer at Galvez-town, a settlement on the Iberville river below Baton Rouge which had been named for Bernardo de Galvez. When the Louisiana Purchase was consumated, Estevan turned over Galvez-town to the United States representative. While some records refer to him as being a captain, other records stamp him as a "*Teniente*" or lieutenant of the Spanish Louisiana regiment. He had risen from the ranks, a rather unusual thing in the Spanish army, and had married a daughter of Don José Moller, a planter, who lived on the American or west bank of the Mississippi river, evidently below the lower Pointe Coupée village.

This commandant, who represented the force and arm of Spain in Feliciana, was not invited to attend any of the meetings of the planters in his district, which is not at all strange; neither was the *cura* in charge of the church of San Francisco asked to attend. This priest, the

32

Cura Francisco Lennán, and the Spanish commander were exceedingly unpopular, the charge frequently being made that between "the Cross and the Crown" the planters were continuously being bled for services of all kinds. Only one of the English-speaking population, so it appears, had anything in common with these two. He was John Murdock, an attorney, who owned a tavern at the "Murdock's ford," the crossing of Thompson's Creek on the Baton Rouge road, the tavern being kept by a man named Horton.

The first news that Governor de Lassus had that an uprising of the planter folk of Feliciana was under way was when Estevan advised him of the circulation of a petition calling for a peoples' convention and that already secret gatherings had taken place.

THE JOHNSON FAMILY

These secret gatherings were held at "Troy" plantation, the home of John Hunter Johnson, a captain in the militia. John was the eldest son of Isaac Johnson, a Britisher, who had come to West Florida about 1775, when West Florida was held by the English. Isaac was the son of the Reverend John Johnson, an Episcopal minister, and Margaret Hunter, both of Liverpool. Soon after his arrival in West Florida, Isaac Johnson settled near Natchez, married Mary Routh, who had floated down the Mississippi river with her two brothers, Job and Jeremiah, from Virginia. In partnership with John H. Mills he went into the sawmill business at Second Creek, and when this was floated away by a spring freshet, he moved to the Saint Francisville section and established "Troy" plantation about the time Mills founded Bayou Sara, as has already been related.

Isaac Johnson became the father of twelve children, rearing five sons and five daughters to maturity. The eldest of this sturdy brood being John Hunter Johnson, who married Thenia Munson. (John's eldest son, named for his grandfather Isaac, and born in 1805, became the first Democratic governor of Louisiana in 1846, its war governor during the hostilities with Mexico, and the first governor of Louisiana born in Feliciana). Other children of Isaac Johnson and Mary Routh were: 2—Ann Waugh Johnson, who married Gilbert Mills, son of John H. Mills, and later became the wife of Moses Semple. 3—Isaac Johnson, Jr., who married Melissa Jane Williams. 4—Mary Johnson, who married Aaron Gorham. 5—Charles Grandpré Johnson, who married first Anna Ruffin Dawson, and later Eliza Eddington, of England. 6.—Carolina Matilda Johnson, who married Benjamin Collins. 7—Joseph Eugenius Johnson, who married Martha Lane. 8—William Gayoso Johnson, who married Eliza Collins Johnson, daughter of William Garrett Johnson, not related. 9—Elizabeth Johnson, who married Thomas

Withers Chinn. The tenth and last child was Martha Johnson, who married Dr. Nathaniel Wells Pope, the friend and clerk of John James Audubon.

Unquestionably John Hunter Johnson was not only the brains and moving spirit, but with his dare-devil brothers, Isaac, Charles and Joseph, became the strong right arm of the rebellion of the Feliciana planters against the Spanish rule in 1810. It was at his plantation that most of the preliminary secret meetings were held, it was he who dictated the wordings of the various proclamations issued, and the demands made by the members of the convention when it held the first open meeting.

While the Feliciana planters were thus quietly organizing, other trouble was brewing at Baton Rouge. Two Frenchmen from New Orleans began holding secret meetings there, practically under the very muzzles of the guns of the fort. They called nearby Frenchmen into parley under pretext of defending themselves from the Spanish but, according to word sent Governor de Lassus by Diego Morphy, Spanish vice-consul at the Crescent City, these French emissaries were in fact planning a revolution for Napoleon Bonaparte; raising a force in West Florida to join forces with others from New Orleans, to capture not only Baton Rouge but Pensacola as well. De Lassus, seeing in these French activities a well-planned propaganda against his jurisdiction in particular and Spain in general, banished the French malcontents and their local followers. The Frenchmen, fleeing Spanish wrath, crossed the Mississippi to Iberville on the American side and there openly threatened to return and overwhelm de Lassus and his entire force. Whereupon, the governor issued a call for the entire territorial militia to take up arms, be prepared for a defense of Spanish soil, and placed the fort in a state of defense.

While de Lassus was in this perturbed state of mind he received a secret dispatch from Don Tomaso Estevan in the Bayou Sara country, advising him of the circulation of an anonymous petition, calling for a popular convention. Estevan coupled these dire tidings with a fervent plea that de Lassus, accompanied by a considerable force, should come at once to Saint Francisville. Deciding that the peril from the French orators at Baton Rouge was more acute than the trouble brewing in Feliciana, de Lassus refused to leave his fort but dispatched two trusted English-speaking "citizens" to consult with Estevan and to urge the planters not to start any disturbance as by so doing they would only favor the enemies of Spain, particularly Napoleon's scheme to repossess the Floridas and then take over Louisiana.

SENORS HICKY AND MATHER

The two messengers were Philip Hicky and George Mather, Sr., both long residents of the district. Parents of both had come to the province when it was under the domination of England and had remained when Spain ousted the British. Hicky was the son of Daniel Hicky of Ennis, County Clare, Ireland, and Martha Scrivner, of Worstershire, England. This couple came to Louisiana and West Florida in 1775 and their one child, Philip, was born at Manchac, June 17, 1778.

Mather's father was James Mather, of Bochin Lane, London, who emigrated to British West Florida in 1777, on the chartered ship "Royal Oak," which also brought Richard Devall, Daniel Hicky, and others. George Mather's sister, Ann, the third daughter of James Mather, married Philip Hicky.

George Mather and Philip Hicky had always been staunch supporters of the Spanish government in West Florida and Hicky, after the death of his father becoming a wealthy man, had, on more than one occasion loaned the Spanish government of the Baton Rouge jurisdiction money to keep up its functions. The Mathers had long been among the more substantial English-born citizens forced to become Spaniards to retain their properties along the Mississippi. Therefore, the two brothers-in-law were friends and advisors that a governor could select with safety to his own interests to go to a disaffected region and urge loyalty in place of revolt.

Before Hicky and Mather could attend to the duties of their errand, John H. Johnson had summoned the principal planters of the Saint Francisville region to "Troy". A few hours later, in a body, they rode along the dusty roads to Bayou Sara where the Spanish commandant Don Tomaso Estevan had his headquarters. They found the right arm of Spain in bed, complaining of a sudden illness (which one of the liberty-demanding planters whispered in an aside to another that it was probably "yellow" fever), but marching into his very bedroom, John Johnson presented a petition which he demanded the official should receive, read and approve. It was to the effect that he, Don Tomaso Estevan, commander of the Bayou Sara and Feliciana district should summon all of the inhabitants of Feliciana to a peoples' convention, that he order all the alcaldes, syndics, militia officers, and the leading inhabitants to form a general meeting "to discuss measures to restore public tranquility."

After a general demurrer, after a plea that he must first consult his superior, Governor de Lassus, after vainly trying to get the determined band of petitioners to put off the matter for a week or two, Estevan signed the call as he was bid and thus saved himself a hurried trip across the Mississippi river to the American side—or into the water!

The date set for the peoples' convention was Saturday, June 23, and to be held at "the farm of Mr. Stirling, some 15 miles from the Mississippi river and about 10 miles below the line of demarcation," according to one report. To another record, it was held "at Saint Francisville." My investigations prove that this first outspoken move for liberty was held at the Stirling place, not at "Wakefield," as some have supposed, but at "Egypt" plantation, first established on Alexander's Creek by Alexander Stirling, which passed to his son, Lewis Stirling, upon his death in 1808. Today "Egypt" is known as "Rosale" plantation. This agrees with "10 miles from the Mississippi river," but not with "15 miles from the line of demarcation."

All was set for the first move; according to one of the physicians of the district "the imposthume [boil] was ready for the lancet!" Messengers dashed to and fro along the roads of the district summoning all who wanted to have a say in the future of Feliciana to be present, at high noon, at the Stirling place on the following Saturday, for then "Vox populi", the voice of the people, would be heard roaring through the hills and dales of flower-spangled Feliciana.

It was in the midst of this activity that Senors Hicky and Mather arrived in the Feliciana district, ready to call the inhabitants together so that they could read them the letters from the Spanish consul at New Orleans, warning of the French plan, and to show these Feliciana folk that any internal disturbance would only favor the enemies of Spain, which was having its own difficulties across the Atlantic; its king, Ferdinand the Seventh, in one of Napoleon's prisons, and the Corsican's. brother seated on the throne of Castile and Leon.. They delivered the message, but—

After interviewing commander Estevan, talking matters over with the curate, Francisco Lennán, and holding a secret meeting "on the square" with the planters planning the convention movement, the two messengers returned to Baton Rouge. They assured the governor that he need have no apprehension over the coming meeting, that Estevan and the priest Lennán were jumping at shadows, that the inhabitants of Feliciana were loyal, and the governor need have no fears over what would eventuate. Hicky denied positively that there was any truth to the statements contained in a letter the frightened cura Lennán had written de Lassus; that the coming meeting of the folk of Feliciana merely cloaked a plan to seize the fort at Baton Rouge and deprive the governor of his command. Hicky and Mather had become, too, apostles of liberty.

Early in May, before matters had reached the crisis stage in West Florida, Governor William C. C. Claiborne of the Territory of Orleans (for as such was Louisiana known before it attained statehood), had left the southland and preceeded to Washington where he immediately went into a series of conferences with President Madison. That matters in West Florida formed the topic of the discussions between the head of the territory and the head of the nation is obvious, and are made certain by the contents of a confidential letter Governor Claiborne wrote in Washington on June 14, and dispatched by messenger to William Wikoff, Jr., an American planter and legislator, or as Claiborne described him in a letter to Secretary of State Robert Smith: "Wam. Wykoff, Jun., is a planter, a native of Penn. and resides on a cotton plantation nearly opposite Baton Rouge, a very honest man, is now and for some time past judge of his parish, speaks English, French and Spanish." Judge Wikoff was related by marriage to the Hicky and Mather families and was quite familiar with conditions on the Spanish side of the big river. First, let us read Governor Claiborne's letter to his friend and confidant, William Wikoff:

GOVERNOR CLAIBORNE'S VIEWS

"By the last accounts from Spain it would seem that all hopes of successful resistance to Bonaparte were at an end. The Supreme Junta was dissolved. Cadiz, the last hold of the patriots, besieged, and there it was that a little local committee exercised the only authority maintained on the Peninsular in the name of Ferdinand," wrote Claiborne.

"You know, that under the Louisiana Convention, we claim as far eastwardly as the Perdido. That claim never has, and never will I trust, be abandoned. But I am persuaded under present circumstances, it would be more pleasing that the taking possession of the country, be preceded by a request from the inhabitants.

"Can no means be devised to *obtain such request?*

"The time may arrive, perhaps it has arrived, when the people of Florida must adopt measures with a view of their present and future security. If Spain has yielded, as is believed, to Bonaparte, the people of Florida will be assailed by a host of intriguers. There will perhaps be a French party and an English party, and a party who would wish to set up for themselves!

"But I hope the good inhabitants, the honest cultivators of the soil, will unite. Silence the factions, and adopt the policy which their best interests advice; to form for themselves an independent government is out of the question! Waving aside other considerations, the paucity of their numbers, their insular situation, and circumscribed limits forbid the idea!

"A connection with France is opposed by all their honest prejudices and would be attended with ruin, and as for the protection of Great Britain, it could not fail to prove to them a curse, for during the contest, with the United

States, which in that case might ensue, Florida would be the seat of war and its entire conquest could not be protracted beyond a few months.

"But the line of conduct which honest policy points out, cannot be mistaken. Nature has decreed the union of Florida with the United States, and the welfare of the inhabitants imperiously demands it.

"From the district it is indeed impossible, that it could for any length of time, remain detached. But to enlarge is useless. I now recollect that when we last conversed on this subject, our wishes, our sentiments, were in union, and therefore it is, that I, with the more confidence, invite you to lose no time in sounding the views of the most influential of your neighbors on the opposite shore, and in giving to them a right direction.

"Your friends and acquaintences, Philip Hicky, George Mather, Colonel Fulton, Mr. Lilley, Mr. Duvall of the Plains, William Barrow, Captain Percy, Captain McDermot, Mr. Brown of Tickfaw, and many others who are known to you, have much at stake, and should take decided measures.

"Impress upon their minds the importance of the crisis, the expediency of scouting everything like French or English influence, and assure them, I pray you, of the friendly disposition of the American government.

"I am aware that among the settlers of Florida, there are persons, who during the American war were disaffected to the United States, and who, probably, may feel some uneasiness at falling under the American government. It may be well to quiet their apprehensions by informing them that the transactions of that day will not be remembered to their injury, that the present is a fit occasion to return to the bosom of their country, and, if embraced with cordiality, the prodigal son mentioned in holy writ did not meet a more heartfelt welcome than they would experience from the American family.

"The most eligible means of obtaining an expression of the wish of the inhabitants of Florida can be best determined by themselves. But were it done through the medium of a convention of delegates, named by the people, it would be more satisfactory. In the event that a convention is called, it is important that every part of the district as far at least as the Perdido be represented, and therefore I feel solicitious that you should be at some pains to prepare for the occasion the minds of the more influential characters in the vicinity of Mobile. Whether this can best be done by yourself in person or by some citizen of Baton Rouge in your confidence, is left to your discretion.

"You will consider this letter as confidential, and in pursuing the object referred to you will act with all the circumspection which its nature requires. You may address me at Washington City where I will remain until the latter part of October."

Although this letter had been written during the middle of June, owing to the delays of transportation of mails in those times, it was some days after the planters had met at Lewis Stirling's place to initiate their own move for independence, that Wikoff received Claiborne's missive, which clearly showed how President Madison regarded West Florida, and that he had not abandoned the claim that West Florida, at least as far east as the Perdido river, belonged to the area purchased from France under the terms of the Purchase.

THE VOICE OF THE PEOPLE

On Saturday, June 23, 1810, a great concourse of inhabitants of Feliciana gathered at "Egypt" plantation. There were more than five hundred Spanish citizens in attendance when the "voice of the people" was raised in one great shout. Ostensibly their object was "to secure themselves against foreign invasion and domestic disturbance", if what the ringleaders said to those assembled on the lawn in front of the plantation home was the truth. These leaders, headed by John Johnson, submitted a prearranged plan and it was adopted *viva voce* and only eleven voices, out of the five hundred, were raised in objection.

Under the plan submitted by those responsible for calling the people together, the inhabitants of Feliciana were asked to "select four of their respectable and influential neighbors" who were in turn empowered to ask each of the remaining districts of Baton Rouge, Ste. Helena, Chifoncté, Christianna, to elect their representatives to a common council. This council of the whole to be invested with the general powers of government, which they were to administer "in a manner best calculated for the common good." Spanish officers then governing the territory would be empowered to continue in office, provided they would submit to the new authority of the people!

The plan was agreed upon with roars of approval. There were only 11 dissenting voices raised in the 500 and more who crowded the lawns in front of "Egypt's" plantation home, and the cheering Feliciana folk selected the four representatives before the meeting was declared ended, and they were: John Hunter Johnson, William Barrow, John Mills, and John Rhea. The people who had delivered the first blow for liberty then wended their way homeward.

Let us be present at this momentous meeting, witness it through the account written by a "gentleman of Pointe Coupée" to "a friend in the Louisiana territory." It was penned the next day and said:

39

"Pointe Coupée, June 24, 1810.

"I yesterday returned from St. Francisville, a little town in the Spanish territory, where I found the whole country in a state of rebellion. A plan had been drawn up by some persons at Baton Rouge for the government of the province. Their names are not known, but it is supposed that Mr. Fulwar Skipwith is at the head. The most important parts of the proposed form of this new constitution are as follows: That the people elect a Governor, Secretary and Council of three to take possession of the country in behalf of Ferdinand VII, if he should again be restored to the throne of old Spain; otherwise they are to hold their offices for life, the Governor to have authority to appoint all inferior officers, Judges, Alcaldes, Syndics, etc., for the administration of justice, with full power to remove them at pleasure, provided a majority of the Council concur. It is in reality, from the apparent intention and meaning of the farmers, nothing more or else than an elective monarchy, giving as ample and uncontrollable powers to their Governor as any the most arbitrary prince in Europe possesses.

"Immediately upon the promulgation of this plan a meeting of the people took place, where a great deal was said upon the subject, pro and con. The crowd was such that I could not get near enough to hear distinctly all the debates, but the final determination was that the people labored under many and weighty grievances from the tyranny and injustice of Spanish officers, that a change was necessary, and that from the known administration of the present government no man can recover his just debts without sacrificing half their value in bribes and presents to the Judges; but the form proposed, if possible, entails upon them greater misery than that under which they now labor. They would, therefore, support it as it now is, until better can be adopted.

"The meeting then broke up, and the Company of Horse, under parade, saluted the Commandant with "God Save Ferdinand VII."

"You will observe that the above is only the resolution of one of the districts in the province; the others may be of a different opinion, and, if so, a civil war will commence without delay.

"When I inform you that almost all West Florida is settled by natives of the United States and since the *French have been driven from Baton Rouge*, which happened about two weeks since, there are not in the whole province one hundred families from a different country."

BATON ROUGE JOINS IN

The news of the action of the Feliciana planters quickly spread and the other districts of the territory were soon asking permission to call similar conventions. On July 6, those in the Baton Rouge district petitioning the chief executive and signing the call were Philip Hicky, George Mather, Joseph Sharp, Samuel Fulton, Fulwar Skipwith, Dr. Andrew Steele, Thomas Lilley, John Davenport, George and William Herries, Philemon Thomas, John Morgan, Edmund Hawes, fourteen in all, all anxious to follow the lead of the Feliciana patriots.

News of the contemplated convention filtered into New Orleans and the newsprints of that city were soon taking cognizance of the unsettled affairs of West Florida. Printed the "Louisiana Gazette" June 27: "Letters have been received today from Bayou Sarah and Baton Rouge, stating that the people of those districts in West Florida had it in contemplation to form a government for themselves; that they had been for sometime without law, or the semblance of government, and that self preservation drove them to the measure they were about to take. We are promised extracts of the letters, which, if handed us, shall be printed tomorrow."

Three days later the "Gazette" stated: "We are not able to give the extracts of the letters on the subject of the commotions in West Florida. The business has assumed a serious shape, and the gentlemen who received the letters, on due consideration, think they ought not to have publicity. We are promised a communication on the subject which will appear Monday."

As promised, in a letter signed "Common Sense," the "Gazette" published July 2, 1810, a long letter from the Bayou Sarah region, which read:

"For the Louisiana Gazette.
"The people composing the district of New Feliciana, which comprehends that part of West Florida, bordering on the river Mississippi and extending eastwardly about one hundred miles, have long wished and expected that the government of the United States, would either by negotiation, or otherwise, get possession of that part of West Florida, which they have claimed under the treaty and purchase of 1803, lying west of the river Perdido. The inhabitants are generally Americans, and many of them have purchased lands and settled in Florida since the cession of Louisiana to the United States; fully impressed with the belief that they would soon find themselves under their former laws and government. They have long anxiously expected to hear of the unfortunate fate of Spain, of her entire subjugation to the arms of France, and in an event of that kind, they have calculated, that either the conqueror of Spain, or Great Britain, the ally of Spain, would claim the Floridas; and they generally revolt at the idea of being placed under the government of either of those great nations.
"The officers who have declared for Ferdinand VII, and now bear the *semblance* of power among the people,

are divided in their attachments. The real Spaniards are few, their zealous attachment to the cause of Spain would induce them to submit to any order from the Spanish Junta, they would willingly pass under the British government, if it was their order. Bonaparte has his friends and emissaries in office, who speak of his imperial greatness, and recommend the people to declare for King Joseph, this, however, is done generally under the *rose*, but it is well known to be a fact. In this distracted state of things, without law or government, the people have thought proper and prudent to hold meetings to consult their general safety.

"The local situation of West Florida, surrounded almost as it is with the laws and government of the United States, and nine-tenths of the inhabitants, being either native born Americans, or strongly attached to the American principles and government, it was reasonable to be expected that they would turn their eyes towards the United States for protection. The inhabitants have never raised a clamor against Spain, or against the Spanish patriots, or the glorious cause they are engaged in; they have been solely guided in all their deliberations by the principles of *self preservation*, the first law of nature. No demogogue or demagogues, who for their own private views, interest or aggrandisement, in my opinion are concerned in the meetings, and should the same unanimity prevail that has so far marked these meetings, there is little doubt that their views and plans will terminate happily. The government of the United States will not, cannot withclaim extends, which as before described, is from the Mississippi to the River Perdido, and in giving that protection, I have no hesitation in saying that my people will cheerfully become citizens of the United States and feel themselves happy in the appellation.

"COMMON SENSE."

Independence Day was celebrated with pomp and gusto in New Orleans, although the editor of the "Louisiana Gazette" noted that there was a lack of warmth and zeal among some of the citizens, particularly those of French sympathies, as witness:

"The anniversary was celebrated in this city, in the years eighteen hundred and four, five and six, with that warmth and zeal that marks us true Americans. The 4th of July, in those years, will be remembered with pride and pleasure; the *Place d'Arms* was covered with regular troops and volunteer militia; firing of cannon, and every demonstration of joy rang through our city, and every American countenance beamed with mirth and gaiety. Since the demon of discord has raised her sneaky head among us, a general apathy prevails to everything that is American; it looks as if we were preparing to change the name of freemen to that of bondmen, as if we were ready and willing to throw ourselves into the arms of some European tyrant. The best tried soundest Americans are laid aside, and the minions of the tyrants, now stand forward

42

as the champions of liberty, but from such liberty, such Gallic liberty, good Lord deliver us."

Below this item was another which pertained to the troubles in Feliciana and West Florida. It read:

"The only news of consequence, by last evening's mail, is the change of government in Carracas. We expect that Mexico will soon follow the example, in fact she ought to have led the way. Our little neighbours (we hope this appellation will not offend them) the Floridians, have anticipated the good cause, and this day, we are informed, they intend declaring themselves free. The fair Goddess of Freedom driven from the one continent, seeks an asylum in another, and happy, thrice happy are we, that she is likely to meet such a cordial reception."

Governor de Lassus did not mull very long over the petitions sent him by the other inhabitants to call an assembly similar to the one held in the Feliciana country so they could select delegates. He replied immediately. He said that as the avowed purpose was to preserve intact the dominions of the Spanish monarchy and sustain Spanish laws, and as such an action would tend to insure the tranquillity and well being of every citizen in the jurisdiction, therefore he freely granted permission to hold such meetings in Baton Rouge, Ste. Helena, Chifoncté, and even sanctioned the meeting already held in Feliciana.

SAMUEL FULTON

With this assurance that their delegate-selecting meeting would be recognized as legal, official, and non-treasonable, the Baton Rouge petitioners assembled at the home of Samuel Fulton in that village. This makes necessary a pause in the recital of events to be introduced Senor Fulton. He was at that time adjutant-general of the West Florida militia and the husband of a daughter of former Governor Carlos de Grande-Pré. Before settling in the Baton Rouge district, Samuel Fulton was one of the French agents in the service of the Directory in its plan to reoccupy Louisiana when the Spanish held it. He visited General George Rogers Clark in 1796, and confirmed the captor of Vincennes in his French sentiment. Later Fulton was at work, with a man named Milfort, among the Creek Indians in an endeavor to help out France's plan to limit the western boundaries of the United States to the Appalachian mountains rather than by the Mississippi river. In August of 1804 we find Fulton in West Florida where, with the assistance of Armand Duplantier and George Dupassau, he assembled a force of some 150 from among the settlers in the Amite and Comite region to balk the Kemper brothers in their revolt, attempt to take the Baton Rouge fort, and make Governor de Grand-Pré a prisoner.

43

That same summer Sam Fulton had been appointed by Governor Claiborne as "a discreet person" to open the mail bags passing through the Spanish territory on their way to New Orleans and distribute the letters in them directed to persons living in West Florida. The appointment was made by the American governor, strange as it seems, upon the advice of President Madison. The two natural postal routes to New Orleans had to pass through Spanish West Florida, one route being from Muscle Shoals on the Tennessee via Natchez, Fort Adams, Saint Francisville, and Baton Rouge. The alternate road was from Muscle Shoals to Mobile, thence to the north of the Pascagoula, and by water through lakes Borgne and Pontchartrain to Bayou Saint John and into New Orleans. In either case, for a bag of mail to reach the Crescent City where the American executive governed, the Spaniards controlled an important part of both routes. A "discreet person" to open the mail bags was necessary.

In spite of his duties as Spanish adjutant general of the West Florida militia, we find among President Madison's private papers a communication from Samuel Fulton, written during the early part of 1810, wherein Fulton confided to Madison his belief that Spain would yield to Bonaparte and that this would so change conditions in West Florida as to bring about British intervention. Consequently if the American government desired to take possession before the British Lion put its paw on the territory, he, Fulton, might be able to render the United States "effective assistance" and would be only too glad to do so.

It can therefore be understood that as the adjutant general of the West Florida militia, which de Lassus would have to depend upon in case of armed revolt, Sam Fulton's defection could seriously embarrass the régime of de Lassus and Spain.

When the petitioners filed out of Sam Fulton's house, July 8, they had named their five delegates to the convention called for by the planters of Feliciana. Those who were to represent the Baton Rouge district were: Philip Hicky, Thomas Lilley, John Morgan, Manuel López, and Edmund Hawes.

ALCALDE SHEPHERD BROWN

The convention idea was not welcomed by everyone in West Florida. The commandant and alcalde in the Ste. Helena district, Shepherd Brown by name, was one of the objectors. He had been receiving rumors of the movement and the desire "for a new order of things," which included the taking over of the reins of government, therefore he was, to say the least, astounded to receive from the governor a written permit to allow the inhabitants of Ste. Helena and Chifoncté to meet and select delegates. Suspicioning that de Lassus had been forced to issue

44

the permits because he was not strong enough to forbid such gatherings or to punish those behind the movement, Brown sent one of his trusted lieutenants, Joseph Thomas, to Baton Rouge to learn from the governor's own lips whether or not he had voluntarily issued the permits or whether they had been extorted.

If the governor was not acting on his "own free will and his course was designed to preserve intact this part of the kingdom and of our loved and worthy sovereign, Don Ferdinand VII, and to sustain his government and wise laws," and the right to meet in convention assembled "had been extorted by fear," then Shepherd Brown declared that the Ste. Helena district which he commanded did not desire a change of any kind, and, if the governor needed help, he, Brown, "could muster in a few hours notice more than five hundred men ready and willing to sacrifice their lives for the honour of the Spanish flag, and who would obey his word!"

The author of these bombastic words was an American-born individual who settled in the West Florida section soon after John McDonough arrived in Louisiana to begin his work of amassing a fortune in the New Orleans trade and in cypress swamps along the Iberville, Amite and Comite rivers. In this latter endeavor McDonough was ably assisted by his confidential agent in West Florida, Shepherd Brown. It was Brown who greased Spanish palms to secure these "worthless" lands for the notorious spendthrift of the Crescent City. No small wonder then Shepherd Brown did not look with friendly eye on any move for any kind of government.

The governor reassured Brown's messenger, wrote the alcalde of Ste. Helena, that he had not been "forced" to permit the meeting, that all who had asked to hold them had done "so with proper respect", that he believed the people not only well disposed towards him but to Spain and their sovereign Ferdinand, and the "real meaning of the coming convention is merely an endeavor on the part of the inhabitants to prove their loyalty to Spain." Which either means de Lassus was a fool, or that he was ready to make a corrupt bargain with the leaders, or that he was craftily playing for time to recruit a sufficiently large force to crush the revolt at one paralyzing blow. Events seem to prove the third suspicion.

Reassured that the governor was not acting under force, Brown issued the call in his district for popular gatherings to elect delegates to the greatly feared convention. As it would be impossible to secure one convenient common meeting place, he divided it into three sections (Ste. Helena at that time took in what is now that parish and Livingston, extending from the northern boundary line to Lake Pontchartrain, and bounded on the west by the Tickfaw and on the east by the "Chifonctè"), two delegates to be chosen from one section, and one from each of the remaining two precincts. Those "elected" were Joseph Thomas, Shepherd Brown's trusted and confidential lieutenant; John W. Leonard, son of Don Gilberto de Leonardo (the father served under de Lassus as *Ministro Interventor y Tesorero*, which means he was the comptroller and treasurer, but when Don Gilberto left the Emerald Isle he was plain Gilbert Leonard and, even when he learned to speak Spanish, he spoke it with a thick Irish brogue); William Spiller and Benjamin O. Williams were the two selected from the outlying precincts of St. Helena. The Chifoncté, or Tanchipaho region sent one delegate only, he was William Cooper, a former "North Carolina Tory" now an adherent of Shepherd Brown.

The date set for the meeting of the convention of delegates was set for July 25, and the designated spot, a plantation on Saints John Plains, or "The Plains," sometimes designated as "Buhler's Plains," but usually written "St. John's Plains." The place was noted for its many massive live oaks about the house and was on the right hand side of the road leading from Baton Rouge to Jackson, La., near the Presbyterian or "Plains" church. According to most accounts it was the home of Richard Devall, although one record states it was the home of Thomas Lilley; their places were not far apart.

While awaiting the action of the other districts the Feliciana ring-leaders were not inactive. They gathered at "Troy" plantation and drew up a tentative code, or constitution, a sort of declaration of purpose to acquaint the people in general as to their aims. Those concerned in confecting this proclamation, as it may best be termed, included John H. Johnson, William Barrow, Judge Rhea, John Mills, Lewis Stirling, *et als.*, but most of the evidence at hand seems to prove that this "constitution" was wholly written by Edward Randolph, of Pinckneyville, a partner of Daniel Clark of New Orleans.

Word of the activities and intentions of the Feliciana patriots filtered into New Orleans and were the subject of conversation in the streets and were also noticed by items in the daily press. In its issue of June 18, the "'Louisiana Gazette" published, under the heading "Extract of a letter from Bayou Sarah, received this day's mail":

> "Since my last to you we have had a general convention of the inhabitants of this district (New-Feliciana) and one sentiment appearing to prevail throughout the whole; the convention proceeded to elect four men to represent this district in a convention held at *Buller's Plains*, for the purpose of redressing the evils attendant on a state which

certainly may with propriety be called anarchy. Dispatches have been forwarded to the other districts of this province, inviting them to concur with us; and when they shall
have chose their representatives, the whole will meet together, not as a Legislative body, but rather as a Committee of Safety. They are to propose such measures to the
Governor, as they may deem most proper for the welfare
of the country, for the preservation of harmony and good
order, and for the execution of impartial justice to all men.
It is presumed they will insist on the judiciary powers being separated from that of the Executive, and something
of trial by jury. Should this be agreed to, the Spanish
laws will most probably be continued in force; but if the
Governor objects to the arrangement and denies the power
of the people (which I think he in honor to himself must
do) then the people will consider themselves at liberty, and
in duty to themselves, bound to act. In addition to a Committee of Safety a Legislative body may be chosen, and it
will follow of course, a new Executive and Judiciary.

"Something of this kind seems indispensably necessary. The credit of the place, as you well know, is ruined
abroad; each individual suffers at home, and, the whole
arises from the want of justice, and of men to execute it.
Who could expect otherwise? When a man has been so
often bribed as to consider justice on either, or neither
side of the question; it must be hard for him after a few
years, to know on which side it really does belong. This
seems to be the case with some of our officers. But we
hope to find men who are not so completely blind, and who
still know something of probity. The four men chosen for
this district, are Captain *John H. Johnson*, Captain *William
Barrow*, *John Ray*, and *John Mills*.

"Since the election the public mind appears to be more
tranquil, but the spirit of independence is still gaining
ground. The support of the mother country being cut off,
and the fact being known that Bonaparte now claims this
province, will rouse the minds of many who have been
heretofore asleep, or scarcely dared to think for themselves. If the United States still pretend any claim on this
place they must not refuse it when it is offered."

The next day's issue contained the following paragraph:

"All the information we have received from West
Florida, corroborate the extract of a letter which we published yesterday, from Bayou Sarah. Deputies have been
named at Baton Rouge, who are gone up to join the general
convention or congress at Buller's Plains. It is generally
understood that the Governor of Baton Rouge is favorable
to the views of the people. We also find that the people
continue to place much dependence on the United States
for protection, at least that part of Florida which has been
claimed by them; they ought not to be too sanguine on this

score, the United States will be (as they have been) very guarded in giving offence to any of the European powers."

THE FIRST PROPOSED CODE

Ten days before that the delegates gathered in convention, assembled as representatives of the people of West Florida, the "Natchez Chronicle", July 17, published in full the tentative constitution or declaration, "code" would be a better world, that Edward Randolph, Johnson, Barrow, Rhea, Mills, Stirling and other Feliciana planters had put to paper in advance of the meeting. Said the "Chronicle", which sent one of its editors to the meeting to report what eventuated:

"The following constitution has been circulated in West Florida, and it is said to be well received in the neighborhood of Baton Rouge. In New-Feliciana, much the most populous, wealthy and important district in the province, we are informed there is considerable diversity of opinion; some of the inhabitants favor the idea of an independent government; a strong party is yet in favor of Ferdinand 7th, while the mass of the inhabitants are desirous of coming under the protection of the United States. From St. Hellena, Tanchipaho and Christianne, we have not yet heard, but presume they would prefer the protection of the United States."

On July 25, the "Louisiana Gazette" republished the Natchez paper's account so that the people of New Orleans would know the aims of the patriots; the "National Intelligencer" picked up the story for the information of the whole nation, and later a clipping sent to England was republished in Yorke's "Weekly Political Review."

If Thomas Jefferson is to be regarded the author of America's famous "declaration," so must Edward Randolph be entitled to a like fame as the author of the first West Florida declaration. Although it was not either the declaration or the constitution finally adopted by the conventionalists, it should be again reprinted in full:

"When the Sovereignty and Independence of a nation have been destroyed by treachery or violence, the political ties which unite its different members are dissolved.

"Distant provinces no longer cherished or protected by the mother country, have a right to institute for themselves such forms of government as they may think conducive to their safety and happiness.

"The lawful Sovereign of Spain, together with his hereditary kingdom in Europe, having fallen under the dominion of a foreign tyrant, by means of treachery and lawless power, the right naturally devolves on the people of the different provinces of that kingdom, placed by nature beyond the grasp of the usurper, to provide for their own security: the allegiance which they owed and preserved with so much fidelity to their lawful sovereign, can never be transferred to the destroyer of their country's indedepence.

"We, therefore, the people of West Florida, exercising the right which incontestibly devolves upon us, declare, that we owe no allegiance to the present ruler of the French nation, or to any King, Prince or Sovereign who may be placed by him on the throne of Spain, and that we will always, and by all means in our power, resist any tyrannical usurpation over us of whatever kind, or by whomsoever the same may be attempted to be exercised for this purpose, and in order more effectually to preserve domestic tranquility, and to secure to ourselves the blessings of peace, liberty and impartial administration of justice, we do ordain and establish the following:

"Article 1. The laws, usages and custom heretofore observed in the administration of justice, and in determining the right of property, shall remain in full force, as far as the situation of the country will allow, until altered or abolished in the manner hereafter provided.

"Article 2. All lawful contracts heretofore made and entered into, shall be binding on the parties according to the true intent and meaning thereof.

"Article 3. The officers of the Militia shall retain their commissions, and the Alcaldes and Syndics of the several divisions shall continue to hold and exercise the duties of their respective offices, having the same jurisdiction as heretofore, until otherwise provided by lawful authority.

"Article 4. One Governor, one Secretary, and three Counsellors of State, shall be immediately chosen by the people, who shall enter upon the duties of their respective offices on the........ day of........ of this present year 1810, after having in the presence of each other taken an oath faithfully to discharge the duties of their respective offices, and to exercise the powers herein granted to them to the best of their judgment for the good of the people.

"Article 5. The supreme executive powers shall be vested in the Governor, who shall also be the commander in chief of all the military force of the Commonwealth, and shall cause the laws to be faithfully and impartially executed, he shall, by and with the consent of the three counsellors of state, or a majority of them, have the power to appoint and commission all officers, civil and military, whose appointments are not herein otherwise provided, and to revoke the commissions of inferior magistrates now in office, or hereafter commissioned by him at pleasure.

49

"Article 6. The legislative power shall be vested in the three counsellors of state, or a majority of them, but no act or resolution passed by them, shall have the force or authority of a law, without being first approved by the Governor.

"Article 7. The legislative council shall meet on their own adjournments, but the Governor shall have the power to convene them at any other time when he thinks it expedient, and they shall cause to be published from time to time, such laws and regulations as may be made for the better Government of the Commonwealth.

"Article 8. The three counsellors of the state shall be conservators of the peace throughout the Commonwealth, and to decide all cases and prosecutions, civil and criminal, which may be instituted by individuals, or on behalf of the Commonwealth, and submitted to their decision. For this purpose, they, or a majority of them, shall hold court four times in every year, at such times, and in such places as shall be provided by law; they shall have, and exercise when in session for that purpose the same jurisdiction, both original and appellate as has been heretofore exercised by the highest authority in the kingdom, and their judgment shall be final.

"Article 9. The Governor, by, and with the advice of the Legislative Council, or a majority of them, shall have power to declare war, levy taxes, regulate commerce, dispose of public lands, grant permissions of residence to emigrants, establish rules for the naturalization of foreigners, form treaties, or enter into confederacy with other states, establish inferior tribunals of justice, provide for the common defense and common welfare, and in general do all acts, and establish such laws and regulations as may be necessary and conducive to the safety and prosperity of the Commonwealth. *Provided Always*, that no law shall be made to have a retrospective effect, or any way to effect the obligation of contracts, and provided, that no man shall be deprived of life, liberty or property without an impartial trial, in which he shall be allowed to examine all the witnesses against him, and produce witnesses in his defence.

"Article 10. It shall be the duty of the Secretary of State, to keep and preserve the acts and laws passed by the Legislature, and the proceedings of the Governor, in his executive department. He shall keep all public records, as well as those now in being, as hereafter to be made, and the seal of the Commonwealth, and shall furnish copies of all public records under the seal of the Commonwealth, when required.

"Article 11. The governor and legislative council shall at any time when they think it expedient, not more distant than three years from the time of entering upon the duties of their respective offices, cause a convention of delegates, chosen by the people in such manner as they shall prescribe by law, to be held at Baton Rouge, which said convention shall have full powers to form a constitution for the better government of this Commonwealth, to establish the future seat of government, and to declare at what time the powers herein granted shall cease, and determine, till what time the seat of government shall remain at Baton Rouge.

"Article 12. The governor shall receive an annual salary of .... for his services, and each of the three counsellors an annual salary of .... for their services, the secretary of state shall receive an annual salary of ...., together with such fees of office as may be allowed and provided by law. The compensation of all inferior officers shall be ascertained and fixed by the legislature, and no officer of this government shall hold any office under, or receive title or pension from any foreign state.

"Article 13. When the present declaration or ordinance shall have been approved and signed by a majority of all the inhabitants within .... it shall have complete effect and operation within the said distrcit, and together with the laws and regulations made in conformity to it, shall be the supreme law of the land. It shall also be extended to any other district or places in West or East Florida, in which it shall be approved and signed by a majority of the people, and to give immediate operation and effect to the same, the following gentlemen are hereby designated to the different offices respectively, and fully authorized and required to exercise the powers, and perform the duties thereof, viz:

"We, the people, do hereby approve and confirm the foregoing declaration and ordinance, in all its parts, and to support it we mutually pledge to each other our lives, our fortunes, and our sacred honor."

While this tentative "code" was never adopted by the convention of the people, it does, however, give us an insight into the desires and intentions of those planning the orderly uprising that ended in a rough and tumble fight.

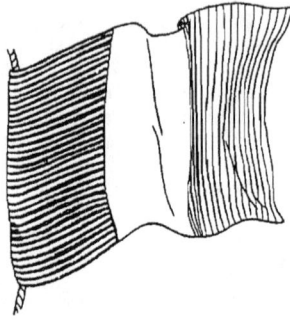

A FLAG THAT NEVER FLEW OVER FELICIANA

The tricolor of Republican France and Napoleon Bonaparte's Empire, first raised in 1794 in France, flew for only 20 days over New Orleans and the rest of Louisiana, but never over West Florida. This flag was designed after the banner of the Netherlands, which had red at the hoist instead of blue.

PART TWO

The Convention

The day set for the meeting of the Convention, July 25, found the delegates from the various districts gathered at Saints John Plains, and the opening meeting was given over to organization. John Rhea, of Feliciana, was unanimously selected as the presiding officer; Dr. Andrew Steele, of Baton Rouge, was made secretary; George Mather, Sr., acted as recorder, and a Feliciana planter named Samuel S. Crocker was designated clerk.

Feliciana was represented by Judge Rhea, John Hunter Johnson, John Mills, and William Barrow. The five delegates from Baton Rouge included Philip Hicky, Thomas Lilley, Edmund Hawes, John Morgan, and Manuel Lopez (the latter, it will be observed, was the only delegate who did not bear an Anglo-Saxon name). The four from Ste. Helena were John W. Leonard, Joseph Thomas, William Spiller, and Benjamin O. Williams. The lone delegate from the Chifoncté district was William Cooper.

"The members naturally hesitated to proceed along the unaccustomed path of self-government," says one account. "Their experience under the Spanish régime and a certain mutual distrust caused them to avoid hasty action until each had disclosed his attitude. Some of them were ready for common action and were doubtless responsible for circulating an anonymous code that had already been favorably received. This was designed to place all political power in the hands of the convention, acting jointly with de Lassus." This "anonymous code" was the so-called constitution or declaration written by Edward Randolph, which had been circulated by the Feliciana ringleaders. As has already been stated this "code" was never adopted, the real declaration and constitution being entirely different documents and adopted later.

The first act of the convention was to pass comprehensive resolutions defining its powers. They were:

"Resolved, That this Convention created by the whole body of the people of the government of Baton Rouge, and by the previous consent of the Governor, is therefore legally constituted to act in all cases of national concern which relate to this province, to provide for publick safety, to create a revenue, and with the consent of the Governor, to create tribunals civil and criminal, and to define their own powers relating to other concerns of the government, when to adjourn, when to meet again, and how long to continue their session.

53

"Resolved, That it is the unanimous wish of this Convention to proceed in all our deliberations for the publick welfare with the entire approbation of his Excellency Carlos de Hault de Lassus, our present Governor, and that we become responsible with him to the superior authorities for the expediency of the measures which may be adopted with his concurrence, that we engage to support him as our Governor, with the emoluments appertaining to his present office, and to give him all the aid in our power in the execution of the duties thereof."

After thus deftly hamstringing Don Carlos with this forced complicity, the delegates called it a day and on Thursday, July 26, got down to business when the several delegates opened their budgets of grievances.

"St. John's Plains, July 26, 1810.
"On motion it was unanimously
"Resolved, That it is the immediate object of this assembly: to promote the safety, honor, and happiness of his Majesty, Ferdinand VII's province of West Florida; to guard against his enemies, both foreign and domestic, to punish wrongs and to correct abuses dangerous to the existence and prosperity of the state.

"Resolved, unanimously, That this Convention consider themselves legally authorized, by decree of his Excellency, hereto prefixed, to exercise the powers and perform the duties expressed in the proceedings of yesterday.

"Ordered, That the Convention do now take into consideration the existing grievances of the country, which require immediate redress, whereupon the following resolutions were unanimously adopted:

"Resolved, That we consider it a grievance that the whole country is a place of refuge for the deserters and fugitives from justice from the neighboring States and Territories, men of character and fortune are prohibited from settling among us, by which means a population is daily increasing, dangerous to the peace and safety of the country, while we have no increase of such as are interested in maintaining order and obedience to the laws. [This was offered by Thomas Lilley and sanctioned by George Harries].

"Resolved, That we consider it a grievance, that in the present defenceless state of the country, when we are by no means secure, either from domestic insurrection or foreign invasion, no sufficient measures are pursued to organize, arm and discipline the militia to act with promptitude in defense of the country. [This was proposed by William Barrow and Philip Hicky jointly].

"Resolved, That we consider it a grievance, that the evil-disposed persons are not deterred from the commission of crimes by the example of speedy and condign punishment of the offenders; there being no tribunal amongst us, competent to give final judgment in criminal cases, by which means the most atrocious criminals either go unpunished or are sent to distant tribunals, so that no advantage is derived from the example of the punishment inflicted. [John Mills and William Cooper backed this grievance].

"Resolved, That we consider it a grievance, that much expense and delay in obtaining justice in civil cases, arises from want of a tribunal among us competent to decide finally on all cases of law and equity; from the too limited jurisdiction of inferior civil magistrates in the several districts of this government; and from the regulation which requires that all process be conducted in a language not understood by a large majority of the people. [John Johnson and William Barrow backed this complaint].

"Resolved, That we consider it a grievance, that abuses and irregularities have been practiced in the office of the Surveyor of the department of the Government for some years past, by which means many cases of litigation are likely to arise, and many of the inhabitants in danger of being deprived of their just claims; and that the boundaries of land, having been made by legal authority, these lands should be resurveyed at any time after, with a view to alter their boundaries. [William Barrow and William Spiller authored this grievance].

"Resolved, That we consider as a grievance, the want, or almost neglect of laws respecting roads, slaves, and all live stock of every description in the country. [This complaint came jointly from Philip Hicky and Joseph Thomas].

"On motion, ordered, That Messers. J. H. Johnson, Thomas Lilley, Philip Hicky, and John Mills, be considered a committee to draft a plan for the redress of grievances, and for the defense and safety of the country, and that they report by bill or otherwise.

"Resolved, That we consider it as a grievance, that no fee-bills are exhibited by officers in the employment of the Government, by which neglect the inhabitants are subjected to impositions and extravagant charges by means of said officers, for their services; and that petitions of pressing importance, when presented, are often neglected, or remain for a long time unanswered. [Philip Hicky and Manuel Lopez insisted on this complaint].

"Resolved, That a uniform standard of weights and measures be established throughout this Province, and that a select committee determine the best mode of carrying the same into effect. [John Leonard and William Spiller insisted on this being included].

"Resolved, That we consider the facility with which the exiled French from our Island of Cuba have found means to introduce themselves into this province, a very serious and alarming grievance, and that prompt measures ought to be resorted to, to prevent their future introduction. [Also by Leonard and Spiller].

"Adjourned until tomorrow at 9 o'clock.

"Friday, July 27th, 1810.

"The Committee assembled. On motion,

"Resolved, That it is a grievance, that a number of the inhabitants, who are, and have been for some years past, resident in this province. are unable to obtain titles to the lands upon which they have settled by permission of the government, in consequence of a mistaken policy or design in the officers of the government and which lands are occupied by his Majesty's subjects, who are willing to come forward in support of the general good and defense of the country. [Benjamin Williams and William Spiller aired this grievance].

"Resolved, That it becomes the duty of this province to lessen as much as possible the burthens of the Mother Country, engaged as she is at present, in a dubious contest for her own preservation; and that provision ought to be made as soon as possible, for defraying the expenses of this department of the Government, from such resources as may be found within the country; that such part of the National Treasury as we might have a claim to hereafter for that purpose, may be employed for more useful and important national objects. [Philip Hicky and Thomas Lilley insisted that this be included among the other protests].

"Resolved, That it be recommended to the Committee appointed to provide for the redress of grievances, to take into consideration the expediency of appointing a Counsellor acquainted with the laws of Castile and the Indies, whose duty it shall be to give his opinion in writing to the Supreme Court of Justice, on all important questions, or points of law which may arise in the discussion of the causes which may be admitted to their decision. [Thomas Lilley and Manuel López backed this recommendation].

"Resolved, That no member of this Convention shall be arrested by any civil process, during the session or pornogation, or when traveling to or from the place of meeting, until final adjournment thereof." [All delegates agreed upon this].

It is worthy of note that neither John Morgan of Baton Rouge nor William Cooper from the Chifoncté district had any grievances to air; they probably agreed upon what some of the others believed needed correction in the government of the whole district.

THE FIRST CONVENTION ENDS

So ended the first meeting the greatly feared and cheered convention of the people. Before adjourning to meet again on the second Monday in August, the members addressed a communication to Governor de Lassus, and appointed a committee consisting of Philip Hicky, Manuel Lopez and Joseph Thomas to present it to him.

This fulsome address advised the governor of the satisfaction the delegates derived from his approval of their meeting and, in the name of their constituents, they thanked him for his efforts "to preserve popular tranquility in a time of general anxiety and alarm." They assured his excellency that the sole object of their deliberations was "to promote the safety, honor, and happiness of our beloved king, Ferdinand VII, to guard against his enemies, foreign and domestic, and to punish wrongs and correct abuses dangerous to the existence and prosperity of the province."

They closed with the hope that their future action would meet with his approval, called attention to the passages in their resolutions which dealt with the powers of government and his salary, notified him of the appointment of a committee that would seek to redress their grievances, and advised him that it was their intention to meet again August 14, to receive the report of said committee and to proceed in the discharge of other duties enjoined by our constituents.

"May God preserve you many years," was the ending.

New Orleans was evidently very much interested in what went on in West Florida as the "Louisiana Gazette" reported every bit of Florida news that came within reach of the typecases. Of the first meeting it printed:

"The convention that met at *Buller's Plains*, previous to their entering on any business, each member took and subscribed an oath of allegiance to Ferdinand the seventh, then their budgets were opened, and on examination it was found that the greatest grievence complained of was the want of a judiciary system and a judge.

"The members comprising this general convention were pretty unanimous in their opinion of clinging close to the Spanish government as long as there were any hopes of their success, and in the meantime to apply to the Governor General of Havanna for redress of grievances, particularly to send them a man learned in the law to hold the scales of justice. Should the Governor General send such a man, it would be a proper precaution to establish a salary for him that will place him above corruption.

"A committee of said convention have been named to draft an address to the Governor General of Havanna; the members are John H. Johnson, John Mills, Philip Hicky, John W. Leonard and Joseph Thomas, Esquires, and Dr. Steele, secretary. The convention is to meet in the latter part of this month to examine the address and give it the finishing touch.

"Governor Folch has arrived at Pensacola, from the Havana, and will, it is said, honor the grand convention by his attendance at their next meeting; whether he intends to approbate or disapprobate, is not known; some say, that he is to take 500 men with him by way of escort. F."

This closing sentence could not have been at all reassuring to those responsible for this first move for liberty. Was Governor Folch actually on his way to Baton Rouge? That was a serious question, especially so to the Feliciana ringleaders.

THE GOVERNOR ACCEPTS

Two days after receipt of the address from the convention delegates, Don Carlos de Hault de Lassus dipped his crow quill into the ink horn and in a lengthy communication informed the delegates that he accepted their terms. The original letter in Spanish and an English translation of it by William Herries of "Montesano," are in existence today and from the original English translation the following is transcribed:

"Gentlemen:

"I have received the 28th of this month by the three Gentlemen named by your deputation Messrs. Philip Hicky Manuel Lopez and Joseph Thomas the address that the assembly celebrated with my permission as directed to me under date of 27th Inst. Being informed of its contents I must express to you how much it tranquilizes me and gives me satisfaction to see the unanimity with which the deputies of the People have acted above all manifesting their Patriotism at the commencement of their deliberations with the object of Promoting the security, Honor and fidelity of this Portion of the Dominions of our beloved King Ferdinand the seventh.

"When I was informed of the movements that existed tending to cause a revolt in this faithful settlement I did not for a moment doubt of the general fidelity of those who have not ceased giving Proofs of it since they have pledged themselves by solem oath to the Spanish Flag. And under this persuasion I dispatched immediately Messrs Geo. Mather and Philip Hicky to Bayou Sarah (from which quarter it appeared came all the alarming news) that in conjunction with the Commandant there should be a general Assembly of the Inhabitants For I hoped that once met together it would calm the weak and put an end to the uneasiness occasioned by perfidious insinuations spread by evil Persons envious of our fidelity and good harmony and from this has followed the present assembly which I have permitted without hesitation, as it is well known, because from its results as I comprehend, we will enjoy a permanent tranquility in this Territory exempt from foreign intreagues that have no other view than the ruin of these good Inhabitants.

"I duly appreciate the thanks that you express to me on the present occasion; But not having been guided by any other idea than the fulfilment of the duties of my honourable Office, to preserve in its integrity this portion of the dominions of his Catholic Majesty, which has been committed to my care, in which as far as possible I have corresponded with my duty, which dispositions I flatter myself will tranquilize the People and with the same they will always find me disposed to contribute with you to preserve the tranquility on all and every occasion where I comprehended they are not in the smallest manner opposed to the existing Laws: orders of my Superiors, and contrary to my instructions which I firmly believe are your instructions, and this belief leads me to think that you will only represent to me the grievances some of you in particular or in general ought to have sustained of which I have not been informed to act in justice I have which I have done on all occasions which have come within my knowledge. But one of the principal and most essential points upon which it is urgent that I should be informed as you must all know, is that every good Inhabitant is obliged by his duty to declare and give me full information (as it is ordered by the Proclamations published in this place and other districts under my command) who may be the author or authors of the seditious *paskinades* ["pasquinade"—a lampoon posted in a public place] tending to make the Settlement Revolt [word missing] others who spread in the different Districts the false and malicious expressions that they were in a real state of insurrection going so far as to express they had fallen into the crime of raising the Standard of Independence in order that ["they" crossed out and "I" set above it] may make known this infernal Project the day on which regulating by my order all the Militias of the districts to receive arms to exercise and be employed in the defense of the Country against the machinations of the French and give convenient dispositions according to the increase these informations may take and which I get from Persons employed by Government in places when they can obtain them with certitude and communicate them to me as they have done till this moment with the greatest exactness.

"With respect to the other objects that you announce to me if they appear of a nature that I accede to their execution you must not entertain the smallest doubt of the satisfaction with which I shall condescend to them. But if they are of such importance as to demand a determination superior to my Powers I shall direct them with the greatest promptitude by the regular channel. Being rightfully persuaded that all you announce to me will be undoubtedly conformable to the Laws under which we live so happy and I shall be ready to receive them with the greatest satisfaction the day that you will mention to me and shall listen to your demands as representatives of these faithful subjects, and as co-operators in the preservation of this Territory to its legitimite Sovereign Ferdinand the Seventh with all his rights and privileges.

"The desire that you manifest to me of having me for your Chief in the name of the People and support my dispositions is extremely greatful to me and if my efforts and wishes for the prosperity of these Inhabitants were even susceptable of being augmented there is no doubt but this should be the moment most propitious as I consider myself always happy to merit the goodwill of a People faithful to their King and his wise Laws. I repeat to you my most sincere thanks for the particular attachments that you may manifest to me in making yourself responsible with me to the Superior Authority, but as by the Royal ordinance, the Chief is the only responsible person for his opperations and dispositions, I cannot accept of your offer notwithstanding that I believe I know the good intentions with which you make it as well as regards the generous demonstrations of supporting my salaries at your expense neither which I can accept of being well Satisfied and honored with the pay that I receive from My Royal Master Ferdinand the Seventh.

"But as I do presume that this proposition originates from a Patriotic offer, when I shall be informed of the amount and full explanation I shall communicate it to the superior authority that they may dispose of it either in defraying the expenses of this Government or any other way that may be considered more convenient. The election that has been made of you to establish your representations please me very well being persons that merit according to my oppinion the just good fame to which they are intitled by their constant Zeal for the general good as well as all the other gentlemen elected by the people of the Assembly. I approve that you should meet again on the second Monday of August and that the committee appointed should remain in session to which I shall make any communications that may be necessary

"God preserve you many years

CARLOS DEHAULT DELASSUS.

"Baton Rouge 30th July 1810

"Messers Thomas Lilley, John H. Johnson, John W. Leonard, Philip Hicky, and John Mills. Members of the Committee by the Deputies of the People with the approbation of the Government."

This answer was promptly dispatched, it appears, as three days later John Mills punctiliously acknowledged its receipt.

"St Johns Plains August 3, 1810

To His Excellency Don Carlos Dehault Delassus, Coll. of the Royal Armies, Governor Civil and Military of the place and Jurisdiction of Baton Rouge, &c.

"Sir

"The undersigned Chairman of the Committee of this Convention of the Delegates of the People, has the Honour to inform your Excellency that he has this moment received your reply of the 30th, ultimo, to their address of the 27th, which shall be laid before the whole body of the Delegates immediately upon their next Meeting.

"In the mean time I cannot but express in the name of
the Committee the great satisfaction they derive from your
Excellency's Communication.

"God preserve you many years

John Mills."

The delegates departed to their several homes at the conclusion
of their labors but during the following two weeks the Feliciana men
were not idle. It was necessary to draw up a comprehensive set of
ordinances and resolutions that the delegates could adopt as future
laws for the province. Much paper and ink was used in the confection
of these ordinances, for it was realized that the tentative code drawn up
by Edward Randolph would not answer all the needs.

WILLIAM BARROW—PATRIOT

William Barrow, after his return to his Feliciana plantation "Locust
Grave", on August 5th, wrote a lengthy communication to his friend, Dr.
J. R. Bedford, of Nashville, Tenn. Barrow confessed that notwithstanding the apparent harmony, which he hoped would continue, the delegates were at a loss as to what course they should adopt. He said that
some were for the United States, some for Great Britain, and others
were for a continuation of the Spanish rule under Ferdinand VII. Therefore, for the present, at least, the delegates had determined to continue
the present Spanish laws but that they should be amended, but with
responsible men of the province put into the offices, and that all inhabitants should be treated with equal justice.

Barrow confided to Doctor Bedford that in the midst of this popular
confusion and ignorance his fellow-citizens wished to know what they
"might reasonably expect from the United States." He declared the
delegates "had no desire to cast a stigma on themselves or risk their
best rights and interests." Barrow admitted that he hoped the measures taken "would quiet the minds of the people and give the leaders
opportunity to determine the best method of procedure." As the United
States had "excited them by laying claim to the territory," Barrow
believed the Washington government was in duty bound to advise the
delegates in the present crisis, and to act as was becoming to "a free
and independent nation." Barrow closed his letter by mentioning a
persistent rumor that Spanish soldiers were being sent to Baton Rouge
from Pensacola by Governor Folch to "restore the old order of things,"
and made no secret of the fact that he and his fellows responsible for
starting the convention movement regarded such a possibility with
proper apprehension. The people have definitely selected their del
gates and Barrow declared he believed the inhabitants would support
their delegates if such danger arose.

Doctor Bedford immediately forwarded this communication to President Madison. It was the second letter from Barrow that the Nashville physician had sent to Washington. Early in June Barrow had confided to Bedford of the unrest in Feliciana and the rest of the province and had stated that he firmly believed the people of the district "were absolved from allegiance to the mother country and had a natural right to assume self-government," and that "in time West Florida must become a part of the United States." To facilitate such an ambitious step, Barrow believed, it might be best, pending action by the Washington government, for the liberty-loving Floridians "to form a temporary independent government," and to "include East Florida, if the latter desired to co-operate."

William Barrow was born in Edgecombe county, North Carolina, in 1765, and accompanied his mother, Olivia Ruffin Barrow, to Feliciana in 1798, where he established "Locust Grove" plantation (now "Highland") under a Spanish grant. Before leaving Carolina he had married Pheraby Hilliard, and on his Feliciana plantation his many children were born, they were: Robert Hilliard Barrow (who married Eliza Pirrie), Ann, or Nancy Barrow; William Ruffin Barrow, Bennett Barrow (died in infancy); Martha Hilliard Barrow (who married Daniel Turnbull), Bennett Hilliard Barrow, and Eliza Eleanor Barrow who married a cousin, William Hill Barrow.

William Barrow became one of the solid men of the Feliciana country. He was of a retiring disposition but proved a tower of strength in the deliberations of the convention. To use his own words to Doctor Bedford "his neighbors had been weak enough to choose him as a delegate" but he showed no sign of weakness in championing the ideal that Feliciana and the rest of West Florida must, in time, become a part of the United States.

There were others who believed that the people desired intervention, that the American eagle must hurry to this territory before the British Lion could retake both the Floridas. In an early issue of the Natchez "Weekly Chronicle" a writer, one evidently familiar with all that was going on "below the line", reviewed the situation and, evidently wishing to prod the Washington government into early action, closed his review with these words:

"Idle demagogues and declaimers may endeavor to alarm the fears of the people and may threaten them with French vengeance, but if the deputies are faithful to Florida, adhere to principle, and pursue a wise and just policy, they will acquire for themselves immortal honor, and secure a free and equitable government to their posterity.

"As far as we have seen an expression of public sentiment, there is not one American heart that does not beat in unison with the people of Florida; and the prayers of seven millions of freemen are daily offered up to this fountain of all good for the civil and political freedom and universal prosperity of our enlightened neighbors. The people of the United States and of Florida have the same object in view, the same end to accomplish. They are all nations of this soil and they must preserve it inviolate. Never must they permit this hallowed haunt of liberty to be polluted by the followers of the Corsican.

"Let the Florida Convention cast a retrospective eye over the miseries of Spain, and remember that these evils have been brought about her by the intrigues of the French, and that torrents of blood, similar to those which have flowed in the mother country, will deluge their happy land the moment they are led astray by the siren songs of Toryism. Let the American Congress and the Florida Convention perfectly understand each other, unite in measures of defense, and plant on the shores of the Atlantic and the Gulf of Mexico, a barrier that will secure us forever against the corrupting influence of French politics. By this means they will not only preserve liberty to themselves, but will transmit it unimpared to their latest posterity."

Governor Holmes of the Mississippi Territory, instructed by Washington to keep an eye on what was going on in West Florida, advised President Madison of the actions of the convention delegates and inclosed in his letter this clipping from the Natchez newspaper. Holmes wrote that it was evident to him that the people of the district desired to join the United States but that "they feared to make known such a desire or to take the necessary step until they knew the attitude of President· Madison," that Governor de Lassus "had only sanctioned something he could not prevent," and ventured to suggest that West Florida could be obtained without any material expense or "even the loss of a single life."

But President Jimmy Madison answered never a word. He and Governor Claiborne continued their discussions of the situation at Washington, but, even though Governor Holmes of Mississippi, and Acting-Governor Thomas Bolling Robinson of Orleans Territory at New Orleans, obeyed his instructions to keep a "wakeful eye" on Baton Rouge, the president sent into the disturbed area secret messengers who fraternalized with the delegates and the people in general. Although he said nothing, Madison was thoroughly alive to what was transpiring.

THE CONVENTION'S SECOND MEETING

When the delegates of the people reassembled in convention, one of the Feliciana delegation was absent. Illness, a fever, kept John H. Johnson confined to "Troy" plantation. Merely as a spectator, Colonel Joshua G. Baker, an officer of the Mississippi Territorial militia, was sent to St. John's Plains as the personal observer of Governor Holmes. His duty was to ascertain the real views of the delegates and those they represented.

On the eve of this second gathering, Monday, August 13, a number of the prominent planters sent an address to their Feliciana representatives so that they might know of the sort of backing they had at home. Addressed to "The members of the Representative Convention assembled at St. John's Plains", it read:

> "The inhabitants of St. Francisville to their representatives assembled at St. Johns Plains, respectfully represent:
> "That we repose every confidence in the laudable desires, patriotic exertions, and *firmness* of our representatives to bring about such a change in the political affairs of our Country—and such a change in men and measures—as will be best adapted to the real interests & happiness of the County—and such as will crown our present exertions, to that effect, with *honor*.
>
> "We desire to express to you, that, being the immediate *representatives of the people* chosen to redress their grievences and to establish a means whereby impartial Justice may be given to all men—and chosen at a time when the political state of the Mother Country renders it necessary that we should act for our selves—we consider you empowered (in the best and only possible manner at present) to act independent of any other authority whatever if that authority refuses to adopt or sanction such measures as you may conceive necessary for our future *welfare* and *respectability*. And we pledge ourselves to support you in whatsoever you may do that shall have a tendency to promote the desirable objects of your delegation.

"August 13th. 1810

"John F. Gillespie	Sam'l S. Crocker
Martin L. Haynie	D. B. Stuart
F. A. Browder	H. Peisee
John P. Conilz	L. A. Smith
Amos Webb	Jos. E. Johnson
James H. Ficklin	James Gray
B. Collins	Isaac A. Smith
James Gentry	William Lyon
William Field	John Browder"

Before arriving at the convention meeting place, Colonel Baker, pausing at Saint Francisville, visited John H. Johnson at "Troy." He told the sick man of his mission and discussed the affairs then agitating the province. After the governor's emissary had left, Johnson, naturally interpreting the visit as displaying the interest of the American government in what was transpiring, wrote Governor Holmes thanking him for his interest and was frank in giving the Mississippi executive his opinion of existing affairs.

"Corrupt and villanious Court sycophants," wrote Johnson, "are enabled to batten on the spoils of the land because so large a portion of the population consisted of American refugees and ignorant time-servers." It was because of these class, went on Johnson, that it was necessary for the delegates to pursue their present "devious methods." The Feliciana planter admitted that the population needed to be placed "under the conduct of a wise guardian who will transform them from slaves to men!"

He was vehement in his assertion that the people of West Florida beheld such a guardian in the United States, their mother country, but at the same time asserted that "two-thirds of the people regarded her tardiness and neglect as worthy only a stepmother." He admitted that those composing the convention's delegates feared Spanish vengeance should they openly break with de Lassus. Therefore, he asked, if in the event of a break "would the United States receive them into her bosom"

"If it is necessary for the convention to formally declare the province independent of Spain and call upon the United States for protection, will it not be proper to insert therein two or three stipulations of consequence to us but not interesting to the United States?" Johnson asked. He declared that these conditions could not be considered "after annexation" but in all other matters the people would "cheerfully submit in all things to the federal constitution." He then went on to explain that "these stipulations" were that British land titles should be disregarded when the same holding was covered by a Spanish title, that actual settlers should be entitled to as much land as the Spanish government had habitually granted, and, with certain exceptions, however, that a general amnesty should be granted all Tories, deserters, and fugitives from American justice. Johnson's proviso regarding the land titles had to do with the fact that some of the original British settlers had abandoned their land after Galvez had won West Florida for Spain, which were later occupied by settlers under Spanish grants, and many feared that original British settlers might endeavor to reobtain them.

The second meeting of the convention delegates lasted only three days and little was accomplished, for it was quite evident that certain of the delegates were merely marking time. One of the tentative measures discussed was the arming of the entire militia, which was then to act under the orders of the convention. When objection was raised to this, the governor was assured that such a measure would prove less important than another ordinance for "the public security and good administration of Justice within the jurisdiction" which they proposed to put in force at the next meeting. The outright request was made that de Lassus approve this particular ordinance without referring the matter to his superior authorities at Pensacola or Havana, as it was the only measure that could save the province "from anarchy and tumult."

Although in their address the delegates told the governor that they believed he would sanction the move, privately they expected no such thing. One of the members is quoted by Cox as writing Acting-Governor Robinson at New Orleans, that: "De Lassus will probably accede to nothing without consulting higher authority, and his refusal might be attended with serious consequences." It was also pointed out "that the majority of office-holders were English in sympathy, and that this constituted the principal obstacle to independence. If the United States did not countenance their efforts, they would send a messenger to England to propose an alliance with that government."

Manuel Lopez, when the members of the convention began to suggest matters other than the preservation of the rights of the King of Spain or the repairs to the fort at Baton Rouge, got up in a huff, left the meeting, and returned to Baton Rouge to warn de Lassus of "the real intentions of the delegates." The governor, who relied on Lopez to translate for him everything that was done by the delegates, prevailed on the Spaniard to return. Realizing then that the governor was becoming suspicious, Philip Hicky and George Mather went to the fort and urged de Lassus to accept the measures of the convention, maintaining that the proposals being adopted were neither disloyal nor unreasonable. They advised he should pay no attention to the many anonymous papers, which they admitted were revolutionary in character, being circulated, nor should he pay any heed to what was printed in the New Orleans and Natchez newsprints. They pointed out to the sadly befuddled executive that the calling of the convention had been the work of the more respectable elements of the population.

Realizing that they could not finish the writing of all the new regulations and ordinances at the second sitting, the delegates adjourned to meet again in August 22. Before departing for their homes they addressed their "demand" communication to de Lassus. Signed by every member of the convention, it read:

> "St. John's Plains, August 15, 1810
> "The Representatives of the people of this jurisdiction in convention assembled have received the communication, which your Excellency was pleased to make to their committee of the date of the 30th ultimo, and have given due consideration to its contents. In obedience to the injunctions of our constituents who are prepared to rally round the standard of their country and provide some efficient remedy for the evils which endanger its existence and prosperity, we have directed our attention to some of the existing grievances which require to be remedied without delay, and after mature deliberation, we have reduced them

to the number and form exhibited in the statement enclosed herewith.

"The plan proposed to be adopted for redress will also be submitted for your consideration by our Committee appointed for that purpose consisting of Messrs John W. Leonard, Manuel Lopez, William Spiller and Joseph Thomas, so soon as a faithful translation thereof can be obtained that your Excellency having all the subjects of deliberations before you in the same order as they have presented themselves to us may discern their connexion, and give to each the consideration which its importance may seem to deserve. We have thought it our duty to lay before you all our proceedings in this manner, that you may have sufficient time for deliberation on subjects so essential to the publick wellfare before making any final decision thereon, and on Wednesday next the 22nd inst we will do ourselves the honor to wait on your Excellency in a body to know your determination.

"You will observe that it is the wish of the Convention with your concurence to establish the *Bill providing for the better administration of Justice within the Jurisdiction of Baton Rouge in West-Florida,* as an Ordinance to have the force and authority of law from the time of our next meeting; and we trust that you will not withold your concurrence from a measure evidently calculated to preserve the peace and promote the prosperity of the province. The initial situation of the country pointed out to the Representatives the necessity of prompt and efficient measures and urges them to solicit your Excellency for a speedy approbation. The danger of delay must be apparent to your discerning mind, hence the necessity for a decision here without reference to higher authority.

"The desire ever manifested by His Majesty's Government for meeting the will of the people is a pledge to you of his approbation of your conduct in relation to our proceedings and the assurance previously given by this Convention of sharing with you all responsibility is again pledged in the most solem manner in case of your co-operation in the only measure which appears to us calculated to save our country from the dreadful scenes of anarchy and tumult.

"We cannot close this address without recommending strongly to your Excellency as a measure of necessary precaution, to arm the whole body of the Militia, to defend our country against its enemies as we are authorized to assure you that no sentiment prevails amongst the inhabitants hostile to the wise laws and government under which they have lived so happily."

TWENTY-ONE GUN SALUTES

Governor de Lassus' lot was not a happy one during these dog days of 1810.

His officers, those constituting the garrison of regular Spanish troops, objected to their chief's course in recognizing or dealing with

67

the members of the so-called peoples' convention. They saw nothing but armed revolt and urged their commander to cease all contact with the delegates. Some of these sessions with the governor were stormy ones but the unhappy executive put a pudgy hand over each ear when the protestations of the Dons wearing the uniform of Spain became too vociferous.

On Sunday night, August 19, de Lassus was host at a dinner he gave in honor of the members of the convention. The banquet was held in the Government House or "Governor's House," which had been erected by Carlos de Grande-Pré, its site was what is now the "corner of Repentence and Convention streets." The governor, in his anxiety to do all honor to the conventionalists, invited other citizens of the province and village to attend, but scenting possible complications, if not actual danger, only a few not directly interested gathered about the festive board.

The governor's entire staff, arrayed in their gaudy uniforms and glittering orders, was in attendance, though with sour faces. They included Don Gilberto de Leonardo, the treasurer; Captain Celestino de Saint-Maxent (he was a brother of Félicité, wife of Don Bernardo de Galvez) second in command; Captain Raphael Croker, the governor's secretary; sub-Lieutenant Louis de Grand-Pré; Lieutenant Juan Metzinger, and Lieutenant Francisco Morejon, and some others. The feast was punctuated by many toasts to His Catholic Majesty Ferdinand VII, hopes were expressed for his speedy restoration to the throne of Spain, and before the feasters staggered to their beds, a salute of twenty-one guns was fired from the guns of the fort—in spite of the plea of the magazine guard, Eulogio de las Casas, that his supply of powder was low and might be needed for other purposes!

Several days later the delegates returned the governor's gesture by a banquet spread at the home of M. Folquier, some distance from Baton Rouge, where, in addition to the customary salute to His Catholic Majesty of Spain, a rousing toast was also drunk to the president of the United States. In addition to these formal feasts, de Lassus gave frequent small dinners, entertaining guests from Feliciana, and usually among those at the governor's board was Philemon Thomas, commander of the militia of the province.

While all was serene on the surface, all was not quiet in the governor's household—his officers were in a near state of mutiny. As a result stormy sessions became the order of the day in the fort. Lieutenant Juan B. A. Metzinger, commandant of artillery, and the magazine guard, Las Cassas, told the governor to his face that they would attend no more peace dinners, and further more, as the store of powder at the fort was being so rapidly eaten away by the firing of twenty-one gun salutes in honor of the delegates, and every time an American gunboat sailed up or down the Mississippi, that they would fire no more! In a rage, de Lassus said they would either fire the cannon, as he directed, or they could consider themselves under arrest for disobeying orders! The harrassed governor, at one rough session with his protesting officers, declared "If I do not rule to suit you, take my baston and govern!"

THE SEDITIOUS BROADSIDE

While the Spaniards were fuming, fretting and fussing with their hard-headed superior, the delegates were whipping their ordinances into shape, as they were many and varied in character they needed lots of writing and much revision. While they were thus preparing the new laws which de Lassus must approve, alarming news was brought into Baton Rouge by one of Captain Tomaso Estevan's soldiers. The commander at Bayou Sarah wrote that John Murdock, so friendly to him and the Spanish regime, had discovered, affixed to a tree in the Saint Francis village, a proclamation most revolutionary in character. Murdock had reported this to a guard but when the soldier reached the tree, the offending broadside had been removed. However, the curate, Francisco Lennán, secured a copy from a parishioner and so Captain Estevan was able to send it on to de Lassus as proof a revolt was being planned.

Estevan also advised that he was in a critical situation and begged the governor to send him a boat so that he and his soldiers "could flee Bayou Sarah" and seek the safety of the Baton Rouge fort. Estevan said he was willing to sacrifice himself but did not want his loyal soldiers to "become victims of public vengeance."

The proclamation that terrorized the Bayou Sarah commander was signed: "A Friend of the People." Its opening sentence said that any man who would destroy the proclamation "deserved to live forever under a despotic government," and the author went on to urge the people of West Florida to "declare themselves independent, just as the people of Spanish America were doing." The anonymous writer drew contrasts between the administration of justice in West Florida and in the United States, which were unfavorable to the Spanish brand. He cited cases of forcible imprisonment from which release could be secured only by bribery. He made sarcastic reference to King Ferdinand VII, "then absent on a visit to his friend "Bonaparte!" He intimated that Floridians should throw off allegiance to him and seek a union with the neighboring American territory, and as the inhabitants had already taken one step towards self-government "NOW was the time to take another." Having elected men recognized as of firm character, just principles, and republican spirit, the people should now further their efforts to the uttermost. "Spanish oppression is no more." The people could now freely communicate with each other and adopt a form of government that would afford them not only protection but liberty. The people were advised to form little parties among their friends and send to their representatives a report of their action, then the members of the convention would know that the people were ready to sustain them in any step towards independence they might elect to make. As the delegates had already heard from those who wished to continue the Spanish system, they should now "be given the views of the friends of liberty and justice." It was promised that all such communications would be kept secret so that their authors need fear no betrayal.

Although the writer of the broadside asserted he "was known to many of his fellow-citizens," he witheld his name purposely. He declared that he, along with others, had long suffered the evils flowing from Spanish despotism, but now, so he informed all who would read, that the party in favor of independence was growing, and that "their brothers of the United States would fervently rejoice in their return to liberty and a system of pure republicanism." He entreated them to repose confidence in their delegates and sustain their actions and thereby avoid the necessity of calling another convention before they were ready to choose an independent legislative body.

As if this was not enough to scare de Lassus and his military officers, on top of the news of the ciruclation this broadside in Feliciana came a secret missive from Shepherd Brown. In it the commandant of the Ste. Helena district confided that he "now distrusted even the delegates he had picked to represent the Ste. Helena and Chifoncté districts in the convention." Also that his people were so aroused over a report that the former Spanish commandant Lieutenant Fráncisco de Hevia was about to leave Pensacola and assume charge of the Tickfaw region that they were about to rebel. Shepherd Brown was also distrustful of his militia officers since they learned of the attitude of the Feliciana people. However, in spite of all this Alcalde Brown "believed" the greater portion of his people would prove loyal should a recourse to arms be the outcome.

Came another missive from the frightened Estevan at Bayou Sarah, carried to the fort by a soldier on a blown and lathered horse. The members of the convention from Feliciana were carrying on what he termed a referendum among the people and this amounted, so the Spanish commander declared, to a "lifting of the mask," for Isaac Johnson had ordered his troop of horsemen to be ready at any hour for a sudden descent upon Baton Rouge. Estevan again declared his life to be in danger and warned the governor that in all probability he would have to take refuge on the American side of the river, consequently de Lassus need not be surprised if the next communication from him would be written at Pointe Coupée!

70

THE SPANISH JUNTA

On Tuesday, August 21, the bewildered governor called a *junta* to meet at the government house to consider the critical situation. The conventionalists were to meet the following day to put the finishing touches on their series of ordinances that in future would govern the province. All of his officers attended the *junta* in a body and each was as concerned as was the governor.

Attending were Don Gilberto de Leonard, the comptroller and treasurer, whose son John was a member of the convention and who, so some of the Spanish officers charged, had gone over to those plotting against the government; Captain Celestino de Saint Maxent, second in command; Captain Raphael Croker, the governor's secretary; Lieutenant Francisco Morejon, Sub-tentente Don Louis Anton de Grand-Pré, Lieutenant Juan Baptiste Antionette Metzinger, in charge of artillery; Sub-lieutenant Antonio Balderas, Lieutenant Manuel Castanos, Don Eulogio de las Casas, the *guarda almacen;* Don Juan Perez, *cabo de sala;* Cadets Don Felipe de Grand-Pré and Don Estevan de Grand-Pré, brothers of Louis and sons of the former governor of Baton Rouge; Don José Maria de la Pena, Don Domingo Ullio, *patron de Falua;* Don Pedro Gondeau, the *cirujano* or surgeon; and Don Santiago Rault, the surgeon of the Feliciana district, who had left Tomas Estevan alone to face the "infuriated Gringos of Feliciana." There were other officers and Dons gathered fearfully in the government house, which was outside the fort, awaiting his excellency's word.

The governor began by explaining why he was agreeing with the requests and demands of the convention delegates, claiming he had adopted such a course to "avoid any calumniating attacks" on his character. He pointed out to his inferiors that he was without proper resources to resist and had endeavored to avoid insults to the flag of Spain. He had warned his superiors at Pensacola and Havana what might happen because he knew he could not depend upon the militia of the province and therefore needed veteran troops at his back. He claimed he had reported the fort in need of repair and the lack of powder but had received neither reenforcements nor a reply to his many letters asking for help. Time was needed for assistance to arrive from Havana.

He reminded his officers that the convention delegates had at least professed loyalty to the Spanish king, and if he did not accept their declarations on face value he would only expose the flag of Spain to greater insults and his officers, soldiers, and himself to violence. These "disturbers of the peace, joined by vicious roving vagabonds," would lay siege to the fort at the first sign of opposition from him and "visit their rage on the peaceful inhabitants." At each salute the artillery in the fort approached uselessness.

Therefore, he told the *junta*, he believed he was acting correctly in appearing to accept the program of the convention and thereby save the province from the horrors of civil strife. As long as he and his officers thought they could safely do so, they should pretend to embrace the provisions of the new ordinances with the exception of accepting the salaries offered, and maintain the situation as it existed "as long as the delegates maintained an appearance of loyalty" and seemed "to be working to preserve the province for Ferdinand VII." On the first indication of a contrary purpose, the governor proposed that he, officers, and soldiers would repair to fort and "defend themselves to the last extremity!"

For two hours discussion raged in the government house. The governor's course did not gain an unqualified approval from his subordinates. Lieutenant Louis de Grand-Pré expressed himself freely, declared if the governor would take the proper steps he still could quell the uprising, and Don Louis offered to lead the troops that would arrest the ringleaders. In this he was backed by Lieutenant Metzinger. But theirs were the only dissenting voices. The others agreed that the crafty action de Lassus counseled was the course of wisdom.

The next day, August 22nd, the delegates met and with only one dissenting vote passed the ordinances and resolutions they had been confecting for weeks. This remarkable document, which consisted of 32 pages, was set up and printed at Natchez, but today only one copy of it appears to be in existence, the one owned by Richmond Favrot of New Orleans.

When Don Carlos de Hault de Lassus attached his name, with its flowing paraph below it, to the ordinances the planters of Feliciana, had won their first step for liberty.

Wrote a correspondent of the "Louisiana Gazette" to that New Orleans newspaper:

"Baton Rouge, August 23.

"I am at this place, where I came to be present at the presentation of our new form of government to Governor Lassus, who yesterday accepted in *toto*. The convention are now sitting with closed doors, making the appointments necessary to carry the new government into effect. The whole proceedings are in the press, and in a few days will be made public—they are such as will tend to the peace, happiness and prosperity of the country.'"

The same day he signed on the dotted line, the governor and the delegates, issued a proclamation to the public. It read:

PROCLAMATION

TO THE INHABITANTS OF THE JURISDICTION OF BATON-ROUGE.

His Excellency Carlos Dehault Delassus, Colonel of the Royal Armies, and Governor Civil and Military of the Place and Jurisdiction of Baton-Rouge, with the Representatives of the people of the said Jurisdiction, in Convention assembled, announce.

THAT the measures proposed to be adopted for the public safety, and for the better administration of justice within the said jurisdiction, are sanctioned and established as ordinances, to have the force and authority of law, within the several districts of this jurisdiction, until the same shall be submitted to the captain-general of the island of Cuba, and until his *decision thereon* shall be known. The said ordinances will be made known in each district, with all possible dispatch, and in the mean time all the good people of this jurisdiction are required to preserve good order, and avoid every movement which may disturb the public tranquility;—It being the only object with both the governor and the representatives, to consult the best interests of the inhabitants. And although it is not intended to mark with severity the authors of the disorder, which has appeared in several parts of the country for some time past, yet all such persons as may be found offending in that manner, after this date, will be punished with the severity which the law prescribes, and which their offences may deserve.

WM. SPILLER,	PHILIP HICKY,
JOHN MILLS,	MANUEL LOPEZ,
JOS. THOMAS,	THOS. LILLEY,
JOHN W. LEONARD,	WM. BARROW,
BENJ. O. WILLIAMS,	EDMD. HAWES.

JNO. RHEA,

CARLOS DEHAULT DELASSUS.

Baton-Rouge, August, 22, 1810.

In addition to the joint proclamation in which they joined their names with that of Governor de Lassus, the members of the Convention believed that the inhabitants of the entire jurisdiction should become acquainted with what they had done and to that end prepared an address August 25, in which they explained what they had done to correct the abuses the people in West Florida had long borne. It read:

"The Convention of your Representatives having assembled agreeable to your commands to wait upon the Governor, and in concert with him to devise some plan for the ridup of existing grievances, and for the safety and defense of the country, think it their duty to state to you the motives by which they have been governed in the discharge of the important trust which was committed to them; that you may form a correct judgment of the regard which they have had for your interests in all their deliberations.

"Being called unexpectedly to act for you in a time of general anxiety, when it was impossible to have a perfect knowledge of your wishes, and without experience in matters appertaining to the discharge of the duties imposed upon us with much diffidence and embarrassment. But all having the same object in view, to preserve the tranquility and secure the prosperity of a country in which we had everything dear to ourselves at stake, we have proceeded with the consoling reflection, that however we might err in the choice of the means for attaining this object, we cannot be suspected of having willfully betrayed or abandoned the interests of our constituents. In this persuasion we have applied ourselves without hesitation according to the best of our judgment to enumerate the most obvious grievances which affect the inhabitans generally, and to provide such remedy for the same as the present exigencies of the country seemed to require, exercising for this purpose the legislative power to a certain extent, without making any unnecessary innovation in the existing laws, or established principles of Government.

"We have thought it necessary in this way to provide for the settlement of the country by persons of reputable character, who may choose to establish themselves here that Physical force of the country may be increased by the advantages which it will offer to the peaceable and industrious of every description, who bringing and acquiring property in the country will become interested in its defense and prosperity.

"We have provided for the organization of the Militia as the only efficient force on which to depend for safety in a way which will enable them to act with promptitude in case of an emergency either to repel invasion or surpass domestic insurrection, a measure of obvious utility, and which our defenseless situation imperiously demands.

"We have provided for the better administration of Justice, by establishing one Superior Tribunal having final jurisdiction for this Department of the Government and one inferior Court in each District, reserving to ourselves the right of nominating the associate judges of the Superior and the Presiding Judges of the inferior tribunals, and securing to the people of each District the right of choosing the magistrates who are to act as associate judges of the inferior courts—by this arrangement it is hoped that the confidence of the people will be secured while the laws are administered by officers of their choice, the unprincipled will be deterred from the commission of crimes by examples of the speedy and condign punishment of the offenders—and an opportunity will be given to all classes, the poor as well as the rich, of prosecuting with effect their just claims, and of obtaining redress for injuries without unnecessary expense or delay.

"Believing it to have been the intention of our Sovereign to grant lands to the industrious cultivators of the soil, who make improvements thereon and support themselves and their families by their industry, we have provided as far as was in our power that no inhabitant of that description should be deprived of his just claim by any intrigues of wealthy speculators or of the improper conduct of officers entrusted with the distribution of the lands of the Royal Domain, and we have thought it our duty as the guardians of the public interest to suspend for the present the power of granting or alienating the lands of the Crown that no actual settler may be injured by grants made after this date, and that no advantage may be taken of the present unfortunate state of Jurisdiction to sell the lands of the Royal Domain for the purpose of enriching a few unprincipled strangers to the prejudice of the public at large.

"And believing it to be our duty to provide some revenue for the support of this Department of the Government, as the depressed state of the mother country prevents us from receiving the customary supplies of money for this purpose, and it would be ungrateful in us not to make some exertion at this moment to lessen her burthens, while she is contending for her existence against enemies so numerour and formidable. Every consideration of duty and interest appeared to dictate this as a measure indispensably necessary, and no other method seemed so just and equitable as that of laying a tax to operate equally on the owners of property in the country, allowing some advantage to the inhabitant who contributes his services for the common defense over the non-resident whose property is protected without any exertion or expense to himself. As this subject could not be reduced to a regular system without much deliberation, the Convention have called themselves at present with laying a tax on real property and slaves which will operate lightly on the largest portion of the inhabitants, the industrious cultivators, who are their country's shield in the day of danger, while the wealthy slave-holder and speculator in lands may afford to pay for the security afforded to their property, and for its increase in value.

"The Governor having concurred with the Convention in establishing the ordinance proposed for the purposes before stated to have the authority of law within this jurisdiction until the decision of the Captain General thereon be made known. The same will be published for the information of all concerned—and the Convention have only to add that they await the expression of the public will to decide how they have acted according to the wishes of their constituents. They wish to be informed whether their conduct be satisfactory to the people, that at some future meeting they may have an opportunity of correcting

75

any of the measures which might be injurious before any
serious evils result from them."

This expression and forerunner of what had been accomplished
made public, the delegates sent the fruits of their labors, the Ordinances, to John W. Winn at Natchez, to be set in type and distributed in
pamphlet form. Seemingly, these ordinances covered every phase of
the series of contentions that had wracked the province for the past
several years, truly an ambitious plan concocted by ambitious men.

To thoroughly understand what these men planned for the people
they represented, the whole series of articles should be read . . . many
as they were . . . as promulgated. Copied from the only known record,
they are:

AN ORDINANCE

*Providing for the Publick Safety, and for the Better Administration of
Justice within the Jurisdiction of Baton-Rouge, in West-Florida.*

Whereas the Good People of this Jurisdiction, ever faithful to
their Legitimate Sovereign, and willing at this eventful period to contribute whatever may be in their power, to maintain the integrity, hon-
or and independence of the Spanish Nation, have a right to enjoy the
privileges of Loyal Subjects, and to exercise the powers which may
be necessary for their preservation:

And whereas, from causes which could not have been foreseen or
avoided, their situation has become extremely perilous, at a time when
they cannot look with confidence to the mother country for protection,
and when internal regulations and powers of the Government are too
imperfect to be relied on, either for preserving domestic tranquility, or
for employing the strength and resources of the country in its defence:

And whereas, the evils and dangers originating from the causes before mentioned, are of such a nature as to make it necessary that the
most prompt and efficient measures be adopted for the preservation of
the province, it becomes lawful and expedient for the people, in conjunction with the chief magistrate of the jurisdiction, to establish such
ordinances as the present exigencies require.

We, therefore, the Representatives of the people of this jurisdiction, in convention assembled, recognizing his Excellency Charles Dehault Delassus, as Governor thereof, and acting with his concurrence,
with a view to preserve and defend this portion of the dominions of
our beloved King, Ferdinand the seventh, and holding ourselves responsible to all superior authorities, deriving their powers from him,
for the rectitude of our intentions and acts, declare ourselves for the
time being, the guardians both of the publick interests, and of the rights
of the individual members of the community, for the whole benefit we
establish this ordinance.

ARTICLE I.

Whereas, it is necessary for the publick safety, that permission be
given to strangers of reputable character to become residents, and en-

joy equal privileges with us, who may thereafter become interested in maintaining order and obedience to the laws.

Section 1. *Be it therefore ordained by the Representatives of the people of the Jurisdiction of Baton Rouge in convention assembled, with the concurrence of the governor thereof, and it is hereby ordained, by the authority of the same,* That from and after the establishment of this ordinance, it shall be lawful for the commandants of the several districts of this jurisdiction, to grant permission to all free persons of good character and peaceable conduct, emigrating from any foreign country whatever, in amity with us, and wishing to establish themselves in any lawful trade or occupation within this jurisdiction, and also professing their willingness to support the laws and government thereof. And all such residents having demeaned themselves in a peaceable and orderly manner, and contributed their due proportion for the support of the Government and defence of the country for two years, shall enjoy thereafter, the same privileges and rights with the present inhabitants.

Section 2. *And be it further ordained,* That with such permission of residence, the said commandants shall also grant permission to all such emigrants as aforesaid, to import and bring into the district, all slaves and other moveable property belonging to them, or which they may have in charge, to be employed or disposed of lawfully, in any manner which to them may seem fit and expedient; the owners or importers of such slaves, or moveable property paying such duties therefor, as may be prescribed by law, or hereinafter ordained.

Section 3. *And be it further ordained,* That it shall be the duty of all such emigrants as aforesaid, within fifteen days after their arrival within any district of this jurisdiction, to report themselves to the commandant thereof, and exhibit to him an accurate statement of the number appertaining to their respective families, or whom they may have in charge, both of free persons and slaves, and to pay for such slaves the lawful duties to the said officer, together with his lawful fees, for granting permission of residence; on failure whereof, the party so offending shall be subject to a fine of twenty dollars, and every slave imported, for whom the duties shall not have been paid as aforesaid, or secured to be paid within six months thereof, shall be confiscated and sold for the benefit of the district.

Section 4. *And be it further ordained,* That no deserter from the armies or navy of any nation in amity with us, or fugitive from justice, or any person bound to service in any foreign state as aforesaid, shall obtain permission of residence within this jurisdiction, or derive any benefit from such permission, if obtained by fraud or in contravention of this ordinance; but any person of that description who may hereafter take refuge within this jurisdiction, or on satisfactory proof thereof being made to the governor or commandant of a district, shall be delivered by either of said officers, to an officer of such foreign state, as shall be duly authorized to demand the same.

ARTICLE II.

For the Organization of the Militia.

Section 1. *And be it further ordained,* That the governor of this jurisdiction shall be the commander in chief of all the militia thereof, and shall commission all officers therein, and have authority to call the whole or any part thereof into actual service, at any time when it may be necessary for the publick safety.

Section 2. *And be it further ordained*, That the militia of this jurisdiction shall be divided into four regiments, which shall be composed of all the free white men above the age of sixteen and under fifty years, civil magistrates, ministers of religion, doctors of physic, millers, keepers of publick ferries, and invalids excepted, who shall be enrolled in the manner herein after prescribed. Those within the district of Baton Rouge shall compose one regiment; those of the district of New Feliciana, one regiment; those of the district of St. Helena, one regiment; and those of the district east of Ponchitoola, including Chiffonta, Bogcheto and Pearl river settlements, to be called the district of St. Ferdinand, one regiment.

Section 3. *And be it further ordained*, That one colonel commandant shall be appointed by this convention, and commissioned by the governor, who shall command the said regiments when formed into one brigade, and there shall be appointed and commissioned in like manner, one colonel and two majors for each regiment.

Section 4. *And be it further ordained*, That there shall be appointed by the colonel commandant, and commissioned by the governor, one brigade inspector, with the rank of major, who shall be aid to the colonel commandant, and under his direction shall appoint a regimental muster in each district, in the month of November, and a muster of each battalion in the month of April annually, at which muster it shall be the duty of all the officers and men belonging to the said regiments and battalions respectively, to attend, armed and equipped in the manner herein after prescribed, and they shall be subject to the orders of the commanding officer of the day, at each of the said musters, during the time of parade.

Section 5. *And be it further ordained*, That it shall be the duty of the colonel commandant to attend personally, together with the brigade major, at each of the said regimental musters, to inspect the discipline and equipment of the troops, and give such orders as he may think proper, to the colonel of the regiment, respecting the manoeuvers of the day.

Section 6. *And be it further ordained*, That the brigade inspector shall attend each battalion muster, and inspect the arms and accoutrements of the troops: He shall moreover receive from the colonels their regimental returns, and transmit a copy thereof to the colonel commandant, who shall cause the same to be laid before the governor.

Section 7. *And be it further ordained*, That it shall be the duty of each colonel, immediately after the receipt of his commission, to nominate the officers of his regimental staff, viz: one adjutant, one surgeon and surgeon's mate, one pay master and one quarter-master, making a return thereof to the governor, who shall commission the said officers accordingly.

Section 8. *And be it further ordained*, That each colonel, together with the two majors of the same regiment, with himself, assembled by him for that purpose, immediately after they shall have been commissioned, shall divide the bounds of the regiment into two battalion districts, as equal in population as may be, assigning one major to each battalion.

Section 9. *And be it further ordained*, That it shall be the duty of each major, under the direction of the colonel, to proceed without delay to lay off the bounds of the several companies within his battalion district, and to advertise the times and places of holding elections for one captain, one first lieutenant and one second lieutenant within the bounds of said company, at not less than three of the most publick places in said bounds, and at least ten days previous to the times, appointed for the said elections.

Section 10. *And be it further ordained*, That each major shall be judge of the elections aforesaid, within his battalion district, and shall report the persons having the greatest number of votes for each of the said offices, to the colonel of the regiment, who shall transmit the same to the governor, whereupon commissions shall be issued by him for the said offices, without delay.

Section 11. *And be it further ordained*, That the field officers of regiments shall have power from time to time to lay off new companies, and divide or alter the bounds of such as may have been established, when they may think proper, causing elections to be held for officers where necessary, in the manner herein before stated.

Section 12. *And be it further ordained*, That it shall be the duty of each captain immediately after the receipt of his commission to appoint any number of sergeants and corporals, not exceeding four, one drummer and one fifer within the bounds of his company, who shall serve for one year, and until others shall be appointed; and to enroll every free able bodied white man within the bounds of his company, between the ages of sixteen and fifty years: He shall also continue from time to time to enroll all such as may remove into the bounds of his company, or attain the age of sixteen years, within the same, who are not exempted from performing militia duty by the ordinance: In all doubtful cases whether with respect to nonage, overage or infirmity, of any person claiming such exemption, the captain shall refer the question to be decided by the next court martial of the battalion, to be held as hereinafter provided.

Section 13. *And be it further ordained*, That each captain shall muster his company once in every month, of every year in which there shall not be a regimental or battalion muster, and shall exercise them under arms at least two hours on each muster day: He shall also note all delinquents, either from nonattendance on muster days, or for appearing without the arms and accoutrements prescribed by this ordinance, and make report thereof to the next court martial; and he shall make an accurate return of the strength arms and accoutrements of his company to the adjutant of the regiment, before the first day of September in every year: At every muster he shall give publick notice of the time and place of holding the next succeeding muster, which shall be deemed sufficient notice for the absentees, as well as those who may be present.

Section 14. *And be it further ordained*, That it shall be the duty of the adjutant of each regiment, with the aid of the sergeant major thereof, to execute the orders of the colonel of commandant of the regiment. The sergeant major shall be appointed by the colonel, he shall obey the orders of the adjutant, and keep a royster of the sergeants of the regiment to which he belongs. It shall be the duty of the adjutant to keep a royster of all the commissioned officers of the regiment, to receive from the captains their company returns, and make therefrom an accurate regimental return, to deliver the same to the commandant of the regiment, on the first day of October in every year.

Section 15. *And be it further ordained*, That one drum major and one fife major for each regiment, shall be appointed by the commandant thereof, whose duty it shall be to conduct the music of the regiment, and previous to each regimental and battalion musters the commandants shall cause to be assembled at such places and times as they may appoint, all commissioned officers and musicians of their respective regiments, for the purpose of training the commissioned officers under the direction of the adjutant of the regiment and the musicians under the direction of the drum and fife majors.

Section 16. *And be it further ordained*, That at every regimental, battalion and company muster, the commanding officer shall have the power to punish all contempts and irregularities, either in the troops or by standards, with a fine not exceeding ten dollars for each offence, or imprisonment under guard during the time of parade, at his discretion.

Section 17. *And be it further ordained*, That commandants of regiments for the regular annual musters shall have at least forty-five days notice of a regimental or battalion muster, adjutants forty days, majors thirty-five days, captains thirty days, non-commissioned officers twenty days, and privates ten days previous notice: But in cases of publick danger, when there may be occasion for extraordinary service, every officer, and non-commissioned officer shall be on the alert, and one day's notice to privates shall be sufficient.

Section 18. *And be it further ordained*, That each commandant of a regiment shall order two courts martial to be held within the bounds of his regiment every year, for the assessment of fines, and to decide on all questions relative to the exemption of any individual from militia duty, according to the provisions of this ordinance. One court martial shall be held not less than ten nor more than fifteen days after the last battalion muster, and the other not less than ten nor more than fifteen days after the regimental muster in every year; there shall be a judge advocate appointed by the commandant of the regiment, who shall act as clerk for the said courts, and prosecute on behalf of the government, and shall within ten days after the adjournment of each court deliver to the commandant of the regiment a statement of all fines imposed by said court, signed by the president thereof, and certified by himself. And every person appealing from the judgment of said court, shall also notify the same by writing to the commandant of the regiment, within ten days after the adjournment of the said court.

Section 19. *And be it further ordained*, That the collection of all fines imposed by any of the said courts, and not remitted by order of the court of appeals, as hereinafter provided, shall be enforced by any alcalde of the district, at the request of the commandant of the regiment, and delivered to the said commandant to be applied to the purchase of drums, fifes and colors, for the use of the regiment.

Section 20. *And be it further ordained*, That any four officers of the regiment, other than field officers, together with the president who shall be a captain, shall constitute a court martial for the assessment of fines; but every commissioned officer under the rank of major shall be entitled to a seat therein. The members of the said court shall in all cases be sworn to discharge their duty faithfully, and shall have power to adjourn from day to day until the business before them is finished.

Section 21. *And be it further ordained,* That for neglect of duty the officers, non-commissioned officers and privates shall forfeit and pay the fines as hereinafter provided, viz: For failing to attend any regimental or battalion muster, or training, an adjutant shall forfeit and pay ten dollars; a captain, five dollars; a subaltern, four dollars; a drum or fife major, three dollars; and any other non-commissioned officer or private, two dollars. For failing to attend any company muster, a captain shall forfeit and pay five dollars; a subaltern, three dollars; and a non-commissioned officer or private, two dollars. For failing to attend the court martial for the assessment of fines, appointed by the commandant of the regiment, a captain shall forfeit and pay three dollars; and a subaltern, three dollars. For failing to give notice of any regimental or battalion muster, or training, an adjutant shall forfeit and pay ten dollars; a captain, five dollars; and a non-commissioned officer, two dollars. For failing to make out and deliver to the proper officer in due time any return, an adjutant shall forfeit and pay five dollars; a captain, three dollars. For failing to enroll the militia of his company, or form them into divisions, or note his delinquents, a captain shall forfeit and pay five dollars. For failing to execute any order of the adjutant respecting musters, train days, or courts for the assessment of fines, a sergeant major shall forfeit and pay three dollars. For failing to keep a royster of the sergeants, two dollars. For failing to notify delinquents to appear at court for the assessment of fines, a sergeant shall forfeit and pay two dollars. And in the absence of a captain the senior subaltern present shall act in his stead, and for any neglect of duty incur the same penalties as a captain.

Section 22. *And be it further ordained,* That within twenty days after the adjournment of each court for the assessment of fines, the field officers of the regiment shall meet as a court martial at the same place where the other courts martial shall have been held, and all persons who may think themselves to have been aggrieved by a sentence of the court for the assessment of fines, may have a rehearing in the said court of appeals, whose judgment shall be final. Notice of the time and place of holding courts martial for the assessment of fines shall be given at each regimental and battalion muster, by the commandant of the regiment, to captains and subalterns, and by the commandants of companies, through the non-commissioned officers, to their respective companies.

Section 23. *And be it further ordained,* That a brigade court martial for the assessment of fines, shall be ordered by the colonel commandant, or by the governor, on the report made to him by a commissioned officer, charging the field officer or the brigade inspector with neglect of duty. The said court consisting of a president, who shall be a colonel, nominated by the officer who shall have ordered the court to be held, a judge advocate appointed by the court, and four field officers at least, (every field officer being entitled to a seat therein) shall be governed by the same rules as have been prescribed for a regimental court martial, for the assessment of fines, and the report of the proceedings of the said court, shall be made to the colonel commandant, for his approbation, unless he be implicated thereby, in which case the report shall be made to the governor; and in either case, it shall be the duty of the officer to whom the report may be made, to certify the judgment of the court, if approved by him, to some civil magistrate, having competent jurisdiction, who shall forthwith enforce the collection of the fines, to be applied to the use of the brigade.

Section 24. *And be it further ordained,* That the colonel commandant, the brigade inspector and field officers, for neglect of duty, shall forfeit and pay the fines hereinafter provided, for each neglect, viz: The colonel commandant, for failing to furnish the brigade inspector with orders for regimental and battalion musters, in due time, twenty-five dollars; for failing to attend a regimental muster, twenty-five dollars; and for failing to forward the brigade return to the governor in due time, ten dollars. The brigade inspector, for failing to give orders to the commandant of a regiment, in due time, for a regimental or battalion muster, ten dollars; for failing to attend a regimental muster, ten dollars; for failing to attend and perform his duty at a battalion muster, ten dollars; for failing to render to the colonel commandant a brigade return, five dollars. The commandant of a regiment, for failing to give notice of, in due time, or to attend a regimental or battalion muster, or training, ten dollars; for failing to appoint a court martial for the assessment of fines, in due time, or to attend as a member of the court of appeals, ten dollars; for failing to transmit the regimental return to the brigade inspector, in due time, five dollars. A major, for failing to attend a regimental or battalion muster, or a court of appeals, five dollars; for failing to perform the duties assigned to him by the eighth, ninth or tenth section of this article, ten dollars.

Section 25. *And be it further ordained,* That every officer holding a commission in the militia, who shall be charged with a high misdemeanor in his office, such as unmilitary conduct, shameful neglect of duty, disobedience of orders, cowardice, appearing, or behaving himself when on duty in an unofficerlike manner, or wilfully injuring those under his command, he shall be liable to be tried by a court martial, and if found guilty, to be sentenced to be reprimanded in orders, or to be removed from office, and declared incapable of holding any military commission under this government for life, or for a term of years, according to the nature and aggravation of his offence.

Section 26. *And be it further ordained,* That all charges of high misdemeanor against any officer above the rank of captain, shall be presented by the officer requesting the arrest to the governor or commander in chief, and against any captain, or officer below the rank of captain, to the colonel commandant, and in either case, the officer to whom the charge may be presented, if it shall appear to him of such a nature as to merit the attention of a court martial, shall cause the accused to be arrested and served with a copy of the charge or charges against him, and also notified of the time and place of his trial. He shall also, by orders under his hand, appoint at least five field officers of the brigade, designating the officer who shall preside, to constitute a court martial for the trial of the accused, at the time and place which he shall have appointed.

Section 27. *And be it further ordained,* That the said court when constituted, shall appoint a judge advocate, whose duties shall be the same as have been prescribed for the same officer in other courts martial, and besides the customary oaths, the judge advocate, and every member of the court shall severally take an oath not to divulge the opinion of any individual member at any time, nor the sentence of the court, unless required to give evidence thereof as a witness in a court of justice, until the same be approved by the officer who shall have ordered the trial.

Section 28. *And be it further ordained.* That every court martial appointed for the trial of any officer for a high misdemeanor shall have power to adjourn from day to day, to issue compulsory process for witnesses for or against the accused, to appoint a provost martial to execute their process, and to send for persons and papers which may be necessary to a fair and impartial decision of the case.

Section 29. *And be it further ordained,* That it shall be the duty of the judge advocate to deliver to the officer who shall have ordered the trial, a fair and accurate statement of all the testimony produced to the court, relative to the charges exhibited and tried, together with the sentence of the court, signed by the members thereof, within five days after the adjournment of the said court; and it shall be the duty of the officer who shall have ordered the trial, to express in writing his approbation of the sentence of the court martial, within ten days after the proceedings thereof shall have been presented to him as aforesaid.

Section 30. *And be it further ordained,* That in all courts martial the oath to the judge advocate shall be administered by the president of the court, and to all other persons by the judge advocate. It shall always be the duty of the officer who shall have appointed the court martial, to approve or disapprove the sentence of such court by him appointed.

Section 31. *And be it further ordained,* That no officer shall be permitted to resign in less than three years from the date of his commission, unless he be rendered incapable of serving by infirmity, of which a court martial shall judge, and in all cases the resignation of any field officer shall be tendered to the colonel commandant, and that of regimental officers, to the commandant of the regiment to which he may belong.

Section 32. *And be it further ordained,* That where two or more commandants of regiments shall have commissions bearing the same date, the seniority of either shall be decided by number of the regiment to which they belong, the first having the preference to the second, &c., the seniority of other officers whose commissions bear the same date, to be decided by lot.

Section 33. *And be it further ordained,* That it shall be lawful for any number of men who may be required to perform military duty, to form themselves in volunteer companies of cavalry, provided there be not more than one company of cavalry of sixty-eight men, for each regiment of six hundred infantry, or in that proportion within the bounds of the brigade; and any such company of cavalry who shall conform to all the regulations prescribed for the government of the same, shall be exempted from the performance of any other militia duty.

Section 34. *And be it further ordained,* That one major of cavalry shall be appointed in the same manner as the other officers of the same grade, and whose duties shall be the same in all respects, but he shall not be attached to any particular regiment; and he shall receive his orders from the colonel commandant through the brigade inspector.

Section 35. *And be it further ordained,* That the several companies of cavalry, shall be governed by the same rules with respect to the election of their officers, musters, returns, courts martial and fines, as have been prescribed for other companies of militia, and shall attend properly equipped at such regimental or battalion muster, as the colonel commandant may from time to time direct.

Section 36. *And be it further ordained,* That every cavalry man shall be equipped with a suitable horse, saddle and bridle, sword, pistols and holsters, cap, boots and spurs, and such uniform as the several companies may establish; and it shall be the duty of each captain to have his company divided by lot or otherwise, into four divisions, as nearly equal as may be, one of which divisions shall be in readiness for actual service at any time when called.

Section 37. *And it shall be ordained*, That it shall be the duty of the brigade inspector with the major of cavalry, immediately after receiving their commissions, to call a muster of each troop of horse now formed within this jurisdiction, and receive the same, enrolling as cavalry all the men that may appear as volunteers for that purpose of the said troops, equipped in the manner herein before specified, forming them into such companies as may be found most conventient and agreeable to the said volunteers; and instructing them to elect and make returns of officers to be commissioned in the same manner as other militia officers.

Section 38. *And be it further ordained*, That all the militia of this jurisdiction, not enrolled in any company of cavalry, shall be armed and equipped, each commissioned officer with a sword, and each non-commissioned officer and private with a good rifle, shot pouch and powder horn, and twenty-four rounds of powder and ball, or a good musket, bayonet and cartridge box, and twenty-four rounds of powder and ball. Every person who shall furnish himself with arms as aforesaid shall forever retain the same, free and exempted from all execution for debt, taxes, fines or any other demand whatever; and those who may not be able to furnish themselves with arms as aforesaid, shall be furnished with the same from the publick arsenal, in such manner as shall be hereafter provided.

Section 39. *And be it further enacted*, That the governor shall have power whenever he may be of opinion that the publick safety requires it, to call out all or any part of the militia, for the defence of the country, or to enforce obedience to the laws, and when in actual service they shall be governed by the same rules and articles of war, and shall receive the same pay and rations as the regular troops in his majesty's service. *Provided*, That no militia man shall be subject on any account to suffer corporal punishment, without the sentence of a court martial.

Section 40. *And be it further ordained*, That one fourth of all the militia of this jurisdiction being warned by their officers for that purpose, shall from and after the organization of each company, hold themselves in readiness for actual service at a moment's warning, at all times, for the space of ninety days, after which another similar portion being warned in like manner, shall do the same duty, and the first shall not be called on again until all the men of each company shall have served in rotation the same length of time, unless there should be occasion for a greater number, or the whole be called into actual service; and any person legally called on to perform a tour of duty, and who snall fail to appear in his place, either in person or by an able bodied substitute, not liable to the then existing call, shall be fined by a court martial, in a sum equal to double the hire of a substitute; which court martial shall be ordered by the commanding officer, immediately after the rendezvous.

Section 41. *And be it further ordained*, That if any man hired as a substitute be called on to take his own place, whilst in service, the man who hired him shall take his place, but the hire shall be refunded; and any man who may be excused from service at a particular time on account of sickness, or any other lawful reason, shall nevertheless be liable to be called at any time, until his proportion of service be performed.

Section 42. *And be it further ordained*, That the brigade inspector shall be allowed five dollars per day, for each day he may be employed in the discharge of the duties of his office, or for every twenty miles which he may travel while employed in performing the same, according to the rules prescribed by this ordinance; and his accounts certified by the colonel commandant, shall be paid from the publick treasury, such certified account being a sufficient warrant to the treasurer for the payment of the same.

Section 43. *And be it further ordained*, That the militia of this jurisdiction being destined exclusively for the defence and the safety of the country, no part thereof shall on any account whatever, be ordered on any service or compelled to go beyond the limits of this jurisdiction.

Section 44. *And be it further ordained*, That the free men of colour may be organized into one or more companies and officered as the commander in chief may direct, and they shall be subject to be called into actual service, or employed in any way within this jurisdiction, at such times and under such regulations as the commander in chief or colonel commandant may think expedient and necessary for the public safety.

ARTICLE III.

For the better Administration of Justice.

Section 1. *And be it further ordained*, That for the better administration of Justice, there shall be one superior tribunal within this jurisdiction, of which the governor when present shall be the presiding judge, and three judges appointed by the convention, viz: One for the district of Baton Rouge, one for the district of New Feliciana, and one for the district of St. Helena and St. Ferdinand, shall be associate judges thereof; and the said court shall have full powers to decide finally on all criminal prosecutions for capital, and other offences not within the jurisdiction of any inferior tribunal, and also to decide finally on all appeals in civil cases.

Section 2. *And be it further ordained*. That the said tribunal shall be styled the superior court of the jurisdiction of Baton Rouge, in West-Florida, and shall hold the sessions in every year at the town of Baton Rouge, commencing on the second Mondays in March, July and November, and continuing in session by adjournments from day to day, Sundays excepted, until all the business before them be finished, attending first to all criminal prosecutions, and afterwards to all appeals in civil cases.

Section 3. *And be it further ordained*, That any two or more of the said judges shall form a court, and in the absence of the governor the senior judge, who may be present at the time and place of holding any session of the court, shall preside therein, and any one of the said judges shall have the power to adjourn the court from day to day for five judicial days, at which time if there be not a number present sufficient to form a court the session shall be clothed and the court adjourned until the next session in course.

Section 4. *And be it further ordained*, That the said court, at their first election, which shall commence on the second Monday of November of this present year, shall appoint one clerk, whose duty it shall be to make and keep in his office a fair and accurate record of all proceedings of the said superior court, to enter in a register kept for that purpose, all petitions of appellants from the inferior tribunals of this jurisdiction, in the order of time as they shall be presented at his office, and to issue all process of the court according to the forms prescribed by law or by this ordinance. He shall also file in his office all documents produced to him relative to any matter of controversy or criminal prosecution pending in said court, and produce the same to the court at the time when such cause or prosecution shall be heard and determined.

Section 5. *And be it further ordained*, That one sheriff shall be appointed by this convention and commissioned by the governor, who shall keep his office at the town of Baton Rouge; and previous to his entering upon the duties thereof, he shall execute and deposit in the office of the clerk of the superior court aforesaid a bond, with four sufficient securities in the sum of ten thousand dollars, conditioned upon the faithful performance of all the duties of his office; the form of which bond shall be prescribed by all the judges of the said superior court at their first session, and they also shall be the judges of the sufficiency of the securities proposed to be given by the sheriff as aforesaid.

Section 6. *And be it further ordained*, That the said sheriff shall appoint one or more deputies in each district, who shall be recommended, each by the court of the district for which he shall be appointed, and it shall be the duty of the sheriff in person, or his deputies, for whose good conduct in all things appertaining to his office, he shall be responsible, to execute all process both of the superior and inferior courts established by this ordinance, to take charge of all persons imprisoned by virtue of any civil or criminal process, and them safely keep as the court may direct until discharged by due course of law, and in general to execute all orders relative to the administration of justice issued by proper authority; for which purpose he shall have the same powers, and enjoy the same privileges and emoluments, as have usually been allowed to similar officers under this government.

Section 7. *And be it further ordained*, That one counsellor learned in the laws of Castile and the Indes, shall be appointed by this convention and commissioned by the governor, whose duty it shall be to attend the several sessions of the said superior court, and give his opinion in writing, when required, by the court on any questions or points of law which may be involved in the discussion of the causes submitted to their decision. The said counsellor shall reside within this jurisdiction, and shall give his opinion in like manner, to any of the inferior tribunals thereof when required, but shall not be permitted to act as counsellor or attorney for either party in any suit at law instituted or pending in any tribunal within this jurisdiction. He shall receive an annual salary of fifteen hundred dollars for his services aforesaid, from the public treasury, and no other compensation thereof under any pretext whatever.

Section 8. *And be it further ordained*, That the said counsellor before entering upon the duties of his office, shall take and subscribe the following oath in presence of the superior tribunal aforesaid, or of the presiding judge thereof: "I, A. B., do *solemnly swear faithfully to discharge the duties of counsellor for the tribunals of justice within the jurisdiction of Baton Rouge, according to the best of my judgment, and that I will not in any case or under any pretext whatever, receive any compensation therefor, other than that which may be allowed by law, and paid from the publick treasury of this jurisdiction. So help me God.*"

Section 9. *And be it further ordained,* That all actions of appeal brought before this tribunal, shall commence by petition, addressed to the court, and presented to the clerk, who shall file the same in his office, and shall deliver to the sheriff a copy thereof, with an order annexed, to the other party in the suit to anwser the same within twenty days thereafter; the said order shall bear test in the name of the presiding judge of the court, and be signed by the clerk; all other process of the court shall be issued in the same form, and all other proceedings conducted as heretofore, except that all judgments shall be pronounced and signed by the presiding judge according to the opinion of a majority of the members present, and except such other changes as may be hereinafter ordained.

Section 10. *And be it further ordained,* That three civil commandants shall be nominated by this convention and commissioned by the governor, viz: One for the district of Baton Rouge; one for the district of New Feliciana; and one for the districts of St. Helena and St. Ferdinand, who shall reside each within the district for which he shall have been appointed, and in all civil cases shall have and exercise the powers and perform the duties heretofore assigned to a commandant of a district within this jurisdiction, together with those of a notary publick for the said district, except in the cases hereinafter mentioned and provided.

Section 11. *And be it further ordained,* That there shall be one district court in and for each of the said districts, those of St. Helena and Tanchipaho including the settlements of Chefuncte, Bogcheto and Pearl River, being considered as one district, of which court the commandant when present shall be the presiding judge, and the alcaldes shall be associate judges thereof, each for the district in which he resides. Any three or more of the said judges shall form a court, and in case of the absence of the commandant from whatever cause at the time of holding any session of the court, the senior alcalde present shall act as presiding judge thereof.

Section 12. *And be it further ordained,* That each of the said district courts shall hold four sessions in every year, at some convenient place within the district for which it shall have been established, viz: For the district of Baton Rouge at the town of Baton Rouge, to commence on the third Mondays of January, April, July and October. For the district of New Feliciana at the town of St. Francisville, to commence on the first Mondays of February, May, August and November. And for the districts of St. Helena and St. Ferdinand, at the habitation of William Spiller, to commence on the first Mondays of January, April, July and October of each year; and each session of the said district courts shall be continued by adjournments from day to day, Sundays excepted, until all the business before them be finished.

Section 13. *And be it further ordained,* That the said district courts shall have original jurisdiction in all cases, civil and criminal, within the districts respectively, for which they shall have been established, not within the jurisdiction of any single alcalde; but in all trials of criminal cases they shall order six free-holders of the vicinity to come and hear the testimony in open court, and to declare upon oath their conviction as to the guilt or innocence of the party accused, who shall be immediately discharged if the said declaration be "not guilty." If the accused be found guilty by the free-holders aforesaid and the court be of the opinion that the offence is of such a nature as to merit capital punishment, or confinement to hard labor for a longer term than six months, or a fine exceeding five hundred dollars, they shall order the prisoner to be conveyed to the fort at Baton Rouge, to abide the judgment of the superior court, giving notice thereof to the governor, and shall transmit all the documents relative to his case, or certified copies thereof to the clerk of the said superior court. In all other cases they shall pronounce such sentence authorized by law as to the nature of each offence may seem to deserve, and cause it to be executed by the proper officer.

Section 14. *And be it further ordained*, That each of the civil commandants aforesaid, shall keep in his office a register, in which he shall enter all civil actions instituted for any amount, which may not come within the jurisdiction of any single alcalde, in order of time as they shall be brought; and at each session of the said district courts, it shall be the duty of each commandant to exhibit to the court in which he may preside the register so made by him as aforesaid, with all the documents relative to the causes or actions instituted at his office and not determined or withdrawn, when each of the said courts shall proceed to hear and decide all the causes aforesaid in the same order as they shall be found on the register of the commandant. *Provided always*, that any cause or action for reasons approved by the court, may be continued from one session to another, until a reasonable time shall have been allowed to the parties to procure all testimony which may be necessary to obtain a fair and impartial decision thereof.

Section 15. *And be it further ordained*, That in all civil actions the judgments of the said district courts shall be final for all sums not exceeding five hundred dollars; but in all cases in which the judgment given by the district court, shall be for a sum exceeding that amount, an appeal shall be allowed at the request of either party, to the superior court, the appellant paying the costs which shall have accrued thereon, and giving sufficient security in the office of the commandant, within fifteen days after such judgment shall have been given, to prosecute the appeal without delay, and abide the decision of the superior tribunal aforesaid.

Section 16. *And be it further ordained*, That the said district courts shall have been established; and also for making and keeping in repair think necessary and conducive to the publick welfare and convenience respecting the government of slaves, and the management of live stock of every description in the several districts respectively, for which they shall have been established; and also for making and keeping in repair publick roads and bridges, causing publick roads to be opened and bridges to be erected where necessary, either through publick or private property, and to establish reasonable tolls where they may think proper, to defray the expense of making and keeping the same in repair. *Provided always*, That where it may be found necessary for the publick convenience to open a public road or erect a bridge in any situation which may occasion injury to an individual inhabitant, it shall be the duty of the court to cause the damages occasioned thereby to such inhabitant to be estimated by six free-holders of the vicinity and paid by the inhabitants of the district. The said district courts shall also have power to give such orders as they may think proper for the erection of publick buildings in their respective districts, and for defraying the expenses thereof by the inhabitants within the same.

Section 17. *And be it further ordained*, That each district court shall appoint one person who shall be sworn to regulate and stamp weights and measures, and establish his fees for the same, to be paid by the owners of such weights and measures as he may examine and seal; and it shall be unlawful for any person to sell any kind of produce or merchandise thereafter by weights or measures inferior to those duly regulated and sealed, under penalty of being fined by the court of the district not exceeding twenty dollars for the first offence and at the discretion of the court for other offences.

Section 18. *And be it further ordained*, That the said district courts shall at their discretion grant licenses to merchants, tavern-keepers, pedlars, and keepers of ferries, and billiard tables and establish the rates and general regulations to be observed by all persons obtaining such licenses. *Provided always*, That the applicant for any license as aforsaid, shall pay to the commandant, or presiding judge of the court, for the benefit of the publick treasury, the tax established by this ordinance on the license for which he applies; and any person who shall be convicted of retailing merchandise or spirituous liquors, or keeping a tavern, a ferry, or a billiard table, and of receiving any emoluments therefor without such license, shall forfeit and pay for the first offence twenty dollars, and for every after offence such fine as the court may impose, one-half of all such fines to be paid to the person who may sue for the same, and the other half to the publick treasury of the district.

Section 19. *And be it further ordained*, That either of the said district courts upon information given them of any person or persons keeping a disorderly house or establishing any institution for the purpose of gambling under whatever name or pretext, within their jurisdiction, shall cause to be arrested such person, or persons, and on conviction of any crime as aforesaid, shall punish all such offenders by fine and imprisonment at their discretion, not exceeding the general powers granted to the district courts in criminal cases.

Section 20. *And be it further ordained*, That twenty-four alcaldes shall be elected by the people of this jurisdiction, and commissioned by the governor, viz: Eight for the district of Baton Rouge, eight for the district of New Feliciana, and eight for the districts of St. Helena and St. Ferdinand, who shall have final jurisdiction in civil cases in which the amount of the matter in dispute does not exceed fifty dollars, and who shall have in all other respects the same powers and emoluments, and perform the same duties as have heretofore been assigned to similar officers under this government.

Section 21. *And be it further ordained*, That the election for the alcaldes aforesaid shall be held in each district on Thursday the 20th day of September next, at such place or places within the same, and according to such regulations as the representation of each district in this convention may determine; and that a return be made within five days thereafter, by the persons appointed to conduct the said elections, of the names of the persons elected to the office of the commander of the district for which they shall have been elected respectively, placing on one roll all the names of the persons elected in one district; and it shall be the duty of each commandant to preserve and file the said roll in his office, and to make a return of the names of the persons elected in the same order, within fifteen days after the receipt thereof to the office of the government at Baton Rouge.

Section 22. *And be it further ordained*, That the commissions shall be issued by the governor in the usual form to each of the alcaldes so elected, within ten days after the return of their names so made as aforesaid to the office of the government, and the seniority of the said alcaldes shall be regulated according to which their names shall be found on the returns made to the commandants of the districts as aforesaid.

Section 23. *And be it further ordained*, That the powers of the present commandants of districts and of the alcaldes and syndics now in office within this jurisdiction, shall cease and determine so soon as the commandants and alcaldes appointed agreeable to the provisions of this ordinance, shall have been duly commissioned; and all civil magistrates appointed under this ordinance, shall continue in office at least one year from the time of their appointment unless sooner removed from office, and until removed by this convention.

Section 24. *And be it further ordained*, That the forms of procedure in all the tribunals of justice within this jurisdiction, not otherwise prescribed by this ordinance, shall be conformable, in all cases, as near as may be, to those heretofore established and practised, except only such changes as may have been rendered necessary by the changes herein ordained, which alteration in the forms of procedure the said tribunals are authorized to make in such manner as to them may appear most convenient to facilitate the distribution of justice.

Section 25. *And be it further ordained*, That in all criminal prosecutions, the accused shall have the privilege of a speedy and public trial, in which he shall be confronted with and allowed to examine all the witnesses against him, and to produce testimony in his defence. He shall also have compulsory process to procure the attendance of witnesses if required, and shall in no case be compelled to give testimony against himself.

Section 26. *And be it further ordained*, That all trials in civil as well as criminal cases shall be public, and all judgments pronounced and signed in open court, by the presiding judge thereof, according to the opinion of the majority of the judges present; that all process shall be conducted and all records made either in the Spanish or English language, as may best suit the convenience of the parties concerned, and that all witnesses may be examined by both parties on all points relative to the matter in controversy.

Section 27. *And be it further ordained*, That each of the courts established by this ordinance shall have the power to appoint one interpreter, who shall be sworn to perform his duties faithfully, and shall receive such compensation therefor, as the court for which he may be appointed shall determine from the publick treasury when employed in the publick service, and from individuals when employed by them in the exercise of his functions.

Section 28. *And be it further ordained*, That the president of any of the courts established by this ordinance, shall have the power to call a session of the court in which he presides, at any time when he may think it expedient, giving three day's notice thereof to every associate judge of such court, by a circular letter addressed to each, in which shall be specified the occasion for which the said session may be called. *Provided always*, that no other business be entered upon at any session so called than that specified in the circular letter of the presiding judge aforesaid.

Section 29. *And be it further ordained*, That when judgment shall be given for debt by any alcalde or court of justice within this jurisdiction, all the legal costs which may have accrued to the plaintiff in prosecuting his suit for the same, shall be taxed by the said officer or court, and the judgment shall be given for the debt and costs so taxed, and after such judgment obtained for any sum now due and payable within this jurisdiction, there shall be a stay of execution allowed to the party who may demand the same for the term of ninety days, when such sum may not exceed one hundred dollars; for the term of one hundred and twenty days, when the sum may be over one hundred dollars and not exceeding three hundred dollars; for the term of six months when the sum may be over three hundred dollars and not exceeding five hundred dollars; and for the term of twelve months when the sum may not exceed five hundred dollars; sufficient security being given for the payment of the debt and costs at the expiration of the time for which the execution may have been stayed in each case as aforesaid.

Section 30. *And be it further ordained*, That it shall be the duty of the superior court of this jurisdiction at their first stated session after the establishment of this ordinance to make a fair and accurate table exhibiting all the fees to which every civil officer of this goverment is entitled by law for his services, in all things relating to his office, and where any civil officer may be required by this ordinance to perform services for which no compensation may be allowed by law or by this ordinance, the said court shall allow such compensation therefor, as to them may appear reasonable and proper, specifying the same in the table aforesaid. And it shall be the duty of the clerk of the said superior court, to furnish to each civil commandant within this jurisdiction, a certified copy of the said table of fees, within ten days after the adjournment of the said first session of the superior court, to be affixed in his office for the inspection of all persons concerned.

Section 31. *And be it further ordained*, That all the civil officers of this jurisdiction who receive compensation for their services other than a fixed salary from the public treasury, shall make fair tables of all the fees to which they are entitled by law for their services; and each officer shall cause to be affixed in some conspicuous place in his office, within one month after the adjournment of the first session of the superior court aforesaid, for the inspection of all persons who may have business in such office, on pain of forfeiting for each day, the same shall be missing through such officer's neglect, the sum of twenty dollars, which shall be paid one-half to any person who shall sue for the same, and the other half to the publick treasury.

Section 32. *And whereas*, difficulties may arise in ascertaining the amount of the perquisites appertaining to the office of the governor of this jurisdiction;

Be it therefore ordained, That from and after the establishment of this ordinance a nett salary of three thousand dollars per annum be allowed to the governor of this jurisdiction, and paid from the publick treasury thereof, as a full compensation for all his services while exercising the said office.

Section 33. *And be it further ordained*, That each of the associate judges of the superior court of the jurisdiction of Baton Rouge shall be allowed an annual salary of six hundred dollars for his services, while exercising the said office, to be paid from the publick treasury of the jurisdiction aforesaid.

Section 84. *And be it further ordained*, That it shall be the duty of the commandant of each district, accompanied by two or more of the alcaldes, as soon as they shall have been commissioned, agreeable to the provisions of this ordinance, to receive all the publick archives within the district in which he may reside, with a proper inventory of the same, and that the commandant of the district of Baton Rouge shall receive and keep the archives of this jurisdiction until they be otherwise disposed of by the superior court.

Section 35. *And be it further ordained*, That all suits now pending before any tribunal within this jurisdiction may either be withdrawn by those who have instituted the same, or transferred to any alcalde or district court, having competent jurisdiction according to the provisions of this ordinance; and to those against whom judgment may have been rendered for debt, and not yet satisfied, the same indulgence shall be given as has been provided and allowed by the 29th section of this article, in cases of judgments hereafter to be given; the time of the stay of execution to be computed from the first session of the district court of the district in which such judgment may have been given. And all persons against whom any criminal prosecution may have been instituted, shall be brought to trial at the first sessions of the respective district courts.

ARTICLE IV.

And, whereas, the irregularities and abuses which have been practiced by some of the officers entrusted with the distribution of lands, and establishing the boundaries thereof, within this jurisdiction, for some years past, may give rise to much litigation, and injustice to the publick, as well as to individuals, if suffered to continue. *And, whereas*, it is the duty of those who exercise the powers of litigation for the publick welfare to prevent as far as possible the evils which might originate from this source, both to the public and the individual inhabitants of the country.

Section 1. *Be it therefore ordained by the authority aforesaid*. That a register of land claims shall be appointed by this convention, and commissioned by the governor, who shall, before entering upon the duties of his office, execute and deposit in the office of the clerk of the superior court of this jurisdiction, a bond with two sufficient securities, approved by the judges of said court, in the sum of ten thousand dollars, conditioned for the faithful performance of all the duties of his office, as prescribed by this ordinance.

Section 2. *And be it further ordained*, That it shall be the duty of the said register of land claims to make and keep in his office at the town of Baton Rouge, a fair and accurate register of all grants or sales of lands made by any officer or tribunal duly authorized to grant, or in any way sell or alienate, the lands of the royal domain within this jurisdiction, and all other documents which may be produced to him by any person or persons, as evidence of any claim or claims for lands in the said jurisdiction, of what nature soever, which they may consider to be vested in them or in any other person, whether residing within this jurisdiction or elsewhere.

Section 3. *And be it further ordained*, That any person claiming lands within the said jurisdiction by virtue of any grant or sale made by any officer or tribunal authorized as aforesaid, and every person claiming lands within the said jurisdiction by any incomplete title of what nature soever, shall before the first day of September of the year one thousand eight hundred and eleven, deliver to the said register of land claims a notice in writing, stating the nature and extent of his claim or claims, together with platt of the said tract or tracts of land so claimed if they have been surveyed by any officer commissioned for that purpose, and shall, on or before the said first day of September of the year aforesaid, deliver to the said register for the purpose of being

92

recorded, every grant, order of survey, deed, conveyance, or other written evidence of his claim: And it shall be the duty of the said register to record the same in books to be kept by him for that purpose within six months after the receipt thereof, each claimant paying to him at the rate of twelve and one-half cents for each hundred words contained in such written evidence of his claim as aforesaid; and the said register shall return to each claimant his original papers deposited at his office as aforesaid, at any time when called for, after same has been recorded.

Section 4. *And be it further ordained*, That any claimant as aforesaid who shall neglect to refuse to deliver such notice in writing of his claim together with a platt, if any there be, or cause to be recorded such written evidence of his claim as aforesaid, all his right, in case his title be incomplete, shall become void, and forever thereafter be barred, nor shall any incomplete grant, warrant, or order of jury, deed of conveyance, or other written evidence which not have been recorded as above directed, ever after be considered or admitted as evidence in any tribunal within this jurisdiction.

Section 5. *And be it further ordained*, That no grant or sale of lands appertaining to the royal domain, within this jurisdiction, which may be made after this date, without the knowledge and approbation of some tribunal established with full powers for that purpose within this jurisdiction, shall be valid, and no such grant or sale shall be received as evidence of title in any tribunal within this jurisdiction, or be admitted to be recorded in the office of the register of land claims established by this ordinance.

Section 6. *And be it further ordained*, That every actual settler who now inhabits and cultivates a tract of land within this jurisdiction, for which he has obtained no complete title, and which has not been legally granted to any other person, shall be entitled to such quantity including his improvements, as has usually been granted to settlers, according to the laws, usages and customs of the Spanish government: And no actual settler as aforesaid shall be deprived of a tract so inhabited and cultivated by him, in consequence of any claim hereafter brought by any person, of which the said inhabitant, has not now or heretofore been notified.

Section 7. *And be it further ordained*, That it shall be the duty of every actual settler as aforesaid to deliver to the register of land claims before the first of September, one thousand eight hundred and eleven, aforesaid, a declaration subscribed and sworn by himself, in presence of some alcalde or civil magistrate of this jurisdiction, stating how long he may have inhabited and cultivated the said tract of land, with the number both of free persons and slaves appertaining to his family, which said declaration shall also be accompanied with the certificate of two or more disinterested persons also sworn, testifying to the truth of the facts stated therein.

Section 8. *And be it further ordained*, That the said settler at the time of making the declaration aforesaid, together with the persons subscribing the said certificates, shall also declare upon oath every claim of any other person, if any there be, for the said tract, of which they or either of them may have been notified before this date.

Section 9. *And be it further ordained*, That it shall be the duty of the register of land claims aforesaid, to record all declarations and certificates made in form as aforesaid, and deliver to him in due time as evidence of the claims of the persons making such declarations, for

93

the tracts by them so inhabited and cultivated as aforesaid; and all such settlers who may refuse or neglect to deliver such evidence of their respective claims to the register on or before the said first day of September, 1811, shall forfeit their said claims, and shall not thereafter be allowed to produce any evidence of the same facts in any tribunal within this jurisdiction for the purpose of establishing their said claims.

Section 10. *And be it further ordained*, That from and after the first day of January, one thousand eight hundred and eleven, the surveyor-general of this province shall reside and keep his office at the town of Baton-Rouge.

ARTICLE V.

Whereas, the publick safety requires that provision be made as soon as possible for defraying the expenses of this department of the government, from such resources as may be found within the country, and that some uniform mode of taxation be established for that purposes.

Section 1. *And be it therefore ordained by the authority aforesaid*, That it shall be the duty of the alcaldes of the several districts of this jurisdiction to make every year, in the month of December, an accurate census of all the inhabitants each for the division in which he may reside, stating therein distinctly every free white person by name, with the number of slaves, and also the number of arpents of land claimed by each within this jurisdiction, causing every person to declare to him upon oath, the whole amount of property claimed by him as aforesaid.

Section 2. *And be it further ordained*, That each of the said alcaldes shall make and return to the commandant of the district in which he resides, a fair transcript of the census so made by him on or before the first day of January in every year, and it shall be the duty of the commandants to make from the returns of the alcaldes a complete census of all the inhabitants and their property as aforesaid, each for the district in which he may reside, and to return the same to the office of the clerk of the superior court for the jurisdiction of Baton-Rouge, on or before the first day of February in every year.

Section 3. *And be it further ordained*, That it shall be the duty of the clerk of the said superior court, to make every year, an accurate table containing the names of all the free inhabitants of this jurisdiction subject to taxation, with the amount of the tax to be paid by each, placed opposite his name, estimating the same from the returns made by the commandants of the districts in the following manner, viz:

For every hundred arpents of land claimed by a resident within this jurisdiction, not exceeding one thousand arpents, four rials; for every hundred arpents claimed by one inhabitant over and above one thousand arpents, one dollar; and for every slave, four rials.

Section 4. *And be it further ordained*, That it shall be the duty of the said clerk of the said superior court, to keep in his office the said table, and to make and deliver to the sheriff of this jurisdiction, a certified copy thereof, on or before the first day of March in every year.

Section 5. *And be it further ordained*, That it shall be the duty of the sheriff to immediately on the receipt thereof, to give notice to the inhabitants by advertisements in the most publick places in each district, mentioning the places and times at which they may attend and pay the said tax to the proper officer; appointing the places not less than three in each district, as convenient as may be for the inhabitants, and the times not more distant than thirty days from the time at which the return of the amount of taxes shall have been made to him by the clerk of the superior court as aforesaid.

Section 6. *And be it further ordained*, That it shall be the duty of the sheriff in person, or by his deputies, to attend at each of the places and times so appointed by him as aforesaid, to receive the said tax, and give receipts for the same, and he shall furnish to every individual inhabitant requesting the same, a fair account of the amount of the tax which he is required to pay, with a receipt of such sum as shall be paid by each, in discharge thereof.

Section 7. *And be it further ordained*, That it shall be the duty of the sheriff in person, or by his deputies within fifteen days after the time appointed for the last meeting aforesaid, to give notice in writing to every inhabitant personally or by leaving the same at the usual place of residence of each inhabitant who shall not have attended at any of the times and places aforesaid, or paid the amount of tax due, stating in such notice the amount due by each; and if the same be not paid within thirty days thereafter, it shall be the duty of the sheriff to seize and sell such goods and chattels of such inhabitants as may be necessary to satisfy and pay the tax aforesaid, with the costs of collecting the same; the proceedings respecting the seizure and sale, being the same in all respects as are directed in cases of debts for the same amount.

Section 8. *And be it further ordained*, That it shall be the duty of the register of the land office for this jurisdiction to make every year an accurate statement of the number of arpents claimed by each and every person not residing within the jurisdiction; and to form a table exhibiting the name of each non-resident as aforesaid, with the number of arpents claimed, and the sum payable by each opposite thereto, estimating the said sum at one dollar, for every hundred arpents claimed by the non-resident.

Section 9. *And be it further ordained*, That the said register shall deposit the table so made in his office, and shall furnish an attested copy thereof to the sheriff at the time in every year in which it is ordained that the return of the amount of taxes due by residents shall be made by the clerk of the superior court.

Section 10. *And be it further ordained*, That it shall be the duty of the sheriff to cause to be published within twenty days thereafter, the names of such non-residents, with the number of arpents claimed by each, and the amount of the taxes due thereon, in such manner as may appear most effectual, to extend the same to the places where such claimants or their agents may reside; with a notice, that if the tax be not paid within six months thereafter, the said lands shall be sold, or such part thereof as may be necessary to pay the tax and costs accrued thereon.

Section 11. *And be it further ordained*, That if the said tax be not paid within the said term of six months thereafter, it shall be the duty of the sheriff to seize and sell such part of the lands belonging to each non-resident as may be sufficient to pay the amount of taxes due thereon, together with all legal costs which may have accrued; the proceedings being the same as are prescribed for the seizure and sale of lands for debt of the same amount.

Section 12. *And be it further ordained*, That until a treasurer be appointed for this jurisdiction, the sheriff shall act as treasurer thereof and shall pay of the publick monies in his possession from time to time all accounts which may be due and payable from the public treasury, and take discharges for the same. *Provided always,* That the said accounts be certified to be truly and justly due, by the superior court, or one of the district courts of this jurisdiction.

Section 13. *And be it further ordained,* That the sheriff shall be allowed for collecting the taxes aforesaid, four per cent. on the amount so collected, and for his services as treasurer, one per cent. on all sums paid by him in discharge of publick debts.

Section 14. *And be it further ordained,* That the civil commandant of each district within this jurisdiction, shall pay every three months into the hands of the sheriff, it being the duty of the sheriff to call upon them for that purpose, all sums received by them for the publick treasury of the jurisdiction, arising from the tax on licenses granted by the district courts, and from the tax on slaves imported into this jurisdiction.

Section 15. *And be it further ordained,* That the said taxes be estblished as follows, that is to say, for every slave imported after this date, above the age of ten years, ten dollars; for every slave imported as aforesaid, under the age of ten years, five dollars.

For a license to retail merchandise at any one specified place within this jurisdiction, ten dollars; for a license to keep a tavern, twenty dollars; for a license to keep a permanent ferry over the Mississippi river, twenty dollars; for a license to keep a ferry over any other river or stream, ten dollars.

For a license to retail merchandise, traveling from place to place, five dollars; and ten dollars for every cart, horse and mule employed in conveying such merchandise.

For a license to keep a billiard table, fifty dollars. *Provided always.* That the said licenses be issued for one year, and to have full force and virtue for that space of time and no longer.

Section 16. *And be it further ordained,* That all fines and forfeitures exacted by any of the district courts or such parts thereof as revert to the publick treasury, by this ordinance, shall be paid to the commandant for the use of the district; and all fines and forfeitures imposed by the superior court, not otherwise directed to be disposed of, shall be paid to the sheriff for the benefit of the publick treasury.

Section 17. *And be it further ordained,* That it shall be the duty of the sheriff to exhibit to the superior court, at each of their stated sessions, a fair and accurate statement of all publick monies received and expended by him, and that the said superior court shall have power at any time to investigate his conduct relative to any or all the duties of his office, and in case of his delinquency to the prejudice of the publick. or of any individual, to give such judgment against him, and to inflict such penalties authorized by the laws, as to them may seem fit and according to justice.

Done in convention at the town of Baton Rouge on the twenty-second day of August, in the year of our Lord one thousand eight hundred and ten.

In testimony whereof, we, the representatives aforesaid, have hereunto in presence of each other, subscribed our names.

JOHN H. JOHNSON,
JOHN MILLS,
WILLIAM BARROW,
For the District of New-Feliciana.

JOHN W. LEONARD,
JOSEPH THOMAS,
BENJ. O. WILLIAM,
     For the District of St. Helena.

PHILIP HICKY,
THOMAS LILLEY,
JOHN MORGAN,
EDMUND HAWES,
     For the District of Baton-Rouge.

WILLIAM COOPER,
     For the District of St. Ferdinand.

CARLOS DEHAULT DELASSUS, Governor.
JOHN RHEA, President.

RESOLUTIONS

Resolved, That all the physicians and surgeons now residing and exercising their professions, with the permission of the government, within this jurisdiction, be formed into a Medical Society, with permission to assemble, from time to time, for the purpose of debating on subjects relating to their professions, and of communicating to each other such interesting cases as may occur in practice. The said society shall hold their first meeting at St. Francisville on the first day of October next; any six or more of them to form a society at the said first meeting; and they shall meet afterwards on their own adjournments. They shall have power to form such bye-laws for the government of the society as to them may seem fit and expedient, not inconsistent with any of the general laws of the country; and they shall form a bill of rates for medical and surgical services, which they shall make publick without unnecessary delay; and the same shall hereafter be recognized by the tribunals of justice within this jurisdiction, as the established rates of the country for such services.

Resolved, That the said medical society be authorized, and required, to choose annually, three or more of their members to form a committee for purpose of examining all persons who may hereafter come within this jurisdiction with a view of exercising the profession of medicine or surgery, or any branch thereof, and of granting licenses to such as they may find sufficiently skilled in the profession which they may propose to exercise as aforesaid; who shall thereafter be members of the said medical society; and any person who shall be found exercising either of said professions within the jurisdiction after this present year, not now exercising the same with the permission of the government, nor duly licensed by the committee of the medical society aforesaid, shall forfeit and pay for each offence, a fine not less than one hundred dollars, nor more than five hundred, at the discretion of the district courts of this jurisdiction; one-half of such fine to be paid to any person who shall sue for the same, and the other half to the civil commandant of the district.

Baton-Rouge, August 22, 1810.

Resolved, That this convention, with the consent of the governor, have power to borrow money on credit to the government and the revenue of the same, whenever the publick service may require.

Baton-Rouge, August 25, 1810.

Resolved, That the inhabitants of towns and villages within this jurisdiction be authorized to form such local regulations within the same as may be conducive to their own convenience and prosperity, not contrary to the general established laws of the country.

Baton-Rouge, August 25, 1810.

WM. SPILLER,	PHILIP HICKY,
JOHN MILLS,	MANUEL LOPEZ,
JOS. THOMAS,	THOS. LILLEY,
JOHN MORGAN,	JNO. H. JOHNSON,
JOHN W. LEONARD,	WM. BARROW,
BENJ. O. WILLIAMS,	EDMD. HAWES.

JOHN RHEA,
CARLOS DEHAULT DELASSUS.

PART THREE

The Revolt

Although successful in obtaining the governor's signature and approbation to their lengthy and all encompassing ordinances, the members of the convention did not immediately return to their homes. Much more had to be done. First and foremost they must select the new officials named by the ordinances who would govern the province "in the name of the people." Care was needed in these selections for, while some of the friends of the governor should be recognized in the appointments, it was vitally necessary that the majority be chosen from among those whole-heartedly in sympathy with the "for freedom" movement.

Forsaking the Saints John Plains for Baton Rouge and holding their meeting in the principal store in the village, one kept by an Irishman named Egan, the delegates, desiring to recognize the valuable services that John H. Johnson had given the convention proceedings, wanted him to take one of the principal judicial offices, but he refused, as did William Barrow and Judge Rhea.

It was the 29th of August before the delegates finished their labors and advised Governor de Lassus of their selections. Transcribed directly from the original document, it reads:

"To His Excellency Charles Dehault Delassus, Colonel of the the Royal Armies, Governor Civil and military of the place and jurisdiction of Baton Rouge, &c.

"Sir:
"The Representatives of the people of this jurisdiction in convention assembled make known to your Excellency that agreeable to the provisions of the 'ordinance providing for public safety, and for the better administration of justice within the Jurisdiction of Baton Rouge in West Florida,' they have made the following appointments, viz:

"Robert Piercy of New Feliciana, Fulwar Skipwith of Baton Rouge, and Shephard Brown of St. Helena, to be associate Judges of the Superior Court; Joseph E. Johnson of New Feliciana, Sheriff; and Andrew Steele of Baton Rouge, Register of land claims for this jurisdiction.

"Gilbert Leonard of Baton Rouge, Bryan McDermott of New Feliciana and Daniel Rainer of St. Helena to be Civil Commandants each for the district in which he resides.

"Officers of Militia
Philemon Thomas, Brigadier General.
Isaac Johnson, Major of Cavalry.

1st. Regiment of Infantry:
Samuel Fulton, Colonel.
George Mather, Junr. first Major.
Reuben Curtis, second Major.

2nd Regiment:
William Spiller, Colonel.
Joseph Thomas, first Major.
Abraham Spears, second Major.

3rd Regiment:
Aquila Whitaker, Colonel.
Robert McCausland, first Major.
John M. Pickford [?], second Major. [His name is
crossed out in the original.]

"Baton Rouge, 25 Augt.
1810."

First, consideration was given the three who were to compose the superior court. The appointment of Shepherd Brown of Tickfaw, the alcalde of the St. Helena district, was unquestionably a sop thrown to Governor deLassus. The delegates were not unanimous in wanting Brown on the bench of the high seat of justice; those from Feliciana were suspicious of him and were outspoken in their belief he would not prove faithful to or sympathetic with the cause of the people. Their suspicions were soon justified.

LIEUTENANT ROBERT PERCY

Robert Percy, chosen as member of the superior court from the Feliciana district, was a retired British naval officer. He was born in Kilkenny, Ireland, in 1762, and the son of Charles Percy, a former British army officer who came to West Florida in 1776 and settled in what is now Wilkinson county, Mississippi. Robert chose the sea for a career and entering the King's navy as a cadet rose to the rank of lieutenant. After the death of his father (who committed suicide by throwing himself into a stream which still bears the name of Percy's Creek), Robert Percy came to Louisiana in 1796 to settle his father's estate and reach a property division with his half brothers and sister, for Charles Percy had married again. Liking this new country, after his return to England Robert Percy obtained a leave of absence from the navy and in 1804 with his wife, Jane Middlemist, and oldest children, he settled in Spanish West Florida. Here, in Feliciana, on the Little Bayou Sarah, he erected "Beech Woods" plantation where he reared his numerous family and left behind him a splendid name borne today by many in Louisiana. Although a sturdy Britisher at heart, Lieutenant Percy became a staunch backer of the Convention movement.

JUDGE FULWAR SKIPWITH

Fulwar Skipwith, whose name later blazed bright in the annals of the tiny Republic of West Florida, was an American and, even in 1810, he was a man of note in national affairs. He had been in the Baton Rouge district only a short time when he was called to the bench. He was born in Dinwiddle county, Virginia, February 21, 1765, and died at "Montesano" plantation, just above Baton Rouge, January 7, 1839, at the age of 74 years. In 1790 Skipwith had been appointed by President George Washington, American consul to a small group of West Indian islands, including Matinique, Guadaloupe, and Sainte Lucie, etc. Ten years later, President Thomas Jefferson made him Consul General of the United States to France, with headquarters in Paris. While carrying on the functions of this office, during the trying days of the French Revolution, the Directory and Empire, the French, displeased with the United States, refused to hold communications with American ambassadors, consequently Skipwith was the sole commercial and diplomatic representative of his country in France, and during the existence of Napoleon's Milan and Berlin decrees, he was compelled to draw heavily upon his private purse to relieve American shipmasters and sailors detained in French ports by the embargoes—a sum, by the way, which he never recovered.

In 1809 Fulwar Skipwith appeared in Spanish West Florida to settle on a plantation on the Montesano Bluffs, near that one operated by the Herries brothers. He had failed to get on harmoniously with General John Armstrong, the American minister to France, so had resigned and left Paris. It was his intention in coming to West Florida to regain his fortune by operating a sheepwalk but George Herries soon convinced him that the operation of a cotton plantation would prove more lucrative, consequently he became a cotton planter. With him came his wife, a Flemish countess named Vanderclooster, his daughter, Lelia, who had been educated in France, and his other children. The daughter, Lelia Skipwith, later became the wife of Thomas Bolling Roberson, who was governor of Louisiana in 1820-24.

Fulwar Skipwith, according to his nephew, was "endowed with more than average intelligence, well cultivated by a collegiate study, and by his cosmopolitan associations in different climes. Of splendid physical development, he was more than six feet tall, straight as an arrow, with exactly enough flesh for his bone and muscle." Another friend wrote that Skipwith was "quite celebrated for his high-bred courtesy, his general literary accomplishments, and his splendid style of living. When he came to West Florida he brought back with him from Paris French *politesse* and French notions and habits. He drove

101

into Baton Rouge from his palatial residence in the country in a splendid coach and four, with outriders and lackeys to match."

Therefore, the planters had picked a distinguished-looking and, mentally and by experience, a well-equipped individual to help Percy and Brown govern the province from the bench of justice.

For the sheriff of the whole province, which now consisted of the districts of Feliciana, Baton Rouge, Ste. Helena, and Saint Ferdinand (this last, named for the Spanish King then in durance vile, was to consist of all territory "east of Ponchitoola, including Chiffonta, Bogcheto and Pearl River settlements"), the delegates had selected a native son of Feliciana, Joseph Eugenius Johnson, a brother of delegate John. The important post of Register of Land Claims was given to Dr. Andrew Steele, who had acted as secretary of the convention.

For the three civil commandants the delegates designated Bryan McDermott for the Feliciana district; Daniel Raynor was selected to preside over the Ste. Helena and Saint Ferdinand districts, and for the Baton Rouge sector the governor's comptroller, Gilbert Leonard.

These selections gave the friends of liberty a two-to-one majority on the high tribunal, and the same advantage among the civil judges, for McDermott and Raynor were heart and soul for the convention. The sheriff and the land office registrar were also "loyal to liberty."

PHILEMON THOMAS

When it came to selecting militia officers the conventionalists took no chances . . . threw no sops! For the commandant, brigadier general they named him, the unanimous choice was Philemon Thomas, later to be termed by Governor Claiborne as the "Ajax of the Revolution." He was a native of Virginia, born in Orange county, Feb. 9, 1764, who at the age of 17 ran away from home to join the American Revolutionary army, in spite of the fact his father, fearing such a move, had locked up his clothes. He bore a distinguished part in the battles of King's Mountain, Eutaw Springs, and Guilford Courthouse, and eight years after he had fled the parental roof to "jine the sodgers" his father and mother beheld a strange young man ride up to the home, dismount and proclaim himself their son Philemon.

In 1805 he moved to West Florida and settled in the Baton Rouge village. He married in Kentucky, first, Elizabeth Craig, daughter of one of the two dissenting ministers whom Patrick Henry defended when charged with preaching the Gospel without a license from the Church of England, and second, Fannie Thomas. His boys were all girls, two of whom married Thomases, and two became Gales. Thomas, who lived at the corner of America and St. Ferdinand streets, was colonel of the militia of the jurisdiction of Baton Rouge, for under the Spanish laws all men were compelled to be part of this citizens corps. He has been described as a Baptist, tall and with a powerful frame, with red hair, and clear blue eyes, and known to be the possessor of unquestioned courage. At the time of these disturbances, according to Henry L. Favrot, Philemon Thomas kept a grocery store or "doggery" and one of the signs on his place of business proclaimed he had "Coughpy for Sail," while another stated there could be found "Akomidation fur Man & Beest." While unlettered there is no doubt that he possessed native military acumen, which stood the revolting planters in good stead.

Thomas was one of the most conspicuous and remarkable of the many taking part in the revolt, according to W. H. Sparks, who in his "The Memories of Fifty Years," which has preserved for us many interesting facts and incidents connected with the revolt, wrote: "He was almost entirely without education; but was gifted with great good sense, a bold and honest soul, and a remarkable natural eloquence. His manner was always natural and genial, never, under any circumstances, embarrassed or affected; and, in whatever company he was thrown, or however much a stranger to company, somehow he became the conspicuous man in a short time. The character in his face, the flash of his eye, the remarkable self-possession, the the natural dignity of department, and his great good sense, attracted and won everyone. In all his transactions, he was the same plain, honest man, never, under any circumstances, deviating from truth—plain, unvarnished truth; rigidly stern in morals, but eminently charitable to the shortcomings of others. He was, from childhood, reared in a new country, amid rude, uncultivated people, and was a noble specimen of a frontier man; without the amenities of cultivated life, or the polish of education, yet with all the virtues of the Christian heart, and these, perhaps, the more prominently, because of the absence of the others. It is frequently remarked of him that he did not think education would have been of any advantage to him. It enabled men, with pretty words, to hide their thoughts, and deceive their fellowmen with a grace and ease he despised; and it might have acted so with him, but it would have made him worse and a more unhappy man. He never did or said anything that he was ashamed to think of. He did not want to conceal his feelings and opinions, because he did not know how to do it; and he was sure if he attempted it he should make a fool of himself; for lies required so much dressing up in pretty words to make them look like the truth, that he should fail for want of words; truth was always prettiest when naked."

Isaac Johnson, who already had recruited the "Bayou Sarah Horse," and was spoiling for an opportunity to display the abilities of his men a-horseback in a brush with the uniformed regular soldiers of Spain, was given the commission of major of cavalry. With Joe Johnson as sheriff of the entire jurisdiction, and Isaac placed in command of the fast-moving fighters of Feliciana, the Johnson family was well represented in this move for independence, even if Brother John, the "brains" of the movement, refused an office. The other militia officers appointed were known and tested "patriots."

LULL BEFORE THE STORM

These important appointments made, the delegates prepared to disperse to their several homes, planning to meet again the first Monday in November. They had assumed control of the purse, the sword, and the scales of justice, giving nothing to Governor de Lassus except an annual salary of three thousand dollars.

What had transpired was immediately transmitted to Washington by Governor Holmes, who had kept in close touch with all going on "below the line." The Mississippi executive informing Secretary of State Robert Smith that, "contrary to general expectations," de Lassus had sanctioned the ordinances of the convention and in so doing had "divested himself of most of the powers of his office, retaining only title and salary." Holmes also wrote it was not necessary to add that "this surrender of authority was not a matter of choice on his part" and predicted, as this apparent harmony was a forced one and that as a majority of the people favored the intervention of the United States, that the agreement would be of short duration. Holmes knew whereof he wrote.

The Mississippi governor believed, as did many others, that the new order of things could not long maintain a separate existence if the inhabitants should finally declare for independence, nor could the leaders of the movement escape the resentment of Spain should that power regain control. Holmes further informed the Washington government that the leaders and the people behind them were determined to hazard everything rather than submit to Spanish officials. There need be no fear of the French, as Napoleon's government was so obnoxious to everyone concerned that it scarcely had an advocate in the province. The friends of Great Britian, however, were numerous, intelligent, and active in seeking proselytes, and were continually representing the commercial advantages to be gained by a union with England, so warned the Mississippi governor.

Before concluding their labors the members of the convention composed a written, but evidently never printed, justification of their activities in meeting and drawing up ordinances for a peoples' government of the province. Their original draft reads:

"To the Inhabitants of the Jurisdiction of Baton Rouge:

"The Convention of your Delegates being about to Adjourn until the first Monday in Nov..feel it their duty to lay before their Constituents the subject of their proceedings. That the impression made on the minds of many by reports in some cases accidental, in others wilfully False, may be removed. When entering upon the important duty assigned to our care, the prospect was awful & embarrassing. The embarrassment of Gov[ernment], owing to the almost total subjection of the Spanish Empire, is well known, and the Leniency of justice, in a manner, dried up; the Spirit of the Law Lost, Corruption had crept into almost every Department. The benevolent intention of our Monarch to grant his Lands to Inhabitants & imigrants of good character had been entirely frustrated, and they have been abandoned as Lawful Pillage to the Wealthy Stranger & indigent Adventurer thro bribery and intrigue. This, as well as other Regulations prevailing, for those of worth among us while the profligate and [lawless] found a ready asylum, and like Birds of Prey Prowle on the peaceful Inhabitants. The arm of Gov[ernment] paralised & a Scene of Chaos and Anarchy approaching.

"In the course of their deliberations the Convention of Delegates have invariably directed their attention to the Public Good. They have endeavoured while correcting abuses to preserve the integrity of the Government. How far they may have met the wishes of their Constituents remains for the expression of the Public Will to decide. The Convention invite this expression. They are anxious to know how far their Conduct gives Satisfaction to the People."

The rough draft was obviously written on the 25th of August, a day that, evidently, found every delegate with a crow quill in his hand and an ink horn at his elbow, busy filling sheets of paper with words.

However, with the news of the adoption of the ordinances and the issuance of the joint proclamation of governor and delegates, a quiet settled over the province, and even in heretofore turbulent Feliciana a decided calm took the place of the storm that had so exercised the planter folk for months. As proof of this the "Louisiana Gazette" published the following extract of a letter:

"Bayou Sarah, Sept. 9th, 1810.

"Confidence is at length restored here. We now have some security for our persons and property, and justice will be administered in due form, and according to our system of laws. The proceedings of the convention so far, have given universal satisfaction, and sanguine expectations are entertained of the happiness we shall enjoy, and the great prosperity of the country under the system adopted.

"I have long wished to have you my neighbor, convinced your removal here would tend greatly to your interest, as it is well known the lands of your low country are not equal to ours for the culture of the cotton tree. A very short time will make the district of Feliciana, the garden spot of the Floridas, possessing the many advantages which it does. Many rich and respectable emigrants are now coming in here, and our lands are augmenting in price. Lands which a short time since were selling at four and five dollars per acre have within a few days been sold at six and seven dollars, and must continue to increase in value; this circumstance alone bespeaks the increasing prosperity of our country."

Which would indicate that the Feliciana folk aside from winning liberty, and the right to happiness, were also going to profit through rising land values.

THE GOVERNOR REJECTS "JUDGE" SKIPWITH

The governor, although he did not hesitate to place his signature and flowing paraph on the many new ordinances, proved to be a trifle stubborn about affirming the selection of the new officers that the delegates had selected to govern the province under the provisions of the ordinances.

On the 25th of August de Lassus penned a communication to the *"Senores diputados"* in which he refused to confirm the appointment of Fulwar Skipwith to the high court, and also balked at giving Philemon Thomas the title of "brigadier general," suggesting that he could retain the title he already had, that of colonel of the militia. His translated words read:

"In reply to your letter of this same date may I explain that the arms stored in this place are intended for use in the defense of this fort and the country, the command of which has been intrusted to me against the enemies of our flag; and you may be assured that, as soon as I am informed of the forces actually in existence and of the individuals who do not have arms to defend the cause of our legitimate sovereign, Ferdinand 7th, I shall make the proper arrangements for them to be so provided and in the manner which you have asked.

"With regards for the plans for the defense, I myself being responsible for them, and the officers of the General Staff having been appointed, and after each of them shall have been installed each in his post, I shall make arrangements for all such dispositions which you do not treat of in your aforementioned letter.

"Inasmuch there has not been presented to me, even in translation, your deliberations, I do not find myself sufficiently well informed regarding them to make replies and observations which might occur to me to promote the general good of this jurisdiction, as I shall duly express to you on the day when they shall be presented to me; nonetheless I approve the suggestions which you make to me that I should give approval to the different officers, civil as well as military, which your second letter dated today contains.

"I must call to your attention that while I believe Don Fulwar Skipwith has all the qualifications necessary to discharge the duties of the post for which you recommend him, our laws prohibit any foreigner who has not resided in the province two years and has not taken the proper oath of loyalty to the government, from enjoying and profiting from the privileges of a subject of Spain, and, additionally, this same Skipwith has stated to me that he would accept no appointment; therefore it is necessary that you elect someone else in his place.

"As there does not exist, and as I myself do not recognize in our military ordinances, the post of 'brigadier general', it appears to me that Mr. Philemon Thomas can take the same post with the title of colonel commandant of the whole militia in this jurisdiction, with the approbation of his Excellency the Captain General.

"God preserve you many years.

                    CARLOS DEHAULT DELASUS."

The refusal of de Lassus to place his official "O. K." on the former American consul at Paris and his further disinclination to invest Philemon Thomas with any title that had "general" to it, especially when the best the governor could do was to rise to the rank of colonel in the armies of Spain, rather nonplussed the convention delegates who were preparing to quit Baton Rouge. Once again the whole was summoned into meeting and, three days later, they answered Don Carlos' letter with a letter of their own. The reader, by this time, will not have failed to gather the impression that all concerned in this remarkable political upheaval delighted to write long letters, filled to the brim with flowery expressions and honeyed words! What must their speeches been!

What the governor had said about Skipwith's standing in the community was true enough. When he arrived in West Florida he applied, as every foreigner had to do, for the right to remain in the province for six months preparatory to taking out regular citizenship papers. For some not known reason, Governor De Lassus had denied Skipwith these documents, although he allowed Skipwith to invest his scanty funds in the "Montesano" plantation, just above the Herries brothers' saw mill and their projected new town. At the time he was named judge he had, in fact, outlived his legal stay.

The delegates did not take kindly to the demand of de Lassus that they select some one else for the high court. They recalled countless other occasions when the established laws of the province had not been so strictly observed in appointing "aliens" to office. In consequence, on August 28th, they sent the governor the following rejoinder:

"The Convention of Representatives in reply to the communication of your Excellency of the 25th Instant have to observe that although it is not intended to make any unnecessary innovations in the existing laws of the country, yet at the present crisis in which the preservation of the Province becomes the primary object of attention, we conceive it our duty to deviate in some points of minor importance from the established laws, when some important advantage may result from the change. The appointment of Mr. Skipwith to be one of the judges of the Superior Court, we consider to be justifiable on this principle, although he be not entitled to that office, from the time of his residence amongst us. To obtain a gentleman of his capacity and good character in that station we believe ourselves justifiable at the present moment in deviating a little from ancient forms.

"The change which you propose of the title of the Commanding officer of the Militia we have no objection to make, as it will in no wise affect the general regulations of the organization of the Militia, to conform in this instance to the established military ordinances of the country."

Recent discovery of papers handled by the delegates indicates that the conventionalists proposed additions to the communication printed in full above for a rough draft, on the back of another letter reads:

"Your Excellency having expressed your readyness to commission the officers of the militia proposed by the Convention on the 24th ult. and a speedy organization of the militia being an object of the first importance for the preservation of the Province, the Committee request your signature to the letter enclosed herewith if the same should meet with your approbation, as an authority for the said officers to exercise their respective offices until commissions can be obtained in due form."

Although the delegates wanted to reorganize and arm the militia, which, according to the new ordinances, would be under the jurisdiction of the convention, it was evident should they press the governor on this point, it might prove disastrous through arousing his suspicions. It will be noted that de Lassus, while he craftily agreed to the proposals of the delegates, always held in reserve the fact that anything he agreed to must have the approbation of the Captain General, the Marquis de Someruelos, in far-off Havana, Cuba. In other words, de Lassus had an ace up his sleeve.

DE LASSUS GETS 6,000 PESOS

About the middle of September a Spanish army officer, Captain Louis Piernas, appeared in Baton Rouge from Pensacola. A few weeks before he had arrived at Pensacola from Havana with fifty thousand *pesos* for Governor Vizente Folch to pay the soldiers serving in West Florida. Folch immediately dispatched Captain Piernas to Baton Rouge with six thousand *pesos* for de Lassus, and instructions to observe conditions which he was to report in detail on his return.

Piernas found Baton Rouge quiet and peaceful. At some length Governor de Lassus explained what he had been forced to do in the circumstances in order to preserve public tranquillity, and that all he had done was to agree with the delegates pending the decision of El Marqués de Someruelos, the captain-general of Cuba. However, other officers of the Baton Rouge garrison told Piernas another story and gave it as their opinion that matters were not as de Lassus represented them to be.

About the time Captain Piernas was preparing for his return trip to Pensacola, Governor de Lassus, in a letter addressed to the whole convention, advised that he desired an important change made in the ordinances. As they were written, in case of his absence or inability to act, the senior judge of the Superior Court would govern. The governor wished that article change so that one of his own military officers would act in his stead should he be compelled to leave the seat of government or suffer any disability. Because the convention as a whole had dispersed, de Lassus sent his demand to the committee, Philip Hicky, Manuel Lopez, and Thomas Lilley, designated to act with the governor in administrative matters until it should reassemble. Wrote the governor:

"Attending to the critical circumstances of this province, and the declaration of the council of the officers of the date of the 21st of August last, with the subjects expressed in my proclamation signed by the representatives of the people on the 22d of the same month; and being assured by all the declarations of the inhabitants who have ever manifested their attachment to our government, that there is no other method to preserve the tranquillity of this territory, against either foreign or domestic enemies, whose preverse machinations were at the point to revolutionize, and kindle the flame of rebellion which would have destroyed this part of the Dominions of His Catholic Majesty Ferdinand 7th, and which through the Divine goodness appears to have subsided since my said proclamation. I find myself imperiously compelled to approve these laws, as I promised in that proclamation, that they may have their complete operation until the approbation of his excellency the Captain-general of the Province: and as the representatives have pledged themselves not to neglect their duty or molest the authorities but on the contrary to support them. Relying on this declaration, thinking it my duty to refuse the salaries offered to me, which I do not accept until the approbation of his Excellency aforesaid, as I have always declared, I will only observe that in case

109

of my absence or infirmity as expressed in the 3d section of the Article providing for the better administration of justice, the senior officer present will of right represent the superior authority in my place.

"And moreover the lands of the Royal domain which may be vacant will be preserved in *statu quo* until the approbation of the Captain-general aforesaid.

"In Baton Rouge signed with my hand and sealed with the seal of my arms and certified by the undersigned Secretary, 12th. Sept. *Anno Domini* 1810.

CARLOS DEHAULT DELASSUS.

Raphael Croker, Secretary."

This move on the part of the governor, to provide that *his* senior officer should act in his stead, so he assured the three committeemen, would make no substantial change in the form of government outlined in the ordinances, consequently he hoped they would agree to it. Unquestionably this sudden move by de Lassus was prompted by something Captain Piernas suggested during their conferences.

However, (so we find in the *Paples de Cuba, Legajo 185*, where complete copies of the correspondence have been preserved), Hicky, Lilley and even Lopez objected to this, pointing out that if one of his military staff was appointed to perform in his absence that such an inferior would perform military as well as judicial functions! This was the one thing that planters objected to! The committee agreed to submit the matter to the whole membership of the convention and pointed out that there was no hurry to do this as the superior tribunal was not scheduled to hold its initial session before the convention would again meet. To this de Lassus, balked in his first intention, acquiesced; although in his letter of reply on the 14th he reiterated his stand not to accept salary until permitted to do so by the Captain-general, and should any vacancy occur on his staff, he agreed that he and the deputies should determine the successor until the convention again met in regular session or the Captain-general should decide otherwise. In this exchange of notes there was the usual and mutual beseeching of the Almighty to "preserve" each "many years!"

When Captain Piernas quitted Baton Rouge he carried with him a long explanatory letter which de Lassus had penned to his superiors. The Spanish army officer also carried another letter back to Pensacola. It had been written by William Cooper, delegate to the convention from the Chefuncté region and dated September 12. In penning his missive Cooper said he felt in duty bound to report the dangerous situation then existing at Baton Rouge. He told of the calling of the convention and how the inhabitants of the Bayou Sarah region, which had been in a rebellious condition since the first of the year, had wanted to declare for independence but that he, with some other members "constituting

110

a vigorous minority," had declared for the Spanish régime. Cooper then charged the majority with making up a code of laws which deprived the Spanish officials of all power, and from that moment on he was certain that "the aim of the malcontents was that of overthrowing the existing system."

Cooper claimed that the people of the province in general, were opposed to this attempt on the part of the Feliciana people, but that de Lassus' agreement had prevented those loyal to Spain from resisting. Therefore, these loyal folk desired the immediate presence of Governor Folch. Cooper warned the Spanish executive that at its next meeting the convention would overthrow the last vestiges of the Spanish system. This was his reason, and the reason of Captain Michael Jones (a "damned old Tory," according to the Feliciana folk), for wanting Folch to hurry with a considerable force "to save the unfortunate but well-disposed inhabitants of the province."

This appeal, which was in Folch's hands the first week in October, determined him to go at once to the disaffected region, and he ordered a force of one hundred and fifty men to prepare to move immediately. But before he could get started distressing tidings came to the govenor of West Florida!

GUILE VS. DUPLICITY

The quiet that pervaded Baton Rouge was, as future events proved, only the calm that precedes the hurricane. Don Carlos was positive that he was cunningly concealing his real sentiments from the conventionalists, while the delegates, although they declared they were satisfied with the adoption of the new laws, felt that, in spite of the time and attention they had given the construction of the ordinances, some other course must be adopted. So both sides sparred for time. Time for what?

Rumors began to steal into the province, into Baton Rouge, into Feliciana, into the Ste. Helena district. From the district where Bill Cooper and Michael Jones were holding forth came the whisper that "the violent aristocrats and the old American Tories" were arming and recruiting men so as to join the force of Spanish soldiers that Folch, at the behest of de Lassus, was then marching on from Pensacola.

At Springfield, John Ballinger, who had recently emigrated there from Kentucky, was told that Michael Jones and William Cooper were "erecting a fort on the Nictalbany" under the instructions of Shepherd Brown so that a fortified base, from which Folch could operate, would be ready when he and his veteran troops arrived. In relaying this news to Philemon Thomas, Ballinger urged that the conventionalists act at once and capture Baton Rouge, and added another rumor, believed by many, that the Spanish governor planned to stir up the slaves, and the Indians would also be urged to rise. Ballinger claimed such news came to him from responsible sources.

Shepherd Brown's conduct was open to suspicion. Designated a member of the high court, he put off his acceptance from day to day. As he procrastinated, Brown moved about the Baton Rouge village smiling and assuring the others that he was in full accord with the new measures. But he would not take the oath of office. Finally he returned to Ste. Helena, telling the governor and close friends that he preferred to retain his office as alcalde of his district. Just before he quitted the fort, in conversation with the commander of the artillery there, he gave it as his opinion "the Bayou Sarah people would be the better for having a little blood drawn."

The actions of de Lassus were also open to suspicion, too, consequently Philip Hicky and George Mather conferred with the governor. Was his procastination in not signing certain documents sent him by the committee of the convention due to any change of mind? Don Carlos blandly denied this was so. Was the governor engaging in double-dealing? No, no—on his honor, no! The delegates had nothing but their suspicions to make them believe that he was.

ESTEVAN IS EVICTED FROM BAYOU SARAH

A week passed. At Bayou Sarah, on the morning of September 20, Major Isaac Johnson called upon Commandant Don Tomas Estevan. Exhibiting written orders from the convention which instructed the Spaniard to turn over all the property and stores held by him and to betake himself and his soliders to Baton Rouge, Major Johnson told "El Capitán" to get busy, whereupon the right arm of Spain did not protest nor did he stand upon the order of his going, but went at once! The next morning, with his "garrison" Francisco Glavan, Manuel Villanueva, Francisco Ximenez, Alexandro Lopez, Manuel Matamoros, and Pasqual Polonesa, we find him going downstream in the *goleta* "Proserpina," and in the prow of the barge was a passenger, the *cura* Francisco Lennán, who had decided that Saint Francisville was no longer a safe place for him. When all reached Baton Rouge, safe and sound, Don Tomas Estevan repaired to the *Real Hospital*, he was sick, he told the physician in charge, and went to bed.

On the night of this same Thursday, the 20th, Governor de Lassus gave another of his "peace dinners" to which he invited the representatives of the convention. Hicky and Lilley were not present but Manuel Lopez attended and among the dozen or so guests were the Mathers, father and son, and "Colonel" Philemon Thomas, who listened to the governor's protestations of friendship with a grim smile and gleaming

112

blue eyes; his red hair seemed redder than usual. Thomas was still smiling when de Lassus ordered another salute of twenty-one guns from the fort to again "commemorate the perfect harmony" existing between the chief executive and the people of Feliciana since he had signed the ordinances.

Philemon Thomas had a reason for smiling. Only that morning some of his trusted men had intercepted a messenger that de Lassus had sent to Shepherd Brown during the night. The dispatch-bearer carried communications that Brown was to forward to Pensacola. In them Governor de Lassus implored Governor Folch to dispatch an armed force to his assistance at once, so that he, de Lassus, could quell an absolute insurrection of His Catholic Majesty's subjects! He informed his superior that he had been deprived of all authority vested in him by the King and had been superseded by self-constituted officers. Although he had not yet been placed in confinement, such a close watch was being kept over him that he feared at any time he would be thrown in goal and the fort occupied.

Don Carlos, in the other letter found on the messenger, urged Shepherd Brown to hurry with his preparations to arm every loyal citizen he could muster, to erect forts, and be ready to lend all assistance possible when he, the governor, would give the word to strike. Then, the ringleaders would be rounded up and punished. At last! Proof of de Lassus' duplicity; proof of Shepherd Brown's treachery!

When these communications were read to General Thomas, for he himself was unable to do so, his lack of education did not prevent him from knowing what to do in the circumstances. He placed the governor's messenger in close confinement, then quietly apprised Philip Hicky of what he had uncovered. Thomas planned to dispatch couriers to the Feliciana district so the leaders of the liberty movement could be informed of the governor's deception and intention of hanging the convention delegates higher than Gilory's kite.

Philip Hicky, however, volunteered to carry the information himself, and was soon in the saddle. When he paused at The Plains and delivered his budget of news to Thomas Lilley and Richard Devall, Lilley joined him. The two galloped their horses over the road, stopping at friendly plantations to exchange their blown mounts for fresh horses, splashed through the ford at Thompson's Creek, and then up the hill to "Troy" plantation.

"STRIKE FOR LIBERTY!"

On the night of September 21, six members of the convention were gathered at "Troy" plantation, just outside Saint Francisville. They were, John Hunter Johnson, William Barrow, John Rhea, John Mills,

113

Thomas Lilley and Philip Hicky. The two latter had delivered their budget of news and echoed Philemon Thomas' warning that their necks were now in danger. They grimly acknowledged that the Spanish governor had outwitted them and therefore they must act quickly. The futility of continuing their mock allegiance to Spain was apparent to each. A quick, decisive blow for liberty must be struck at once, even if they had not yet secured muskets from the fort for the militia. Pistols, fowling pieces, knives were at hand, with stout arms, and stout hearts behind the arms, to wield them. Post haste messengers were supplied with fresh horses and sent back to Thomas with the convention's orders. These orders were that he should arm all the men available and storm the fort at Baton Rouge as quickly as forces could be assembled, the latter to be done secretly. The militia leader was assured he could expect armed assistance from Feliciana to join him in the attack.

From now on it was to be war! The sword was to take the place of the crow quill!

Saturday, September 22, was a day of activity in and about Baton Rouge. While the governor bustled about the fort and the village, Philemon Thomas dispatched riders to Daniel Raynor in Ste. Helena ordering him to amass loyal planters and march to an appointed place just outside the village.

In the Feliciana country Major Isaac Johnson and Captain Lewellyn C. Griffith rounded up their dragoons and early that day the clattering hoofs of their mounts on the dusty road leading to Baton Rouge gave notice that the "Bayou Sarah Horse" was on its way. At the head of the column rode a flag-bearer. The banner that waved in the early morning breeze from the staff he carried was a strange one, all blue, like the azure of the sky, in its center a single five-pointed gleaming white star. It had been made, several days before, by Isaac Johnson's wife, Melissa, and represented the "five points of fellowship" under which the Feliciana planters had first gathered in secret session to confect their plans for liberty in West Florida.

While the Feliciana dragoons were on their way, Philemon Thomas himself went to Springfield as fast as horseflesh could take him there and assisted John Ballinger to muster the grenadier company. When this "army" took up the line of march, forty-four armed men tramped behind their commander as he turned back towards Baton Rouge, all "fit to fight a battle for the freedom of the world."

It was an hour after midnight before two columns met just outside the village. Impatiently Commander Thomas awaited the arrival of the third column due from Ste. Helena. His present army consisted of the

114

21 mounted men from Feliciana, there were 44 from Springfield, and eight or ten "patriotic gentlemen" who brought the effective force up to about 75 men. Additional men from Ste. Helena were on their way but whether they would arrive before daylight was problematical. A few of the Ste. Helena patriots had arrived on their piney-woods tackies. They were headed by a quaint character named Larry Moore, who was spoiling for a chance to fist-fight those in the fort. It might be pointed out that neither Mr. Moore or his companions ever referred to Spaniards, officials or private citizens, as Dons or Hidalgos. To these hardy sons of the piney woods such humans were either "yaller bellies" or "pukes".

THE FORT AT BATON ROUGE

While the patriots were secretly gathering and making ready for the onslaught, Spanish officers in the fort were making that place ready for any possible trouble. Early Saturday morning a horseman had dashed into the village seeking the governor, he told Lieutenant Morejon that he had been sent from Bayou Sarah to advise the authorities that the Feliciana people were arming and securing horses for a descent on the fort. In the late afternoon another messenger, dispatched by John Murdock, arrived and informed the governor of the suspicious movements of those who had backed the convention. To make sure his message would reach the governor, Murdock had sent another courier by water. Quietly the fort was put in readiness to receive the delegation with appropriate ceremonies.

The fort at Baton Rouge was situated on a piece of ground that overlooked the Mississippi river, an elevation ten or fifteen feet higher than the surrounding land. The fort was surrounded by high cypress pickets, which were set so they slanted outwardly, and then enclosed about three acres of ground. Behind them banks of clay, nearly as high as the cypress pickets had been thrown up so as to form a solid rampart. The stockade itself was square with four small bastions at the corners. The *fosse* or ditch, about nine feet deep and fifteen feet wide, was dry but it would hinder, in spite of its lack of water, an attacking party from investing the fort on the land side. The fort would prove, to a force not supplied with artillery, a difficult nut to crack.

There were several well-appearing houses within the enclosure, one being a rather substantial blockhouse. Facing the river were mounted about a score of guns, all apparently in good condition, whose mouths gaped on the turgid flow of the mighty Mississippi; scattered about the grounds were a number of rusty old cannon, of many fashions and of varying calibres, mounted on decrepit carriages, the whole looking for all the world like a gathering of cripples home from the wars.

115

But the main gates, which faced south and the village, were flanked by four cannon, which Lieutenant Metzinger saw were well loaded with grape. Any attack from the land side would result in the charging columns being swept with a hail of lead. It was from the direction of the village that an attack, if any, would be made, so the soldiers decided and they were prepared.

Surrounding the parade ground were the blockhouse, with many musket portals; a well-buttressed arsenal, and a thick walled storehouse. In the center of the *presidio* or parade ground rose the tall white-painted staff from which floated the red and yellow banner of Spain.

If there was blood to be let, then the soldiers of Castile and Leon were ready to let it, and let it flow from the bodies of those who would dare flout the dignity and authority of His Catholic Majesty, Ferdinand VII, of Spain!

LOUIS DE GRAND-PRE—CREOLE

On this September Saturday, while the Dons were on the *qui ve vive* for eventualities, Sub-Lieutenant Don Louis Antonio de Grand-Pré, eldest son of the late governor Don Carlos de Grand-Pré, left the fort and was rowed across the river to the American side. He went to the plantation of Don Pedro Favrot, a former French and Spanish army officer, where he had promised to spend the Sabbath.

Don Pedro Favrot, (in the days of the French domination of Louisiana he was called Pierre Joseph de Favrot), was a native of Louisiana, who served in the French colonial army until his native land was ceded to Spain. In 1778 he was allowed to hold his same commission in the Spanish colonial army and was in charge of Fort Saint Philip on the Mississippi in 1803, when the Louisiana Purchase was consummated and the province passed under the control of the United States. Thereupon Don Pedro forsook his military career, retired to a plantation he had purchased on the west bank of the Mississippi nearly opposite Baton Rouge, and with his wife and children prepared to live out the rest of his life in peace and contentment as an American citizen.

His eldest child was Joséphine, described as a beautiful and talented Creole. Her bethrothed was young Louis de Grand-Pré. They were childhood sweethearts, for Carlos de Grand-Pré and her father had been companions-in-arms in both the French and Spanish colonial troops. Joséphine Favrot and Don Louis were Louisiana-born French Creoles and pardonably proud of this distinction. When Louis announced the fact he would be unable to pay his regular Sunday visit to the Favrot plantation, regret was expressed, and the young officer in the service of Spain was urged to stay for the night.

116

Don Louis said that, that as much as he desired to remain and court his lady love, his duty made it imperitive that he return to the fort for, should anything occur in his absence, he would never forgive himself. The Favrots pointed out to him that he was too loyal to the Spain that had cast such a stigma on the name of his honored father. To this Louis replied that he must prove by his devotion to the Spanish cause that the charges against his father had been baseless. So he ordered his men to row him back to the fort where he arrived soon after darkness fell.

Upon reaching the fort, Don Louis sought out his friend Lieutenant Metzinger, the artillery officer. He was told that everything was quiet and, in the estimation of all in charge of the fort, the reported uprising would prove untrue. All the regular soldiers were instructed to sleep on their arms, however, and the night guard was cautioned to be extra alert and report any suspicious movements. The sentinels paraded the ramparts and Metzinger saw to it that the guns were in readiness to repel any attack.

At midnight, when the sentries patrolling the ramparts were calling into the star-studded night: *"Ave Maria purisima! Las doce de la noche y sereno. Salve Espana!"* a third messenger from John Murdock reached the fort. He was in search of Tomaso Estevan and was conducted to the bedside of the former commandant of Bayou Sarah, who was being treated in the *Real Hospital*. Murdock's message was to the effect that he had positive information that the Feliciana mounted men, under Major Isaac Johnson and Captain Griffith, had left Sain Francisville to attack on the fort. The sentinels were reenforced, the guard called out, artillerymen were ordered to their guns, officers sleeping outside the stockade were summoned to the fort, and word was sent to de Lassus, who was abed in his house, which was only two hundred paces away.

A half hour later the governor was at his post where he waited from two in the morning until nearly four. A slight fog was rising from the surface of the river. Anxiously the officers paced up and down the stockade. Would there be an attack? Scarcely at night, they reasoned, and besides, it was now Sunday; would the Feliciana planters desecrate the Sabbath by war? Unthinkable!

The governor, after satisfying himself that the guards were alert, returned to his house and his interrupted sleep.

"HURRAH FOR WASHINGTON!"

Meanwhile, on the outskirts of the village, in the dark, the forces of the patriots were gathering. The Ste. Helena contingent was slow in arriving and the leader feared the sun would be up before they would join his forces. Philemon Thomas had marched his Springfield foot soldiers forty miles in the space of thirteen hours. Isaac Johnson, with his one score and one of mounted men, had reached the designated rendezvous on time and with him rode a number of planters and convention delegates who had hastily armed themselves with pistols and fowling pieces. The delegates were as ready to participate in the coming physical encounter as they were to write laws.

How was he to crack the fort with the least harm to his men? This was Philemon Thomas' problem at that time. Informed of the preparations made within the fort to receive his forces, he realized that to march directly on the stockade and force the main gate would merely mean his men would be raked by a killing fire from the four cannon whose grape-filled muzzles faced the port. Thomas' force was small, not many more than sixty-odd, he was without artillery, and he knew that the Sapnish inside the fort would have the advantage should he elect to take the place by storm.

At this point Larry Moore, a Kentuckian by birth, and settler in the Ste. Helena district, a close friend of Philemon Thomas, as illiterate as he was bold, but as cunning as a piney-woods fox, spoke up and claimed he knew how to "git inter thet dinged ol' fort." He explained that the cows, which supplied the garrison with fresh milk, always entered and left the fort through an opening in the cypress palisades on the river side. As this opening was opposite the commons, Larry claimed that those on horseback could sneak in. "Ef them cows kin git in thar an' outen again, I knows my pony kin tote me in the same way, an' do h'it as easy as fallin' offen a log."

Isaac Johnson was immediately interested and he secured permission from the commander to try entering the fort by this round-about ruse. Led by the tobacco-chewing Larry Moore, the Bayou Sarah cavalry set off to circle the fort, approach it by the river bluffs, and approach the fort by the cow path and enter it through the broken cypress pickets, while the defenders were keeping vigilant watch on the main gate.

In single file the horesmen urged their mounts up the steep river bluff and threaded their mounts through the herd of feeding milk-cows; the cow path was distinct in spite of the thickening fog that hung close to the surface of the wide Mississippi, for day was about to break. The opening in the cypress palisades was found just as Larry Moore had predicted and so quietly did the horsemen make their way into the fort that they were lined up on the edge of the parade ground before the sentry, Corporal José de la Polvora, who first heard the stamping of horses hooves, cried: *"Ole! Qué es eso!"* Getting no reply to his inquiry, the sentry yelled *"Quien vive?"* and then, like rapid shots, the shrill *"Alerta! Alerta! Alerta!"* of the other sentinels tore into the black morning air to apprise the rest of the garrison that the Gringos were *inside* the fort!

Sharp commands in purest Castilian ordered out the guard, and Louis de Grand-Pré dashed into the guardhouse and then out of it with the *Cuerpo de Guardia* at his back. The intrepid young Creole made straight for the line of mounted men now forming the width of the parade ground. Waving his sword and bidding his men follow, Don Louis reached the invaders. *"Mio amigos"*, he called in Spanish, "my friends we are more numerous than you; we do not want to hurt you!" As he spoke, he started slashing with his sabre, at the flanks of the horses within reach of his blade as though to turn them back the way they had come.

But the mounted men only urged their hoses on towards the block-house. Don Louis ran back to his guardsmen, and as he reached them he shouted *"Fuego! Fuego!"*

Obeying the order to fire, the soldiers put up their muskets and discharged a volley at the oncoming mounted men. Horses reared and whinnied in pain, but not a Bayou Sarah man was struck by a flying ball. Then, for the first time since entering the fort, Isaac Johnson voiced an order, "Shoot 'em down!" From the men on horseback came the answering hail of lead. The brave young leader of the Spanish guard fell with four balls in his body. Lieutenant Juan Metzinger, endeavoring to wheel his guns into a new position, was struck twice, a bullet punctured his sword arm, while a pistol ball fractured his wrist.

Breaking their silence, whooping with might and main, and shouting "Hurrah for Washington!", Isaac Johnson and his men from Feliciana dashed forward, leaping their mounts over the prostrate forms of the Spanish dead and wounded, for six of the defenders of the fort were rolling and threshing about in the dust of the parade.

Artillerymen, endeavoring to face their guns in the opposite direction, scattered before the earth-shaking throb of galloping hooves. In a trice the gates were reached and the Spanish foot soldiers guarding the main port were soon madly fleeing for the safety of the guardhouse. To throw open the gates was the work of a few seconds and Philemon Thomas, followed by his foot soldiers, came boiling into the fort. At the first cry from the fort, the shrill *"Alertas!"* of the sentinels informing them that the horsemen sneaking into the fort via the back way had been discovered and then the sound of firing, sent the whole patriot force in a mad rush for the fort to engage in the mélee.

Governor de Lassus entered the fort to find the whole patriotic force of about 65 men gathered about the blockhouse busily making Spanish soldiers prisoners. Ordered to hand over his sword, the gov-

119

ernor refused so one of the Feliciana invaders, who had just wrested
a musket from a captured Spanish soldier, knocked de Lassus down
with the butt, and would have run the bayonet through him had not
Philemon Thomas intervened. As the dazed governor rose to his feet
another Bayou Sarah patriot discharged a pistol so close to his bald
head, that the power of Spain in the jurisdiction of Baton Rouge near
to swooned from fright.

The Spanish defenders were demoralized, not only by the night attack, but by the violation of the recognized rules of warfare, "the capture
of a fort by cavalry alone!" These Gringos! The jubilant captors had no
time to discuss the amenities. Spanish soldiers had to be disarmed and
herded into the guardhouse. The ex-governor was also locked up. Then
a hasty survey was made of the attacking force. Not a man had been
killed, not a man wounded!

Tenderly, the pain-wracked Louis de Grand-Pré was carried into
the hospital and a surgeon summoned to attend his hurts. The young
Creole's order to his men, *"Fire! Fire!"*, had proved his own death
warrant. He had been struck twice in the arm, a ball had broken his
thigh, and another had punctured his chest. The victors also carried
into the hospital, which had been hastily deserted at the first sound of
firing by "sick" Don Tomaso Estevan, a dead soldier, Manuel Matamoros,
one of Estevan's force at Bayou Sarah; and two badly wounded soldiers,
Francisco Ximenes and Corporal Andres Martinez.

THE LONE STAR RISES

Just as the coming of daylight was being indicated by a pinkish
glow in the eastern sky a member of the Bayou Sarah Horse called
Isaac Johnson's attention to the red and yellow banner still floating
over the fort that had been taken by force from Spain. It was quickly
lowered and Isaac attached his flag to the halyards and a new ensign
rose to the top of the staff, the banner blue with a single white five-
pointed star. Wild cheers greeted it!

To the very day, exactly thirty-one years before, on September 23,
1779, Spain, represented by the stripling Don Bernardo de Galvez, had
forced the capitulation of Colonel Alexander Dickson and his force of
regular British troops and had taken possession of this very fortification. Spain's emblem of sovereignty had then replaced the crosses of
Saint George and Saint Andrew, the British Union Jack. The Latin had
triumphed over the Anglo-Saxon. On this same date, in 1810, the Anglo-
Saxons had turned the tables. Certainly, the 23rd day of September
should always be printed on Baton Rouge's calendar in bright red
figures.

The Lone Star flag unfurled to the river's breezes for the first time, Major Isaac Johnson, in obedience to Philemon Thomas' command, sprang to his horse and made off. He was followed by Larry Moore, Captain Griffith and practically every man of his troop. As he dashed through the gates of the fort and into the village, his men, who for the first time in the annals of war had captured a fort a-horesback, were behind him—whooping, yelling, discharging pistols, and "hurrahing for Washington." Trailing ignominiously behind the flying feet of Isaac Johnson's horse, and in the dust of the roadway, was the red and yellow Spanish banner that had flaunted its folds over the Baton Rouge fort a short hour before.

As the cavalcade swarmed into the village in the wake of the desecrated banner, inhabitants were told, with a wealth of expletives, of the fall of the fort, and the Bayou Sarah troopers warned all to surrender to the new masters, to the delegates of the convention, to the Voice of the People! The sun came up over the tops of the forest trees that girded Baton Rouge in the east. A new day had come with its rising—a new Republic had been born!

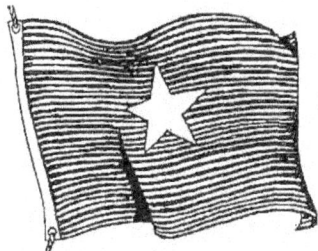

THE SEVENTH FLAG

The flag that succeeded the Lone Star Flag of independent West Florida had fifteen stripes and fifteen stars; the return to the original design of 13 stripes was not made until 1818. The 15 stars shown on the first "Stars and Stripes" to fly over Feliciana included the thirteen original states plus Vermont and Kentucky.

PART FOUR

The Republic

The government house outside the fort did not fail to receive the attention of the hilarious patriots and in it Isaac Johnson's men found and pried open a strong box, the chief item being the six thousand *pesos* which Captain Piernas had brought on from Pensacola to pay the garrison. His Excellency had evidently "forgotten" to distribute the coin or he had some other reason for withholding pay from those under him. The finders cheered their discovery but delivered the money to "Gin'ral" Thomas who had it counted in the presence of captured Spanish officers.

Diligent search was made for the governor's secretary, Captain Raphael Croker, but the searchers soon discovered that that hated official had vanished. Don Pedro Favrot, in a letter to the Marquis de Someruelos, Captain General at Cuba, in which he described in detail the taking of the fort and the death of de Grand-Pré, gave his views as to what caused the revolt [this letter, together with testimony of Spanish soldiers, and manuscripts of those taking part in the assault, was used as a basis for my description of the actual taking of the fort in the preceding chapter. S. C. A.]. Wrote Favrot: "Don Carlos de Lassus, who was in his lodgings outside the fort, at the sound of firing, ran to the fort calling to Rafael 'El Famoso' Croker to follow him. But the secretary made a half turn to the right and abandoned his commander, ran to the river bank, where finding a skiff he crossed to the other side of the Mississippi, made his way to the residence of an Acadian, rented a horse, and at full speed arrived at the house of his father-in-law about 12 leagues away." Dona Croker, left behind and alone, later complained that the patriots had harrassed her while searching the house for her husband for, in spite of her denials, they believed he was concealed there—under the bed or somewhere else.

The *Cura* Francisco Lennán was another who slipped out of Baton Rouge during the excitement. He reached the home of Captain Celestino de Saint Maxent at Manchac, then crossed the river to Croker's father-in-law's plantation on the American side of the Mississippi, then made his way to New Orleans, and wound up at Pensacola. Don Tomaso Estevan, the erstwhile commandant of the Bayou Sarah region, in spite of his "illness," also succeeded in eluding the patriots and reaching the American side of the Mississippi river, galloped fearfully to father-in-law Muller's plantation, a favorite rendezvous of former Spanish masters.

122

As soon after he was in possession of the fort, Philemon Thomas issued a formal order to the inhabitants of the village demanding they deliver their arms. As posted it read:

"By Philemon Thomas, Esqr., Colonel Commander and of the Militia of this Jurisdiction and of the Fort of Baton Rouge, a Proclamation:

"All the inhabitants of the village adjacent to the Fort are required to deliver to me all firearms and other offensive weapons which may be in their possession without delay, on which condition they will be allowed to remain in quiet possession of their property and will be protected in the enjoyment of all privileges to which they may be entitled by the laws of the country and the ordinances of the Convention.

"Given under my hand at head quarters in the fort of Baton Rouge this 23rd. day of September 1810.

PHILN THOMAS
Coll Comindant of the Jurisdiction of
the force of Baton Rouge."

All the regular Spanish soldiers had not succeeded in getting to the safety of the American side of the Mississippi river in the darkness and more than a score were imprisoned in the fort as quickly as they were apprehended and disarmed. They were later released and the majority found their way to Pensacola via New Orleans. The members of the militia who had remained loyal to the Spanish cause were stripped of their firearms and confined to their homes. Their late ruler, Don Carlos de Lassus, fuming and quite apprehensive as to his fate, was lodged in the *juzgado*, or as we would now say it, "in the hoose gow."

The Convention delegates soon gathered to consider what was best for them to do in the new position of authority and responsibility thrust upon them so suddenly, and gave attention to official reports from the commander of the forces that had successfully stormed the fort, and James Nelson, who made an inventory of the arms, munitions, and stores taken. Taken from the original document, Thomas' report read:

"Headquarters Fort of Baton
Rouge Septr 24th 1810
"Sir
"In obedience to the order of the Convention Bearing date of the 22d inst I directed Major Johnson to assemble such of the Cavalry as might be ready at hand, and marched immediately for the Fort of Baton Rouge. I then proceeded to Springfield where I found forty four of the Grenadier Company commanded by Coll Ballenger awaiting the orders of the Convention; at one oclock in the morning of the 23d we joined Major Johnson and Captn Griffith, with 21 of the Bayou Sarah Cavalry, and five or six other patriotic Gentelmen joined us on our march. At four oclock the

same morning we made the attack. My orders were not to fire, till we received a shot from the Garrison, and to cry out in French and English 'Ground your arms and you shall not be hurt;' this order was strictly attended to by the Volunteers, till we received a fire of Musketry from the guard House where the Governor was, which was briskly returned by the Volunteers. We received no Damage on our part. Of the Governor's Troops Lieutt Grand Pré was mortally wounded. Lieut J. B. Metzinger, comt. of Artillery was also wounded, 1 private killed and four badly wounded, we took twenty-one prisoners among who is Coll Delassus. The rest of the Garrison escaped by flight; the Magazines &c found on the Garrison have been reported to you by James Neilson, Esq., who was appointed for that purpose.

"The various and complicated Duties devolving on me from the pressing circumstances of the moment, forbid a more particular communication.

"The firmness and moderation of the Volunteers who made the attack, was fully equal to the best Disciplined Troops. Whole Companys are flocking to our standard daily, and the Harmony and Patriotism that prevails in the Garrison, must be highly gratifying to every friend of the Country.

"Accept Sir for yourself & your Body assurances of my high Esteem & Regard—

(Signed) PHILN THOMAS
Commander in Chief
of the Fort of Baton Rouge
and its Dependencies."

"The Honble John Rhea
President of the Convention."

While the members of the Convention were busy with their plans for governing the now freed jurisdiction, the rank and file of patriots in the fort prepared an address, advising the delegates of the people of their loyalty to the cause. They assured the conventionalists:

"To the Honorable the Representatives of the free people of West Florida in Convention Assembled:

"The Volunteers now occupying the Fort of Baton Rouge are highly gratified at the presence of your honorable body, whom we recognize as the legimate organs of of the Sovereign People—

"We acknowledge your honors as the Rulers of the Country. We acknowledge no others unless they derive authority from you.

"We have on a former occasion expressed our Confidence & Tendered you our Support and recent events have no doubt fully Proved the reality of our professions—and we again, in the most solemn manner, on the honor of soldiers—renew that pledge.

"Peace is desirable to all on honorable & safe principles. But when Goaded by oppression, Borne down by Subaltern Tyrants, Insulted & Betrayed; and an infernal

124

Machine at work to Rivet on us Eternal chains—we flew
to arms in obedience to your orders, and we Trust your
Honorable body will never allow the sword to be sheathed
till the work of Regeneration is complete, & the rights,
Liberties, and properties of our citizens secured by a free
Representative Government and Equal laws.

"Signed at Head Quarters, fort of Baton Rouge
Sept 25th 1810

> Philn. Thomas, Col. Comdt.
> Wm. Kirkland, Colo.
> Benja. P. Thomas, B. Inft.
> John Ballinger, Capt., in behalf of himself
> & Company.
> Robt. McCausland, Maj.
> Robert Young, Major.
> Lewellyn C. Griffith, Captn. dragoons, for
> self and Company.
> L. Z. Foochtell, Capt. Batonrug Company,
> for him Self and ¾ of the Company.
> David T. W. Cook, Capt. P. T. of 3 Regmt.,
> New Feliciana.
> John Dorch, Capt. P. T. of 3 Regmt., New
> Feliciana.
>
> M. L. T. Caynie, Surgeon General for the
> Surgical Department and Commander
> of the Provost Guard."

At the first sitting, the delegates decided upon a preliminary proclamation or resolution declaring West Florida a *Free and Independent
State*. Several handwritten copies were made, and one of them, together with a letter to the American governor of the Mississippi Territory was dispatched to Natchez by Abner L. Duncan. This first liberty
resolution, read:

> "*By the Representatives of the People of West-Florida, in
> Convention Assembled.*
>
> "A PROCLAMATION
>
> "The several districts of West-Florida having been de-
> clared *a Free and Independent State*, by a solem act of this
> convention, made and published this day, we hasten to con-
> gratulate our fellow-citizens on this fortunate event, and to
> assure them that nothing shall be wanting on our part, in
> order to secure to our constituents and to our country, the
> blessings of liberty and equal rights, and to establish those
> rights on the most permanent foundation. In the mean
> time the laws heretofore observed in the administration of
> justice, and the determining the right of property, remain
> in full force as far as the situation of the country will per-
> mit. The ordinances and resolutions adopted by the Con-
> vention, with the concurrence of the Governor, on the 22d
> day August last, are considered as law, agreeably to the
> proclamation of that date, excepting only that the powers
> vested in the Governor, by that ordinance, shall be exer-
> cised by this Convention, for the time being, and until

125

some permanent regulations be made for the better government of this commonwealth.

> "Done in Convention, at the town of Baton Rouge, on Wednesday the 26th day of September, in the year of our Lord one thousand eight hundred and ten, and the independence of Florida, the first.
>
> JOHN RHEA, *President*."

The other letter, which Duncan placed in Governor Holmes' hands, read:

> "To his Excellency David Holmes Governor of the Mississippi Territory:
>
> "Sir
>
> "We have been abandoned and betrayed by our Gov. Delassus who is now anxiously awaiting the arrival of Gov. Folch and avowedly with the determination of cooperating with him in any manner he may direct. Folch is beyond all doubt on his march toward Baton Rouge and not without support. The enclosed Resolution and order taken on it will best show our situation and determination to resist oppression. We cannot but cherish the hope that our neighboring brethren will be put in motion to our succor, indeed we all feel that the faith of our mother country stands pledged for our protection and support. In a day or two we calculate opening the pleas and of forwarding to your Excellency an unqualified declaration of Independence with such an appeal to our parent country as will at once free them from any fear of being [word undecipherable] and prove our unalterable determination to assert our rights as an integral part of the United States. Any body of Militia put immediately in motion even under the pretext of preserving the tranquility of your own territory could not fail to favor our cause, it would give a check to the Spanish and serve to animate the honest though timid Americans. If the gun battery could be prevailed upon to drop down to the neighborhood of Baton Rouge the Dons would be paralized.
>
> "The term 'a Confederation' fixed to the cause will explain our schemes and wants more fully.
>
> John Rhea, President."

THE DECLARATION OF INDEPENDENCE

While the foregoing appeal was being hurried "above the line" to Governor Holmes, the members of the Convention finally decided upon the wording of their formal declaration of independence. Finished to their satisfaction, it was signed, September 26, 1810, by John Rhea, as president, Andrew Steele, as secretary of the Convention, and the other members of the Convention, all save Bill Cooper and Benjamin O. Williams. On Saturday, the day before the taking of the fort, Williams had sent John Rhea his resignation as a delegate from Ste. Helena, the gist of what he said in his letter was that his "local situation not permitting my longer attendance as a representative for this District, in the Convention."

Finally signed and sealed, the Declaration of Independence of the people of West Florida was given to the world. It meant as much to these liberty-loving folk of the South as did a similar document signed and sealed in the city of Philadelphia on that historic fourth day of July, 1776. While it was not as long as the avowal written in the Quaker City, but it was to the point, as you can read for yourself:

"*By the Representatives of the People of West-Florida, in Convention Assembled:*

"A DECLARATION

"It is known to the world with how much fidelity the good people of the Territory have professed and maintained allegiance to their legitimate Sovereign, while any hope remained of receiving from him protection for their property and their lives.

"Without making any unnecessary innovation in the established principals of the Government, we had voluntarily adopted certain regulations, in concert with our First Magistrate, for the express purpose of preserving this Territory, and showing our attachment to the Government which had heretofore protected us. This compact, which was entered into with good faith on our part, will forever remain an honorable testimony of our upright intentions and inviolable fidelity to our King and parent country, while so much as a shadow of legitimate authority remained to be exercised over us. We sought only a speedy remedy for such evils as seemed to endanger our existence and prosperity, and were encouraged by our Governor with solemn promises of assistance and cooperation. But those measures which were intended for our preservation he has endeavored to pervert into an engine of destruction, by encouraging, in the most perfidious manner, the violation of ordinances sanctioned and established by himself as the law of the land.

"Being thus left without any hope of protection from the mother country, betrayed by a magistrate whose duty it was to have provided for the safety and tranquility of the people and Government committed to his charge, and exposed to all the evils of a state of anarchy, which we have long endeavoured to avert, it becomes our duty to provide for our own security, as a free and independent State, absolved from all allegiance to a Government which no longer protects us.

"We, therefore, the Representatives aforesaid, appealing to the Supreme Ruler of the world for the rectitude of our intentions, do solemnly publish and declare the several and distinct districts comprising this Tettitory of West Florida to be *a free and independent State;* that they have a right to institute for themselves such form of government as they may think conducive to their safety and happiness; to form treaties; to establish commerce; to provide for their common defense; and to do all acts which may, of right, be done by a sovereign and independent nation; at the same time declaring all acts within the said Territory of West Florida, after this date, by any tribunals or authorities not deriving their powers from the people, agreebly to the provisions established by this Convention, to be null and void; and calling upon all foreign nations to respect this our declaration, acknowledging our independence, and giving us such aid as may be consistent with the laws and usages of nations."

With utmost dispatch this formal declaration was enclosed in letters addressed to the governors of the Orleans and Mississippi territories. Read the letter to Claiborne:

"To His Excely the Governor of the Orleans Tettiory:
"Sir:

"We, the Delegates of the People of this State have the honor to enclose to you an official copy of their Act of Independence requesting that it may be forthwith transmitted by you to the President of the United States with the expression of their most confident and most ardent hope, that it may accord with the policy of the Government, as it does with the safety and happiness of the people of the United States, to take the present Government and People of this State under their immediate and special protection as an integral and inalienable portion of the United States.

"The Convention and their constituents of the State of Florida rest in the firm persuasion that the blood which flows in the veins of their constituents will remind the Government and People of the United States that they are their children, that they have been acknowledged as such by the most solem act of the Congress of the United States, and that so long as Independence and the Rights of Man shall be maintained and cherished by the American Union, the good people of this State cannot be abandoned, or exposed, to the violence of force of any foreign or domestic foe.

"The Convention beg you to receive for yourself and to assure the President of their high respect and consideration.

JOHN RHEA, President.

Governor Holmes promptly acknowledge receipt of the Convention's communications but all he permitted himself to say was that the declaration would be promptly sent on to Washington. No reply was received from Claiborne, because that executive was then in the capital of the United States. Replied Holmes:

"Town of Washington
30th Sept. 1810
"Sir:
"I have the honor to acknowledge the receipt of your
letter of the 26th inst. inclosing a copy of the Declaration
of Independence by the Convention of West Florida. You
and your colleagues may rest assured that no time will be
lost by me in forwarding these important documents to the
President of the United States. In the meantime let me
be early informed of every occurrence that may take place
interesting to the inhabitants of your Government, whether
they arise from internal of external sources. I shall leave
this place on Thursday next for the county of Wilkinson.
On Saturday I shall be at the General Headqts near the
Court House. After that day address your communications
to me at this place. I have the honor to be with great
respect for you and your colleagues.
Your obdt.
DAVID HOLMES.
"JOHN RHEA, Esq.,
"President of the Convention of West Florida,
Baton Rouge."

The Mississippi executive, it will be noticed, did not reply to the
plea that United States troops be sent into the district. His letter,
written from the "Town of Washington", was penned at the village of
that name a few miles from Natchez, then the capital of the Mississippi
territory. Holmes, however, did order out the American soldiers.
Regulars under Colonel Thomas P. Cushing were sent to the border
to protect American interests in the neighborhood of Pinckneyville and
the territorial militia was ordered to be in readiness for any emergency.

THE EULOGY OF A BRAVE CREOLE

The day after the capture of the fort, the mortally wounded Don
Louis de Grand-Pré died in the arms of Philogene Favrot. A romantic
idyl regarding this young Louisianian and his lovely betrothed, remains
to be told. At four in the morning, the very time that the fort was
taken by the patriots, Joséphine Favrot awoke everyone in her father's
home by her screams. Hastening to her bedroom, her father, mother,
and brothers found her pacing up and down her bedroom shivering in
terror and hysterically declaring that she had seen, in a vivid vision,
men on horesback entering the fort, Louis de Grande-Pré covered with
blood defening his post, and calling for her!

The members of the family unsuccessfully endeavored to quiet her,
and when daylight came, in answer to her pleas that she must go to
Baton Rouge because her lover was calling her, her father and brother
Philogene agreed to take her there so she could be convinced her dream
was only a dream.

As they approached the fort in their skiff, Don Pedro Favrot and
his son were astonished to see that a strange blue flag with a single

white star had replaced the Spanish banner. Hurrying ashore the Favrots learned of the happenings of the night, of Don Louis' plight, and that Joséphine's uncanny vision had been more than a figment of her imagination.

Louis de Grand-Pré lived until two in the morning on Monday. His childhood sweetheart was sobbing at his side as the young soldier, supported by the arms of his chum, Philogene Favrot, breathed his last. The victors of the battle buried their brave foeman with full military honors just outside the fort he had vainly tried to defend.

A touching eulogy from the pen of Don Pedro Favrot on the intrepid Creole who had 'given his life to prove his father had not been a traitor to the Spanish cause later appeared in the New Orleans' newspapers. Said the "Louisiana Courier" October 29:

> "One of the inhabitants of this country, in sending us a few verses composed to honor the memory of his young and generous friend, asks us to pay a tribute to those virtues, which even his enemies took pleasure in according to him: as we would only weaken the expression, noble and touching, of the regrets and of his profund sorrow . . . we think it impossible to make a more complete eulogy than did his true friend . . . we therefore publish a part of his letter and likewise the piece of poetry that he was kind enough to send to us:

> "M. Louis de Grand-Pré, has just met his death, victim of his devotion to the Spanish cause, and of military bravery. He died . . . due to the many wounds received in the defense of Baton Rouge. He died with the calm and serenity of a great soul, and his last moments placed the seal to the nobleness of his character. So deeply ensconced in his generous heart was the memory of the atrocious persecutions which his honored father had recently suffered at the hands of the Spanish Service, that he actually seemed to forget that this fact had poisoned and doubtlessly shortened his days; he would not heed the words of honor, and this valorous Creole wanted to prove that those of his blood had never known intrigue or treachery . . . but that they knew to pardon, or to die, having fought, for the cause to which they had pledged themselves . . . This martyr, or better still this example of honor was but 23 years old, he breathed his last September 24, at two in the morning, in the arms of my eldest son, midst the regrets and lamentations of his family and numerous friends . . . The loss of this man was even regretted by his enemies, who gave testimonies of veneration by funeral honors, characterized by sadness and mourning."

The verse signed by a friend of Louis de Grande-Pré, in testimony of the deep regret that his death caused him, in French follows:

130

"Un seul trepas ternit votre victoire
En y mêlantela plus juste douleur
Louis de Grandpré guidé par sa valeur,
De blessures courbé, tombe convert de gloire.
Jeune heros, que ce beau devouement
Jette d'éclat sur ton dernier moment!
Au milieu des regrets qu'on donne à ta mémoire,
On ne peut s'empêcher d'envier ton trépas,
Modèle de l'honneur tu vivras dans l'histoire
Entre Jumonville et d'Assas."

Or in English:

"A lone death held all your victory
Mingling with it the most just of pain,
Louis de Grand-Pré, guided by his valor,
Covered with wound, fell, covered with glory.
A hero . . . to whom such devotion gave eclat
To his last moments!
Amidst regrets which one lavishes on your memory
One cannot but envy your death;
Model of Honor . . . you will live in history
Between Jumonville and d'Assas."

Jeséphine Favrot never married, she remained true to her dead lover, and throughout a long life was wedded only to her art, her brush and pencil depicting the lovely flowers that grew in profusion all about the Favrot plantation.

WHAT THE NEW ORLEANS PAPERS PRINTED

The action of the West Florida patriots in throwing off the yoke of Spain was applauded everywhere above and below "the line." The Natchez newsprints devoted considerable space to the happenings, while the New Orleans dailies set in type all the news obtainable. One or two of the articles appearing in the "Louisiana Gazette" are of interest, if for no other reason than to show how "hot news" was handled in those far-off days.

The first information that New Orleans had of the uprising, aside from the buzzing that went on in the coffee-houses and on street corners, was found in the "Louisiana Gazette", Wednesday, Sept. 26:

"A rumor was afloat this morning, that the inhabitants of Bayou Sarah had marched down to Baton Rouge in hostile array . . . that Col. *Lassus* has opposed them, but was overpowered after several being killed and wounded . . . that Col. *Lassus* was in close confinement . . . that the American flag was displayed over the fort, &c., &c.

"We are fearful the rumor is nearly true. Letters we are told are in the city which state the whole affair. Tomorrow, perhaps, we shall be able to give correct information. . . . Reports say, that a son of the late Governor *Grand Pré*, has been wounded."

The next morning the "Gazette" concluded the news was important enough to justify a one-column head. Said the issue of Sept. 27:

THE FLORIDIAN WAR!

"In confirmation of the rumor of yesterday we are informed that letters in the city from Baton Rouge state, that the attack was made on the fort, between two and three oclock on Sunday morning last, that General *Philemon Thomas*, commanded the militia who made the attack . . . that at eight olock the American flag was hoisted. The information does not say, whether the General summoned fort to surrender before he commenced the attack or not."

It was not until Friday, the 28th, that the "Louisiana Courier" realized the importance of the news for tucked away in one column was:

"Private letters from Baton Rouge announce that 50 inhabitants of Bayou Sarah had left that place in the night and had taken possession of the fort of the port. It is feared that this event will be attended with serious consequences; two or three persons have been wounded, and amongst the number the son of the late governor; De Lassus, the actual governor, is, it said, imprisoned in the fort."

For several days following these first publications the New Orleans newsprints were devoid of any mention of the startling events that had taken place up the river, but on Wednesday, October 3, the "Gazette" said:

"We find the rumor of last week, (as it relates to the taking of the fort at Baton Rouge) to be true. Young Mr. *Grand Pré* died of the wounds he received a short time after the affair. Gen. Thomas commands, and we are informed, is at the head of the executive, Gov. Lassus being in close confinement. The greater part of the Spaniards made their escape, and numbers have arrived in this city. At first there was danger apprehended from the people of the Amite and Comite, but when the mail passed everything was tranquil, and active preparations were being made for defense. The convention, under whose orders Gen. Thomas has acted and continues to act, are determined on supporting their independence.

"We are not able to state with accuracy the reasons why the convention deposed Gov. Lassus. It is said it was in consequence of his procrastination of some executive acts, and that he intended to impede the progress of the new system until he could receive force from Gov. Folch to destroy it in *toto*.

"It is strongly impressed on the minds of the foreigners in this city, both Spaniards and French, that the United States government are at the bottom of this revolution. We are not in the cabinet secrets, nor at headquarters, but as Americans, and judging from our own feelings, we have no hesitation in saying, that the impressions are wrong and without any foundation, and have originated from jealously alone."

FORMING A NEW GOVERNMENT

Meanwhile, at the seat of trouble, the members of the Convention were kept active arranging for a defense of the territory just won at the point of the sword. Fears of reprisals by Folch and his columns of marching men were uppermost and a flood of wild rumors and a decided lack of extra information kept these new masters of West Florida in constant apprehension.

News of the success of the patriot force in storming the Baton Rouge fort in the dead of morning, the raising of an independent flag, and the general hip-hip-hurrah welling in every American's heart over the coup, sent men of all classes flocking to the fort to support "the American cause" by enlisting "under the Star." So depleted were many families on the United States' side of the border of their "men folks" that pleas were hurried to the Mississippi executive to furnish them with protection in case there might be "another San Domingo" uprising of negroes. The rather lawless character of many of the men rushing to Baton Rouge to join in the contemplated onslaught against the Dons in the rest of the province was a matter of serious apprehension, for many were deserters from the U. S. army and navy, or had other good and sufficient reasons for fleeing American courts of justice.

Substantiated rumors were to the effect that Alcalde Shepherd Brown, and "that damned old Tory" Captain Michael Jones, were actively recruiting settlers still favorable to the Spanish regime so that they could act in concert with Governor Folch and his regulars coming from Pensacola. The very day the Spanish Governor of West Florida received word of the fall of the Baton Rouge fort and the imprisonment of Governor de Lassus, Brown wrote him that he and his "fellow loyalists" were determined to oppose the "rebels" until Folch would arrive and, so said Brown, if Folch would come in person, he "would find 500 loyal settlers to help him reestablish the royal authority."

While Folch planned an early relief of de Lassus, as a matter of fact he never left Pensacola. He asked Cuba for men and money for the purpose but so delayed from day to day holding long-winded councils-of-war and *juntas* that by the time he was ready to start westward other events convinced him that such a relief expedition would be useless, and that West Florida, from the Pearl to the Mississippi, at least, was gone from Spain forever. However, the patriots in Baton Rouge did not know this; what they did know was that Shepherd Brown and Michael Jones were arming and defying and flouting the new authority, and such news was not received with good grace by the members of the force guarding the captured fort. They had won one battle and yearned for more worlds to conquer; wouldn't the Convention do something about it? To spur the delegates into action, the patriot soldiers formed themselves into a body, designated Colonel Bill Kirkland president, and Captain John Ballinger, as clerk, and then confected an address. If the Convention delegates could write addresses, proclamations, ordinances, codes, and such, what was to prevent the fighting men from doing the same, Not a thing! So this is what they wrote:

"To the Honorable the Representatives of the People of West Florida, in convention assembled:

"The officers in the fort of Baton Rouge have appointed Genl. P. Thomas to wait on your honors to consult the most proper measures for restoring tranquility in St. Helena. He is in possession of the views of the officers, and the information necessary for effecting the object must belong to your body. We are uninformed and forbear to make remarks.

"Done at headquarters, Fort of Baton Rouge, September, 29, 1810.

WM. KIRKLAND, Colo., President.

"Attest:

J. BALLINGER, Capt. Inft., Clerk."

The prayers for orders to capture Shepherd Brown, Bill Cooper, and Michael Jones and scatter the forces they were forming to resist the new masters of West Florida were quickly given. On the first day of October the punitive expedition set forth in the direction of Ste. Helena. In the van were the Feliciana Dragoons, led by Major Isaac Johnson and Captain Llewellyn Colville Griffith. The Springfield grenadiers were under the command of Major Robert McCausland, while Colonel Kimball headed another detachment of foot soldiers. Exactly what was done on this expedition to "quiet matters" in the eastern section of the new republic, and how Shepherd Brown and Michael Jones were tamed is set forth in General Thomas' report:

"Head Quarters fort of Baton Rouge
Octr 9th 1810

"Sir,

"Pursuant to the orders I received from your honors, I commenced my march for the District of St. Helena on the first day of October. On the third I crossed the Amite at Major Curtains at the Head of about four Hundred men. I had previously wrote to Michael Jones Requesting an Interview with him, he met me at Well's six miles East of the Amite, and tendered a proposition for a Union between the several Districts, signed by himself and others. But his conduct was such as to preclude an Idea of Negociation. However on the Same Evening he surrendered his men at discretion & signed the Declaration of Independence. The same evening I dispatched an advanced Guard under Major Johnson of the Cavalry & Major McCastland of the Infantry to endeavour by a forced march to surprise Brown & Cooper in their fort at Springfield. But the fort was evacuated ten Hours before their arrival. On the 5th I dispatched a considerable force to the Tansapaho & Chefuncta under the Command of Colo Kimball from him I have received no dispatches But expect intelligence which when Recd will be communicated without delay.

"I continued at Springfield the 5th & 6th in order to intercept straggling Parties of Brown's men & to see & inform the people of the principles and Wish of the Convention. Everything appears Tranquil & the great Body of the People really disposed to defend our Cause, a company of Volunteers is formed at Springfield. They have elected Samuel Baldwin their Capt which appointment together with the Lieuts which may be hereafter elected I wish confirmed. I returned by way of Brown's plantation & the Spanish settlements—they all appeared friendly.

(Signed)   Philn Thomas, B. D. General.
"The honorable president of the Convention."

THE BROWN SHEPHERD FLEES HIS FLOCK

Shepherd Brown, failing to raise his boasted "500" and very apprehensive of his own skin, advised his few, about 80, followers to disperse and save themselves, when he was apprised of the coming of General Thomas and his force of four hundred men. Brown set the "loyalists" a good example by fleeing on a boat bound for New Orleans. He was overtaken before he could get into neutral territory and sent to the fort at Baton Rouge to keep de Lassus company.

When the Lone Star patriots appeared before the fort on the Nictalbany, the defenders fled before the rapid approach of the Feliciana Dragoons. Although Brown had slipped away, William Cooper was captured, and later the patriots destroyed his stock and other property, the animus they displayed against him was twofold, his record as a former and notorious Tory back in North Carolina, and his desertion of the proceeding of the Convention after being elected as the lone delegate of the Chifoncté district. Before the punitive force returned to Baton Rouge, Cooper was killed trying to escape.

With William Cooper dead, Michael Jones, a penitent convert to the cause of Independence, and Shepherd Brown locked up in the fort with his former superior, all opposition to the Convention came to an abrupt end in Ste. Helena. Captain Samuel Baldwin, who had been designated by General Thomas as a sort of peace officer, recruited and equipped a considerable force and ruled with a rigid hand, and slapped irons on all men in the district who would not sign the Convention's declaration of Independence.

With insurrection smothered the Convention could now get down to the business of creating a new nation. At Pensacola the Spanish authorities believed that they could soon retake the lost territory on the Mississippi River when the inhabitants of the jurisdiction learned they had become tax-payers under the ordinances of the Convention. This was something the Spanish regime had not required for the money to run the government came from the Crown and the officials secured their extra money in other ways. Evidently there was some such thought in the master minds of the Convention for on October 5, when General Thomas was sending Shepherd Brown scuttling through the cypress swamps like a frightened rabbit, the ordinances adopted in August, which fixed taxes on slaves imported into the district, were repealed and the taxes on lands reduced, as witness the text of these important resolutions are:

"*In the Convention of the State of Florida, at the town of Baton Rouge assembled, October 5th, 1810.*

"On motion, *Resolved*, That so much of the ordinance of this Convention, of the 22d of August last, as relates to the tax on slaves imported into the commonwealth, be repealed, and the same is hereby repealed accordingly. And all persons residing within this commonwealth, or allowed by the said ordinance to obtain permission of residence within the same, shall be allowed to import into this commonwealth, all slaves belonging to them, without paying any tax or duty therefore, whatever, anything contained in said ordinance to the contrary notwithstanding.

"On motion, *Resolved*. That so much of the ordinance of this convention, of the 22d of August last, as relates to the tax on lands, be amended in such manner that all lands within this commonwealth being reduced to three classes, those of the first quality be subject to a tax of six rials per hundred arpents; those of the second four rials; and those of the third quality, two rials per hundred arpents. And it shall be the duty of the several Alcaldes, each for the division in which he resides, to estimate the quality of the lands subject to taxation within his division, both of residents and non-residents, and to express the quality of each tract, on the return made by him of taxable property, to the commandant of the district, who shall make his return in the same manner to the clerk of the Superior Court. And it shall be the duty of the Alcaldes aforesaid, each for the division in which he resides, to make a return of the land as of non-residents, at the same times, and in the same manner, classing them accordingly to quality, as the lands of the inhabitants of the country.

"By order of the Convention

JOHN RHEA, *President*".

However, there was another important matter for the Conventionalists to consider: Would they continue as an independent republic or fly to the bosom of the United States, be received by that great republic as one of its own children and as such receive protection? While sentiment in the Baton Rouge jurisdiction was overwhelmingly for annexation to the United States, the proponents of such a move were divided as to the terms upon which it should be brought about. Finally, on October 10, John Rhea attached his signature to a letter sent Secretary of State Robert Smith for transmissal to President Madison, in it he established the contentions of the convention for annexation.

"The Convention of the State of Florida have already transmitted official copy of their act of independence, through His Excellency Governor Holmes, to the President of the United States, accompanied with the expression of their hope and desire that this Commonwealth may be immediately acknowledged and protected by the Government of the United States, as an integral part of the American Union. On a subject so interesting to the community represented by us, it is necessary that we should have the most direct and unequivocal assurances of the views and wishes of the American Government without delay, since our weak and unprotected situation will oblige us to look to some foreign Government for support, should it be refused to us by the country which we have considered as our parent State.

"We therefore make this direct appeal through you to the President and General Government of the American States, to solicit that immediate protection to which we consider ourselves entitled; and, to obtain a speedy and favorable decision, we offer the following consiedrations:

"1st.—The Government of the United States, in their instructions to the Envoys Extraordinary at Paris in March, 1806, authorized the purchase of West Florida, directing them at the same time to engage France to intercede with the Cabinet of Spain to relinquish any claim to the Territory which now forms this Commonwealth.

"2nd.—In all diplomatic correspondence with American ministers abroad, the Government of the United States have spoken of West Florida as a part of the Louisiana cession. They have legislated for the country as part of their own territory, and have deferred to take position of it, in expectation that Spain might be induced to relinquish her claim by amicable negotiation.

"3rd.—The American Government has already refused to accredit any minister from the Spanish Junta, which body was certainly more legally organized as the representative of the sovereignty, than that now called the Regency of Spain. Therefore, the United States cannot but regard any force or authority emanating from them, with an intention to subjugate us, as they would an invasion of their territory by a foreign enemy.

"4th.—The Emperor of France has invited Spanish Americans to declare their independence rather than to remain in subjection to the old Spanish Government; therefore, an acknowledgment of our independence by the United States could not be complained of by France, or involve the American Government in any contest with that power.

"5th.—Neither can it afford any just cause of complaint to Great Britain, although she be the ally of Spain, that the United States should acknowledge and support our independence, as this measure was necessary to save the country from falling into the hands of the French exiles from the island of Cuba, and other Partisans of Bonaparte, who are now the eternal enemies of Great Britain.

"Should the United States be induced by these, or any other considerations, to acknowledge our claims to their protection as an integral part of their territory, or otherwise, we feel it our duty to claim for our constituents an immediate admission into the Union as an independent State, or as a Territory of the United States, with permission to establish our own form of government, or be united with one of the neighboring Territories, or a part of one of them, in such manner as to form a State. Should it be thought proper to annex us to one of the neighboring Territories or a part of one of them, the inhabitants of the Commonwealth would prefer being annexed to the Island of Orleans; and, in the meanwhile, until a State government should be established, that they should be governed by the ordinances already enacted by this Convention, and by further regulations hereafter.

"The claim which we have to the soil or unlocated lands within this Commonwealth will not, it is presumed, be contested by the United States, as they have tactically acquiesced in the claim of France, or Spain, for seven years; and the restrictions of the several embargo and non-intercourse laws might fairly be construed, if not as a relinquishment of their claim, yet as at least sufficient to entitle the people of this Commonwealth (who have wrested the Government and country from Spain at the risk of their lives and fortunes) to all the unlocated lands. It will strike the American Government that the moneys arising from the sales of these lands, applied as they will be to improving the internal communications of the country, opening canals, etc., will, in fact, be adding to the prosperity and strength of the Federal Union. To fulfill with good faith our promises and engagements to the inhabitants of this country, it will be our duty to stipulate for an unqualified pardon for all deserters now residing within this Commonwealth, together with an exemption from further service in the army or navy of the United States."

The delegates decided, for the present, not to change the frame of the government they had prepared with their set of ordinances with the exception that the Convention as a whole would assume the powers granted to the deposed Governor de Lassus. Anxiously they awaited a response to their appeals to President Madison for annexation to the United States. It was also decided that the present force of five to six hundred armed men was too large to maintain, so reduced the force to one hundred and four regular soldiers to keep order at the fort under the command of Captain John Ballinger.

A committee of "Publick Safety" was appointed, John H. Johnson, Edmund Hawes, and John W. Leonard, and given the power to draft a new constitution while the rest of the members were in recess. The convention at that time consisted of: from Feliciana, John Rhea, John Hunter Johnson, John Mills and William Barrow; from Baton Rouge, Philip Hicky, Thomas Lilley, John Morgan and Edmund Hawes; from Ste. Helena. John W. Leonard and Joseph Thomas were the only representatives, for Benjamin O. William, evidently getting what is known today as "cold feet", sent the Convention his resignation on Saturday, the eve of the capture of the fort.

However, on the date of their adjournment, October 10, the members of the convention issued an address to the people inhabiting the Mobile and Pensacola district, still held by the Spanish, and first calling attention to the fact that distance had prevented them calling the citizens of this section of West Florida into the common deliberation, announced that they had appointed as commissioners Reuben Kemper and Joseph White "to bring about united action with their brethren" and, although they had not "yet ventured to legislate for these unrepresented districts, the object of the Convention was to secure the liberty and happiness of the people of West Florida." Therefore, it was requested that the citizens of Mobile and Pensacola authorize the Convention to act for them or to send their own deputies to join that body. The request ended with the promise of good faith in all measures that would serve the common good.

Reuben Kemper spoiling to get even with the Spanish, for he hated them as much as any man is capable of hatred, immediately repaired to the eastern country along the gulf with the promise that "The Star would rise and shine" with his coming. His mission failed, as has already been related in my "The Story of the Kemper Brothers," and it was not until years later that the section east of Mobile fell under the dominition of the United States.

The Convention was not due to go into session until the 24th of October to receive the report of John H. Johnson and his two co-delegates on the progress they had made in preparing a constitution of the new Republic of West Florida. Before the delegates gathered again a number of things happened. The most important was an attempt to release former Governor de Lassus and Shepherd Brown from their confinement in the Baton Rouge fort. The attempt was engineered by Captain David T. W. Cook, who commanded the third regiment from Feliciana.

MUTINY IN THE FORT

Said the "Louisiana Gazette" of this frustrated attempt to free de Lassus:

> "On the night of the 16th inst. a mutiny was discovered in the fort at Baton Rouge. A newly appointed captain, who calls himself *Cook*, had it in contemplation to liberate Col. Lassus, and take possession of the fort. The Convention got information of it and ordered down the dragoons from Bayou Sarah, who arrived in time to save the fort. Captain Cook and two of his subaltrons were cashiered and ordered out of Florida, and everything is now tranquil."

From above the line, where close watch was kept on all transpiring within the new republic, letters were sent to New Orleans to apprise the citizens there of the state of affairs. Below is a typical expression from Pinckneyville, printed in the "Gazette" of October 20th:

> "On my return from Baton Rouge I found your letter, and would willingly answer all your interrogations could I possess the facts. In a summary way let me tell you that the people of West Florida have done right in throwing off all allegiance to a Prince that could not give them any relief. The double dealing of Col. *Lassus* and *Shepherd Brown*, convinced the members of the Convention they had nothing to depend on from them, on the contrary it is pretty well ascertained that a plan was laying to secretly seize the most influential members of the Convention and carry them off to Pensacola, and perhaps to Havana.

> "I have seen and conversed with almost all the best informed men, and they appear to have great confidence in the government of the United States, and I do most sincerely wish they may not be disappointed; but I have many doubts on that subject. The timid, temporizing disposition of our executive, give but little reason to suppose they would risk anything even to protect our own rights; and in this case, to give offense to the great Emperor, would be a serious thing. Could our executive obtain his permission, most probably they would give those people succour.

> "The Convention has enlisted two complete companies for six months, who are stationed in the fort at Baton Rouge, and the militia are all ordered home."

Others seized their pens, either to lampoon the Spanish defenders, or to extravagantly praise the captors. No more interesting recital of what occured during those strenuous September and October days was ever set to paper than a parody of Biblical narratives written by one Jonathan Longstreth. This young man at the time of the disturbances was teaching school in the house of Thomas Lilley, at the Saints John Plains, and in all probability, was an eyewitness to the deliberations of the original Convention. In a paper dedicated to Philip Hicky, who long owned the original, devoted to the Grand Sanhedrine ["Great Sanhedrin", an ancient Jewish assembly or council of 71 members] the young schoolmaster wrote:

A LA HOLY WRIT

"THE BOOK OF THE CHRONICLES OF THE GRAND SANHEDRINE of the verdant country bordering on the Great Father of Rivers, to the eastward, and extending even into the Tanchepaho, as thou goest towards the sunrising.

CHAPTER I.

"1. And it came to pass, Charles the Gawlite [Chas. de Hault de Lassus] was Governor of the verdant country, and Stephen, the lawyer [Don Thomas Estevan, commandant at Bayou Sarah], had charge of the fertile land of Sarah, that the people were sorely oppressed for want of upright judges and just judgements.

"2. And they spake, one unto another, in this wise: 'go to, let us assemble together as one man, and enquire from whence this great evil proceedeth,' and they did so.

"3. And the people of the land of Sarah said, let us appoint some of our Elders and fathers of the people to meet the Elders and fathers of our brethren from the South and from the East, at the House of Richard the Albionite [Richard Devall], who dwelleth in the plain country.

"4. So they appointed John [Rhea] the President, John the Hunter, [John Hunter Johnson], John the Millwright [John Mills], and William the Barrowthite [Wm. Barrow], members of the Grand Sanhedrine.

"5. Now, when Philip the Troublesome [Philip A. Gray, an alcalde of the St. Helena district] heard of these things, he was filled with indignation, and saddled his horse, and journeyed into the South country to give an account thereof to Charles the Gawlite, if, peradventure, he might prevent the meeting of the Grand Sanhedrine.

"6. But Philip spoke not the words of truth and soberness; he endeavored to influence the wrath of Charles the Gawlite against the Elders and wise men of the land of Sarah—for he was thought to be malicious.

"7. Now, when Charles, the Gawlite, [probably meant for "Gaulite", a native of ancient Gaul, or France], heard these things, he was grieved in spirit, and sent forth George the Bald [Geo. Mather], and Philip the Amiable [Phillip Hicky], into the land of Sarah, to enquire and see if these things were so, and bring him word again.

141

"8. And it came to pass when George the Bald, and Philip the Amiable, came to the land of Sarah, they were smitten with the just complaints of the people against Stephen the Lawyer, and his scribe, John the Murdockite [John Murdock], forasmuch as they loved filthy lucre more than justice and just judgement.

"9. Therefore, they returned, and told Charles the Gawlite of those things which they had seen and heard, and he said, 'My bowels doth yearn with compassion for this people; let the Sanhedrine assemble, and I will assist them in doing justice and establishing sound judgement.' Howbeit, he dissembled unto them.

"10. Then he gave commandment, and the people of the South assembled, and appointed Philip the Amiable, Thomas the Lilly of the Vale, [Thomas Lilley], Manuel the Iberian [Manuel Lopez], Edmund the Hawthite [Edmund Hawes], and John the Morganite [John Morgan], to be members of the Grand Sanhedrine.

"11. Charles the Gawlite, also sent to the Brown Shepherd [Shepherd Brown], to whom he had given command of the country of Helenites, to assemble the people entrusted to his care, that they might appoint deputies to attend the Grand Sanhedrine; but the Shepherd obeyed him not.

"12. Now, the Brown Shepherd was a man of proud and haughty spirit; great in his own conceit, and mighty in his own eyes, fond of filthy lucre, and fearful if justice and sound judgement prevailed, they might extend to his own government, weaken his power, and deprive him of some of the honor and profit he thought due unto himself alone.

"13. He, therefore, sent a writing unto Charles the Gawlite, in this wise: 'The Brown Shepherd unto Charles the Gawlite, greetings, and at such a time. Be it known unto the most noble Charles, that my heart is with thy heart; if what thou hast written unto me be of thy own free will, I will most assuredly obey thee; but if thou hast writ to me in this wise for fear of the people, I will come and assist thee with five hundred men, and compel them to submit unto thee.'

"14. Then Charles the Gawlite, returned him an answer: 'What I have written, I have written.' On which the Brown Shepherd gave commandment to Helenites, and they assembled together, and appointed Joseph the Thomasite [Joseph Thomas], John of Leon [John W. Leonard], William the Spillhite [William Spiller], and Benjamin the Willhite [Benjamin O. Williams] to attend the Grand Sandhedrine.

"15. Now, the Tanchepahoites likewise assembled, by the commandment of Charles the Gawlite, and appointed William the Belialite [William Cooper], their representatives to the Sanhedrine. Now, William was a great man among the sons of Belial, and had, for a long time, been a man of renown in evil deeds.

"16. Now, it came to pass, when the Grand Sanhedrine, attended by Andrew the Scribe [Dr. Andrew Steele], and George the Recorder [Geo. Mather], met and conferred together, they found much cause for complaint against the officers which Charles the Gawlite had set over the people; therefore, they removed them, and appointd others to rule the people in their stead.

"17. They also made several new laws and ordinances, for the better government of the people, to all which proceedings Charles the Gawlite gave his assent, and signed his name; but in all these things he dissembled for his heart was full of guile.

142

"18. Now, when Vincent the Folchite [Gov. Folch, of Pensacola], who abided in a stronghold in the East, in the country of the Pensacolians, heard these things, he waxed exceeding wroth, and swore, in his anger, to destroy the whole Sanhedrine; but not having men of war wherewith to accomplish it, he sent to Charles the Gawlite six thousand pieces of silver, to the end that he might have men wherewith to destroy the whole of them together, with their laws and ordinances.

"19. And William the Belialite, and Michael the Thunder [Michael Jones], and the Brown Shepherd, made a league with each other, and gathered unto themselves a host of sons of Belial, and set their faces to oppose the Grand Sanhedrine; they also sent a message to Charles the Gawlite, full of high-sounding words, promising to make the Grand Sanhedrines all captives, and deliver them bound into his hands, for such and such a portion of the six thousand pieces of silver.

"20. But when the Grand Sanhedrine discovered the malice of their enemies, and the great evil intended against them, they gave the commandment unto, Philemon, the chief captain of their host [Philemon Thomas], gathered together a few lion-like men, and traveled all that night. A little before the dawn of day, they came to the stronghold on the bank of the Father of the Rivers, where Charles the Gawlite lay entrenched with his men, thinking himself secure.

"21. Then Philemon, the chief captain, together with the captains and men of war that were with him, broke into the stronghold, and took Charles the Gawlite, with a number of his men, captives; of the residue, some they slew, some they wounded, and the rest escaped by flight."

ST. FRANCISVILLE THE NEW CAPITAL

It was the 24th of October before the members of the Convention again gathered received a report from Johnson, Hawes and Leonard, who had been instructed to draw up their new constitution. The result of their labors was one frankly based upon that of the United States which was to go into force the following month. The convention thereupon appointed an executive committee of five consisting of John H. Johnson, John Mills, William Barrow, from Feliciana, and Philip Hicky and John Morgan of Baton Rouge to conduct the affairs of the new nation, for no news was forthcoming from Washington in reply to their plea to Jimmy Madison that the United States adopt them.

The new steering committee selected Saint Francisville as the seat of government and from this capital issued orders. Captain John Ballinger was ordered to keep safe all "state prisoners", maintain strict discipline amongst the 115 soldiers guarding the fort, and was cautioned to be on guard against any surprise attack. He was instructed to salute all American gunboats passing up and down the Mississippi, but at the same time to transfer six pieces of artillery, 200 muskets, and necessary munitions to the new capital city.

On October 26 the Convention issued another declaration of independence, and on the following day adopted a constitution. It provided for a "governor" to be elected by a general assembly biennially, and the government of the republic to be divided into three branches: legislative, executive, and judicial. The legislature to consist of a senate and house of representatives, with the representatives to be chosen annually; and the senators, triennially. The new state was divided into five districts—"Baton Rouge, New Feliciana, St. Helena, St. Ferdinand, and Mobile." Each district was entitled to one senator and three representatives, with the exception of Feliciana, which was allowed a single senator and four representatives. Said the proclamation: "The first general assembly shall meet at Saint Francisville on the third Monday of November next, and shall choose a governor on the second day after a quorum of both houses shall be formed."

On the tenth day of November Feliciana made its selection and designated John, Rhea as senator, and selected John H. Johnson, William Barrow, Lewellyn C. Griffith, and John Scott the representatives.

On the 12th of November orders were given General Thomas to organize a force of 618 militia to perform service in any part of the territory and to proceed, when ready, to capture Mobile and hoist the Lone Star over that gulf port. That accomplished, Thomas and his army was to reduce Pensacola. Not all of the delegates were favorable to this campaign along the gulf, they preferred to await the action of President Madison upon their request for annexation to the United States.

On the day set, Monday, November 19, the infant government met in the new state capital. The senators and delegates were faced with a new situation, for on that very day word came from Natchez that the United States was about to take action: "We understand from a source that may be relied upon, that orders have been received by the commanding officer at the Cantonment Washington, near this place, Natchez, to hold the army in readiness to march at a moment's warning. The order, we learn, enters into such details, as to indicate a speedy movement", read the New Orleans "Gazette's" story.

When met, the senators made John W. Leonard president *pro tempore* of the upper house, while Dudley L. Avery was selected as speaker of the House of Representatives, these two evidently the selection of the Baton Rouge and Ste. Helena districts. On the following day, the 20th, Fulwar Skipwith was elected by the whole assembly as "governor of the State."

THE NEW GOVERNOR SPEAKS

Philemon Thomas was placed in command of the army; C. M. Audibert, Samuel Baldwin, and John Mills were appointed navy agents; a committee of safety, with John H. Johnson, as chairman, was also designated, and an expedition of 400 effective men, to join forces with the regular forces of the state, under the command of Colonel William Kirkland, was ordered to reduce the forts at Mobile and Pensacola.

Fulwar Skipwith, who maintained his elevation to supreme command was not of his seeking, said that he supported the West Florida declaration of independence from principle and because he believed that this was the best way to turn the captured province over to the United States. He accepted the governorship, not from vanity, but because he hoped with the aid of the others in the movement to avoid anarchy and confusion until annexation could be consumated. In his inaugural address Skipwith advised the legislative assembly to adopt a better judicial system, an improved militia establishment, a more just system of representation, and apportionment of taxes. He told the members of the legislature they had a natural right to independence, and gave it as his belief that neither gain nor the implied promise of protection had led them to take the momentous step they had taken.

"Whenever the voice of justice and humanity can be heard, our declaration and our just rights will be respected. But the blood that flows in our veins like the tributary streams which form and sustain the Father of Rivers encircling our delightful country will return, if not impeded, to the heart of our parent country. The genius of Washington, the immortal founder of the liberties of America, stimulates that return, and would frown upon our cause should we attempt to change its course."

During the first weeks of his government, Skipwith personally directed the preparations for the dispatch of the patriot force to wrest the remainder of West Florida from the Dons. There was great excitement prevailing at Saint Francisville and Baton Rouge as volunteers were recruited and marched away to join the regular forces to be assembled at John Stuart's plantation preparatory to going overland to raise the Lone Star over the fortifications along the gulf.

To understand the spirit that animated these "sons of liberty" one needs only listen to the song they sang as they marched away from Baton Rouge, leaving Lieutenant Charles Grandpré Johnson, (brother of John, Isaac, and Joseph) in charge of the fort with a garrison of twenty-five men.

The song that the patriotic gun-toters sang carried a French title and, in consequence, the pronunciation of *"Vive la"* should be given as "Vive-a-lay" to fit the meter and rime correctly. Now, you sing the stirring march-tune:

"VIVE LA"

The Song of the West Floridian Army in 1810.

1.

West Floriday was once invaded.
Gen'ral Thomas sot it free.
With powder an' ball he skeered 'em all,
When he planted the flag of liberty.

CHORUS

Vive la the new convention.
Vive la the rights of man.
Vive la West Floriday.
The new convention is the plan.

2.

Michael Jones, that damn'd old tory
Unto our gen'ral thus did say—
Gen'ral Thomas I respct you
And with your troops I'd like to stay.

CHORUS

3.

Lissen to our answer—
We all know how black's your heart.
We all know you are a traitor.
Mount your horse and do depart.

CHORUS

4.

Shepherd Brown, that great commander,
Thought to fright our troops away.
But he turned his face to the cypress swamp
When he heard the shouts of *Vive la*.

CHORUS

5.

Houra, brave boys don't make wry faces
The Tickfaw boys they all have fled.
Colonel Kimball made them tremble
And he sheathed his sword in a tory's bed.

CHORUS

6.

West Floriday, that lovely nation,
Free from king and tyranny,
Thru' the world shall be respected
For her true love of Liberty.

We can drink and not get drunk.
We can fight and not be slain.
We can go to Pensacola
And can be welcomed back again.

CHORUS, ETC.

But the West Floridian army was not destined to come to grips with the Spanish soldiers along the gulf. In Washington, with Governor Claiborne at his very elbow, President James Madison at last was prepared to act. Dispatch riders flying over the Natchez trace had carried word to him of the *coup* of the Feliciana patriots, the fall of the fort at Baton Rouge, and the copies of the acts of the Convention and their ringing declarations of independence. Jimmy Madison determined not to await the action of Congress and lay the matter before that body, because five weeks must intervene before the nation's lawmakers would go into session. He determined to act at once to prevent foreign intervention as well as to maintain order.

Therefore, on October 27, while the Floridians were still wrestling with their plans for self-government, Madison issued his proclamation declaring that West Florida formed a part of the Louisiana Purchase! After a wait of seven long years, the United States had tardily claimed its own!

The president ordered Governor Claiborne to return forthwith to the scene of action, take possession of West Florida, invite the people to respect him, obey the laws of the United States, and to preserve order. To do the latter Claiborne would have the backing of the United States army.

Another new day was about to dawn for Feliciana and the rest of the West Florida.

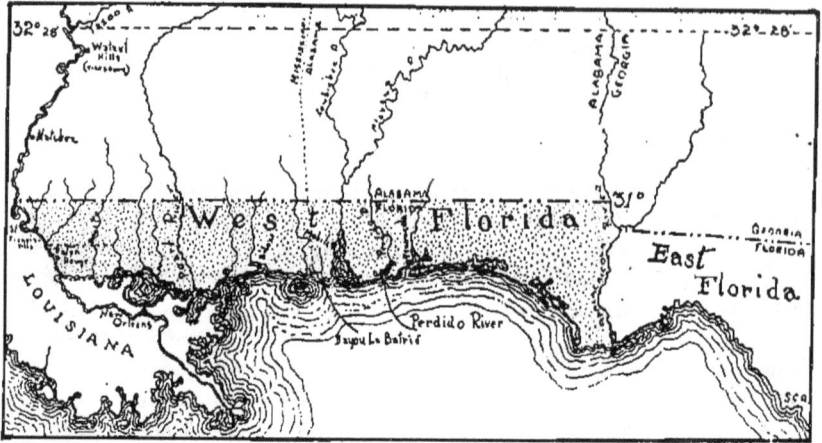

THE THEATRE OF ACTION

BRITISH West Florida, acquired from France 1763 by treaty. King George III named the new English territory when he designated the River Apalachicola as the dividing line between "East and West Florida." In 1767 the northern boundary of West Florida was fixed at the 32nd degree 28 minutes line, at the mouth of the Yazoo River, east to Apalachicola.

SPANISH West Florida was acquired through Governor Bernardo de Galvez's conquest over the British when he captured Baton Rouge and Natchez, 1779; Mobile, 1780; and Pensacola, 1781. The treaty of peace between Spain and England gave both Floridas to Spain, while all territory north of 31st degree parallel was awarded the new United States. This Spain protested, claiming the boundary north to the junction of the Yazoo and the Mississippi, and the controversy over the land it had taken from Great Britain at point of bayonet was not ended until 1795, when a treaty with the United States fixed the boundary at the 31st degree line. The Dons did not actually leave the territory "above the line" until January 1798.

INDEPENDENT West Florida, won by revolt of September 23, 1810, included all the territory from the Mississippi to the Perdido river. Possession was taken only to a point west of Mobile by the Lone Star Flag.

UNITED STATES West Florida, possession taken December 7, 1810 through presidential proclamation. Actual territory seized only to Bayou La Batrié, just west of Mobile. The United States did not take over Mobile until April 15, 1813. East Florida was purchased from Spain in 1819 for $1,000,000. The formal transfer of East Florida (the present state of Florida) was not made until July 17, 1821.

PART FIVE

The County

It was Saturday, the first day of December, 1810, when William Charles Cole Claiborne, governor of the Territory of Orleans, after a hurried overland journey from Washington, D. C., reached Washington, T. M., the tiny Mississippi village then the capital of that territory. He wrote Secretary of State Robert Smith:

"Near Natchez Dec. 1, '10.

"I arrived here this morning and lost no time in communicating to *Gov. Holmes* the orders of the President, and in advising him as to the best means of carrying the same into immediate effect. He accorded with me in the opinion that a great majority of the inhabitants of the District of Baton Rouge, would receive with pleasure the American authorities. But to guard against the intrigues of certain individuals believed to be hostile to the United States, and a few adventurers from the Territories of Orleans and Mississippi of desperate character and fortunes, who have lately joined the convention army, it was deemed advisable to order a Detachment of Troops to descend the River close in my rear, and to place the whole effective force in this territory in a situation to move at a moment's warning & to be used hereafter as the occasion may require.

"In the mean time the proclamation of the president is in the hands of the printer; and I am making the other necessary preparations to depart in the morning of the 3rd instant. In descending the River I shall call at Fort Adams, from whence I shall dispatch messengers to Florida, with instructions to distribute the president's proclamation, to ascertain the general sentiments of the people, and particularly the Leaders."

Governor Claiborne ordered Colonel Leonard Covington to detach for immediate service a force of about 300 effective men, including a detachment of artillerists with two field pieces, to proceed without delay to the post at Pointe Coupée and there await his further instructions. A barge was to be in readiness for him at Fort Adams and two subaltern officers were to be detailed to accompany him on his mission to take possession of West Florida.

On Monday the printer had the proclamations printed. Claiborne immediately saw to the distribution of the printed sheets and left in his barge for Fort Adams. He was not well when he arrived at the frontier post but wrote back to Washington that he was "deeply im-

149

pressed with the delicacy, the importance of the operation before me, and you may rely on my discretion. The instructions of the president, will be held continually in view, and in obeying them you may be assured that no blood will be shed, if it can be possibly avoided."

After finishing his message to the president, Claiborne dispatched two messengers, Audley L. Osborne to Saint Francisville, and William King to Baton Rouge, with copies of Madison's proclamation. Then he crossed the river to Pointe Coupée where he met by appointment William Wikoff, and by aid of other friends prepared to contact the West Florida legislature which, according to information given him, was then in session at Saint Francisville "exercising legislature powers."

The proclamation that Osborne and King carried with them for distribution in the "Republic of West Florida" read:

By the President of the United States of America.

A PROCLAMATION.

"*Whereas* the territory south of the Mississippi Territory and eastward of the river Mississippi, and extending to the river Perdido, of which possession was not delivered to the United States in pursuance of the treaty concluded at Paris on the 30th. of April, 1803, has at all times, as is well known, been considered and claimed by them as being within the colony of Louisiana conveyed by the said treaty in the same extent that it had in the hands of Spain and that it had when France originally possessed it; and

"*Whereas* the acquiescence of the United States in the temporary continuance of the said territory under the Spanish authority was not the result of any distrust of their title, as has been particularly evinced by the general tenor of their laws and by the distinction made in the application of those laws between that territory and foreign countries, but was occasioned by their conciliatory views and by a confidence in the justice of their cause and in the success of candid discussion and amicable negotiation with a just and friendly power; and

"*Whereas* a satisfactory adjustment, too long delayed, without the fault of the United States, has for some time been entirely suspended by events over which they had no control; and

"*Whereas* a crisis has at length arrived subversive of the order of things under the Spanish authorities, whereby a failure of the United States to take the said territory into its possession may lead to events ultimately contravening the views of both parties, whilst in the meantime the tranquility and security of our adjoining territories are endangered and new facilities given to violations of our revenue and commercial laws and of those prohibiting the introduction of slaves:

"Considering, moreover, that under these peculiar and imperative circumstances a forbearance on the part of the

150

United States to occupy the territory in question, and hereby guard against the confusions and contingencies which threaten it, might be construed into a derelection of their title or an insensibility to the importance of the stake; considering that in the hands of the United States it will not cease to be a subject of fair and friendly negotiation and adjustment; considering, finally, that the acts of Congress, though contemplating a present possession by a foreign authority, have contemplated also an eventual possession of the said territory by the United States, and are accordingly so framed as in that case to extend in their operation to the same.

"Now be it known that I, James Madison, President of the United States of America, in pursuance to these weighty and urgent considerations, have deemed it right and requisite that possession should be taken of the said territory in the name and behalf of the United States. William C. C. Claiborne, governor of the Orleans Territory, of which the said territory is to be taken as part, will accordingly proceed to execute the same and to exercise over the same Territory the authority and functions legally appertaining to his office; and the good people inhabiting the same are invited and enjoined to pay due respect to him in that character, to be obedient to the laws, to maintain order, to cherish harmony, and in every manner to conduct themselves as peaceable citizens, under full assurance that they will be protected in the enjoyment of their liberty, property, and religion.

"In testimony whereof I have caused the seal of the United States to be hereunto affixed, and signed the same with my hand.

Done at the City of Washington, the 27th day [SEAL] of October, A. D. 1810, and in the thirty-fifth year of the Independence of the said United States.

JAMES MADISON.

By the President:

R. SMITH,
Secretary of State."

By this proclamation, which Henry Adams designated as one of the most remarkable documents in the archives of the United States government, Madison had authorized, by a few strokes of his pen, the seizure of territory belonging to "a just and friendly power", having legislated for a foreign people without consulting their wishes, sent a sharp message to the Conventionalists through Governor Holmes, to the effect that their independence was an impertinence, and that their designs on public lands were something worse.

The news that the United States had claimed West Florida, after seven years of dilly-dallying, reached the members of the General Assembly and came up for consideration immediately. On the 5th of December the members of the whole assembly passed the following resolution:

"*Whereas*, information has been received that his excellency, Wm. C. C. Claiborne, Governor of the Territory of Orleans, with an armed force is now in the neighborhood of this Territory, and that certain proclamations have been distributed by his orders, bearing the signature of the President of the United States, calling upon the inhabitants of this state to receive and respect the said Wm. C. C. Claiborne as the governor and to consider themselves to owe allegiance and subjection to the government of the United States: *Resolved*, that the governor be requested to dispatch an agent immediately to the headquarters of the said Wm. C. C. Claiborne, with instructions to demand of him an explicit avowal of his views and intentions, and of the orders he may have received from the President of the United States with regard to this state, and by what authority he has given orders for the distribution of the aforesaid proclamation within the same.

JOHN W. LEONARD,
President *pro tem.* of the Senate.

Skipwith designated John H. Johnson as the messenger of the West Florida Assembly and addressed the members with a stirring speech in which he referred to their previous willingness to be received as a separate state or territory or to become a part of either Orleans or Mississippi, and he resented the fact that Madison had shown such little deference to the already installed authorities. He declared that in the steps they had taken they had acted wholly within their rights and, so they felt, in accord with the wishes of the American people. In bitterly resenting the president's proclamation Skipwith asked the members of the Assembly to unite with him "in expressing towards the proclamation the mutual sentiments and honest feelings of freemen." He declared they had a right to "self-government, despite the imperative tone in which the president summoned them to submit to the Orleans governor."

SKIPWITH DEFYS CLAIBORNE

The members of the General Assembly thereupon declared that the form of annexation that had been proposed by the Convention was the only one that could give the United States a perfect title to the territory and, while they were ready to unite with the people of Orleans Territory, they would not betray their constituents and dishonor their cause by accepting President Madison's proposals. They assured Governor Skipwith that they were ready "to unite with him in proper resistance."

While the assembly was fuming and calling Jimmy Madison harsh names, Governor Claiborne arrived in a barge at Pointe Coupée with two army officers and 33 regulars, where he was joined by Governor Holmes and Audley L. Osborn, the latter his messenger to the Feliciana country with the presidential proclamation. Holmes had passed through Saint Francisville and told Claiborne that his arrival and contemplated action was the subject of general conversation. Many had sided with Skipwith in being dissatisfied with the tenor of the proclamation and while he, Holmes, had explained it satisfactorily to some, Governor Skipwith refused to be mollified and, accompanied by three or four members of the Assembly, had left Saint Francisville for Baton Rouge.

When John Johnson greeted Claiborne at Pointe Coupée the Feliciana leader said that he, personally, was gratified with the terms of the proclamation but said, so Claiborne wrote Madison, "he was charged with a message from Governor Skipwith which he held in his hand and gave me. I told Johnson that, as a citizen, Skipwith would be respected but I would not recognize him as governor and commander in chief, nor enter into correspondence with him but that he, Johnson, had my permission and was requested to say to the people that I came among them with views most friendly. The president's proclamation, which they had seen, was my authority, and that I would proceed immediately to discharge my duties required of me."

To this Johnson replied: "Governor Skipwith has charged me verbally to inform you that *he has retired to the fort of Baton Rouge, and rather than surrender the Country unconditionally and without terms, he would, with 20 men only, if a greater force could not be procured surround the Flag Staff and die in defense of the Lone Star flag!*"

Claiborne says he made no reply to this verbal message from Skipwith but requested Johnson to repeat the words. After he had done so, Johnson again took the opportunity to express his devotion to the United States government and urged Claiborne to cross to Saint Francisville where he would find a troop of militia cavalry, a company of Riflemen and a concourse of citizens who would welcome his arrival in the territory and would, with pleasure, recognize Claiborne as their governor.

THE FALLING STAR

Audley L. Osborne was sent across the river to ascertain whether or not Johnson had correctly felt the public pulse. On his return he reported that the presence of Governor Claiborne would give the inhabitants great satisfaction. "I will further state to your excellency," said Osborne, "that the great point, at which the disaffected seem to stickle, is, that the *State of Florida* should be *treated with* as an *in-*

dependent nation, and that certain terms *should* be granted to them by your excellency before they *could submit* to become citizens of the United States, and come under your authority." Thereupon, accompanied by Governor Holmes, John H. Johnson, Colonel Covington, and his armed escort, Claiborne crossed the river. From his own pen we can learn how he was received and what he did:

> "I was met by citizens at the beach and escorted by cavalry and militia to the town. There I saw a pavilion waving which was said to be the Colors of the State of Florida. The militia formed around the staff, I appeared in center and the proclamation being read by a citizen, I said to militia, 'that having come among them as their Governor and Commander in Chief charged by the President of the U. S. to protect them in the enjoyment of their liberty, property, and religion, I had only to observe that it would be my pride and glory to discharge with fidelity so high a trust.' The flag of Florida was then ordered by me to be taken down, which was done, the Militia and Citizens cheering (as a mark of respect) as it descended. I then ordered a flag of the United States, which I had taken from my barge, to be reared, which was also done amid the huzzas of the Militia and Citizens."

And so the Star fell in Feliciana at the very spot that witnessed its rising, and for the first time, December 7, 1810, the stars and stripes of the United States flew over West Florida soil.

Independence was lost but independence was gained—if such a paradoxical situation can be so expressed.

COUNTY OF FELICIANA PROCLAIMED

Once established in Saint Francisville, Claiborne set about to prove himself the chief executive and boss of this new United States possession.

His very first official act was the drawing up and making public an ordinance designating the late Spanish holdings below the 31o line, from the mighty Mississippi eastward to the purling Perdido river, its shores on the south lapped by the blue green waters of the Gulf of Mexico— the County of Feliciana. Let us read it:

ORDINANCE

By William Charles Cole Claiborne, Governor of the
Territory of Orleans.

To all who shall see these presents greeting:
Be it known by the virtues of the powers in me vested, I do hereby order and ordain that so much of the Territory of Orleans as lies 'south of the Mississipi Territory, and Eastward of the river Mississippi, and extending to the

154

Perdido' shall constitute one county, to be known and called by the name of FELICIANA.

> Given under my hand and the seal of the town of St. Francisville, in the territory aforesaid, one thousand eight hundred and ten and in the thirty-fifth year of the Independence of the U. States of America.
>
> Wm. C. C. CLAIBORNE.

This accomplished the new governor gave his attention to the more pressing business of conciliating the objecting officials of the now defunct Free State of West Florida. Claiborne wrote the president on this subject the very day he raised the flag of the United States over Saint Francisville and it is interesting to note his reactions to the events of that day. So let us look over his shoulder as he takes crow quill in hand and follow the inked words:

> "This part of the *District of Florida the most populous*, is believed attached to the United States and to be greatly pleased with the event of the day. How far a like disposition may manifest itself at the town of Baton Rouge and its vicinity, remains yet to be seen. No efforts which my *Country's honor* or *my own* permit will remain unessayed to induce Mr. Skipwith to abandon his ill-judged and rash purposes; Nor am I without strong hopes of succeeding. But if conciliatory measures should obstinately fail, *the troops of the Untied States will be commanded to take the fort.*
>
> "I am not advised of the terms which Mr. Skipwith would propose, but among other things it is said he would wish a *formal recognition of all the sales of lands under Spanish authorities;* the payment of debts contracted by the constitution; and not only a pardon for the deserters, but their discharge from the service of the U. S. The fort at Baton Rouge is garrisoned for the most part by Deserters, with them Mr. Skipwith may hope to make a desperate defense, but he ought not to expect that it is in their power, with him at their Head, to command terms. I have already said, that as related to Deserters, such as were found in the District should meet no punishment, but on the contrary should receive lenient treatment until the will of the president be known and I was full persuaded a pardon would be extended them, but, if they wish mercy, *not to remain in arms.*"

As indicated in this letter to Madison, the new executive did not wish to have his occupation of the Baton Rouge fort bring on trouble. The declaration of Skipwith and some of the other members of the West Florida General Assembly that they "were determined sooner to perish under the falling star of Florida than to submit to the sacrifice and disgrace of any of their followers, not even the deserters from the American army, or suffer themselves to be given up to any Foreign

155

Power," determined Claiborne on sending peace messengers ahead of his own armed approach. He wisely chose Governor David Holmes, together with "a few gentlemen of respectability" from St. Francisville, and Isaac Johnson's Feliciana Dragoons as escort, to conciliate those who were loud in their intention of refusing to accept President Madison's sudden and stunning move. So, a-horseback, the peace party took to the long and dusty road that led over Thompson's Creek, through the Plains, and thence to Baton Rouge where the Lone Star still waved over the fort perched on the banks of the turgid Mississippi.

Skipwith had arrived at the Baton Rouge fort the day before Holmes and his escort got there. The "governor" of West Florida found that Captain John Ballinger, in command of the forces in the fort, had arrested Claiborne's messenger, William King, for distributing Madison's proclamation, Ballinger believing Mr. King was distributing a forgery designed by the Spanish to throw the Floridians into confusion. Skipwith at once ordered that King be released and then sat himself down to crow quill and paper and eased his badly lacerated feeling by a long letter to President Madison, in which he admitted that he personally desired to maintain peace and order in West Florida while working for its "honorable return to the bosom of the parent country," but at the same time he strove to "secure for the United States a fair and legitimate title" to West Florida. He warned the president that he and his liberty-loving associates would resist dishonor, repel any wanton outrage to their feelings," and would assert the rights of their adopted country should circumstances require it.

The next day, however, when Holmes entered Baton Rouge and went into conference with him and Ballinger, Skipwith exhibited a change of demeanor when Ballinger expressed his willingness to surrendered the fort to the American forces. As they left the meeting place word was brought to Holmes and Skipwith that five American gunboats carrying Colonel Covington's regulars and Governor Claiborne had been sighted two miles up the river and the soldiers were landing. When Holmes met Claiborne he handed the Orleans excutive a letter from Skipwith expressing his gratification over the prospect of West Florida being annexed to the United States, but he defended his course and again protested against Claiborne's methods as an outrage against the Lone Star Flag and the constitution of West Florida.

Nor would he give an order to the Florida troops to lower their own flag, but he directed them not to resist the American forces; "as a native of the United States he would never sign an order that would lead to the shedding of a single drop of American blood!"

FIFTEEN STARS OVER BATON ROUGE

Let us again rely upon Claiborne's own words in picturing the scene that saw the final "falling of the Star" and the first raising of the flag of fifteen stars and fifteen stripes over Baton Rouge:

"My last letter informed you that peaceable possession was taken on the 10th of the Town, Fort and District of Baton Rouge in the name and in behalf of the United States . . . I had reasons to apprehend resistance, and was prepared to meet it; But on landing near the Town the agreeable intelligence was brought to me that the armed Citizens (called here the Convention Troops) were ready to retire from the Fort, and to acknowledge the authority of the United States. It was not understood by me that terms were insisted on; but a wish was expressed that the Florida flag might *be treated with respect*, and the *deserters unmolested*. In answer I requested that the fort be evacuated at half past two o'clock, and that the citizens should march out and stack their arms.

"As to the flag I readily assented that on striking it, such evidences of respect might be shown as the armed citizens of the Fort thought proper. And with regard to the deserters I stated, that, they should remain undisturbed, until the president's pleasure respecting them should be made known. At three the fort was taken possession of by a Detachment of United States troops.

"Mr. Skipwith's conduct continues correct. When I first apprized him of the proclamation his feelings were, I presume, wounded, and betrayed him into some imprudence of expression. But from what I have since learned, the Union of Florida with the United States has always been his avowed object, and he now professes to be much gratified by the late event, and to be sincerely disposed to contribute to the general welfare.

"I have seen and conversed with Gen. Thomas, the Ajax of the late revolution, & who has always been esteemed an honest man; He declared that the great object he had in view was now accomplished and that no man more than himself rejoiced in taking possesion of the Country by the U. S. I find that the most *influential* among the convention party are very generally the friends of the United States. There are others, who are hand and heart devoted to the British interests and whenever occasion favors it, by their acts evince their dislike of American institutions."

A PART OF THE PURCHASE—AT LAST

So, after an existence of 74 days, a short life but a merry one, the stout little republic of West Florida had ceased to be one of the nations of the world. The closing scenes that marked the demise of this Tom Thumb republic were as dramatic as those that had witnessed

157

its birth. Exactly at two-thirty in the afternoon of December tenth, the whole force of four hundred men (for the expeditionary force that had started eastward to subject the land beyond the Pearl had marched back) with their muskets at shoulder, gathered about the white staff in the center of the parade in the fort. As the Lone Star descended the pole the muskets crashed out a volley. Then, in obedience to low commands the men tramped out of the gates and formed in line in the esplanade, stacked their arms, laid off their accoutrements, and were marched by their officers into the village and were dismissed.

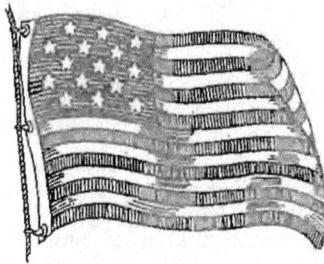

THE SIXTH FLAG

The flag that succeeded the Lone Star flag of Independent West Florida had fifteen stripes and fifteen stars; the return to the original design of thirteen stripes was not made until 1818. The 15 stars shown on the first "Stars and Stripes" to fly over Feliciana included the original thirteen states plus Vermont and Kentucky.

A half hour later, led by Colonel Leonard Covington and Lieutenant Colonel Zebulon Montgomery Pike, the United States troops marched into the deserted fortification and formed a hollow square about the bare staff. Governor Claiborne, accompanied by Governor David Holmes, and a few citizens, raised his hand in command and a color sergeant fixed the halyards to a new banner and a flag of fifteen stars and fifteen stripes rose into the blue of the sky. When it reached the peak a crashing volley from the muskets of the uniformed soldiers, and twenty-one measured blasts from a field piece, mingled with the cheers from the members of the late garrison, saluted the new emblem of sovereignty.

Indecision, strife, delay, bloodshed was over—West Florida *was*, after seven long years, actually a part of the Louisiana Purchase!

CLAIBORNE'S TROUBLES BEGIN

No sooner had Claiborne established himself as governor of this new part of his territory than his other troubles began. He must im-

158

mediately provide for self-government. His first act was to name the new area and as we have seen he proclaimed everything below the Mississippi Territory's southern boundary from the Mississippi to the Perdido rivers, "The Country of Feliciana."

It was necessary that judges for the different parishes be selected to rule under the judicial system of the United States and, of course, there was a rush of would-be judges. His selection as judge of East Baton Rouge parish was George Mather, Sr., an Englishman by birth, who for 35 years had been an inhabitant of Baton Rouge and New Orleans. Doctor Andrew Steele was temporarily made judge of Feliciana parish, but for the parishes of St. Helena and St. Tammany (for such was the name Claiborne fastened on the section formerly called Chifuncté and then St. Ferdinand) he did not indicate a choice. "There is in that quarter a great scarcity of talent, and the number of virtuous men (I fear) is not as great as I could wish," he complained.

Nor did the new executive have the privilege of releasing Don Carlos de Lassus from "durance vile," for the day before Claiborne reached Baton Rouge, Skipwith freed the former Spanish governor, and de Lassus immediately went across the river to friends living in Pointe Coupée. "He is greatly chagrined at the loss of the Fort and Country," wrote Claiborne, "and is so apprehensive that his misfortunes will be looked upon as crimes by his Government, that he seems desirous to remain for the present under the protection of the United States."

Don Carlos had reason for such fears, as he was afterwards court martialed and sentenced to death, but he did not die for he refused to attend the court martial and remained in New Orleans, at the home of his sister, the wife of Pierre Derbigny, (afterwards a governor of Louisiana). A year after he had been deposed as governor, he married Adélaïde Féliciana Mariana Leonard, daughter of Gilbert Leonard and sister of John W. Leonard. Carlos de Lassus never returned to Spanish soil. He lived for a while in New Orleans, then took up his residence in Saint Louis, where he had once governed, but later returned to the Crescent City where he remained a conspicuous figure until his death in 1842 in his seventy-eighth year. He left a single child, his son, Charles Auguste de Hault de Lassus, who married into the Blanque family and left many descendants in New Orleans bearing his name.

PORTRAIT OF A GOVERNOR

Claiborne, wanting to do something handsome for Fulwar Skipwith, offered him the post of justice of the peace in Baton Rouge, but the late governor of West Florida refused the post. In later years he became registrar of the land office at Montpelier, serving as a clearing house for all land claims west of the Pearl river. Following the events concerned with the days of the West Florida Republic Skipwith returned to his "Montesano" plantation where he raised cotton and recovered the fortune he lost in France. In his late years on the plantation, he and his wife, the Flemish Countess Vandenclooster, were "not living together as harmoniously as two cooing doves," and his children, in these domestic broils, took sides with the mother, so wrote Henry Skipwith, of Clinton, his nephew, who also describes his uncle in the following priceless pen-etching:

"Fulwar Skipwith retained to the last one of the charcteristics most essential to a ruler of families or States. He was the most methodical man in his habits I ever met. From early morn to dewy eve he was out on foot attending personally to all the plantation affairs. At candle-light he and his young associate would meet by the parlor fireside, on each side of which was a chair of some fancy model for his nephew, and on the opposite side was a cushioned big-armed, high-backed veritable chair of state, and when the governor reclined himself cosily in his old familiar seat, memories of Marly, Versailles, Paris, Bonaparte, Barras, Sieyes, and Talleyrand flowed from his mouth in polished phrase as smoothly as water from a gurgling fountain.

"On one side of the chair of state was placed a small round table on which his servants had placed a long candle in a high candlestick, a large decanter of water, a sugar dish and tongs, a decanter holding a quart of whiskey, and a large meerschaum, by the side of which reposed a tiny tobacco pouch. On the other side of the chair of state was placed a basket full of seed-cotton and an empty basket to hold the cotton seed when picked. To pick that basket of cotton was the task of the evening. He might engage in animated narratives of interviews with the First Consul or the Emperor, or with some other great men of those days of great deeds, but the cotton picking went on mechanically and monotonously all the same. He never paused in his task while drawing the most fascinating pictures selected from the wildest panorama ever enacted on the human stage. He did not even pause in his task of cotton picking to mix himself a drink. That indispensible part of the drama devolved upon his young relative who had become familiar with the properties of whiskey, sugar, and water by nightly practice in mixing for the old gentleman.

"As the night wore on the results began to be more clearly developed. The candle was flickering in its socket. The water decanter was empty, the sugar dish was empty, the whiskey decanter was empty, the tobacco pouch was empty, and the basket of seed-cotton was empty. But the basket of picked seed was nearly full, and the Governor was quite full!

"Nevertheless, after bidding his nephew a ceremonious good night, he would back himself out of the room with all the grace of a courier of the *ancient régime*. When the curtain dropped on this last act of the mighty drama, he was as majestic, dignified, and graceful in his carriage, he was as logical and entertaining in his pictures drawn from memory, as he was at the start; neither time, talk, or whiskey had the power to unsteady the legs of the late Governor of West Florida!

"To the very last he was in act, in deed, and in graceful carriage the Consul of the Republic and the Governor of the free and independent State of West Florida."

THE FELICIANA VIEW

A day or two after Claiborne took charge and West Florida became a part of the United States, the anonymous but verbose correspondent of the "Louisiana Gazette," that very informative "Bayou Sarah Planter," sent the New Orleans newspaper the following resumé:

"When revolutions convulse a country, it is very difficult to trace the cause of its original source; the recent but small revolution in West Florida needs explanation—feeling myself sufficiently furnished with information on the subject, I offer to the public, through your Gazette, a narrative of facts as they have occurred. As I am little acquainted with writing for public prints, pardon will be granted me for the many inaccuracies which may appear in my detail, when I pledge myself for the truth of my statement.

"From the spring of 1808, immediately after the capture of Charles the fourth, and his son, Ferdinand the seventh, by the Corsican tyrant, a general distrust and want of confidence was mutually evinced between the Executive of Baton Rouge and the people. The people had long thought that the Governor, who had all powers, executive and judicial in his hands, like scales inclined to the side from which he received most; this opinion was supported by strong evidence. Governor Grand Pre then presided as Governor. He was suspected of favoring the views of the usurper Napoleon, and was ordered to the Havana, where he paid the debt of nature. Here let me say in honor of his memory, that he was a soldier, a man gentlemanly in his manners, and possessed handsome talents.

"Colonel Lassus succeeded Grand Pre, and the people had hopes of some change in their favor, but alas! they were deceived. Lassus had long practiced in the Spanish school of bribery and had studied duplicity, which he practiced like a proficient in the art. He promised everything and performed nothing. Timid, fearful and intriguing; he held out to the people everything, while he was using all his diplomatic powers to crush their hopes and views.

"The public are well acquainted with the different meetings of the convention, all of which General Lassus went with them hand in hand apparently. The new system of jurisprudence was among the first objects of the convention.

161

The judges named to associate with Gov. Lassus were, Fulwar Skipwith, Robert Percy, and Shepherd Brown, the latter named gentleman, it appears, was in all the secrets and intrigues of Lassus; he procrastinated his acceptance from time to time. Nature had done well for this man; fitted him well for intrigue. With a constant smile upon his countenance, he kept the members of the convention in full belief that he was a great admirer of their new measures, that he would most willingly go with them in all the proposed reform. This was in the latter part of the month August or the beginning of September. The members of the convention fully impressed with the belief that everything was tranquil, that all classes of virtuous good citizens were disposed to accede to their regulations, adjourned, leaving a committee at Baton Rouge to attend to the business that immediately related to the reform; such as the organization of the militia, taxation, &c.

"When Gov. Lassus was called upon for his signature in any case by the committee, he always made some plausible cause of delay—in the meantime his friend Shepherd Brown quit Baton Rouge without accepting his appointment as judge, retaining his old appointment as civil commandant of St. Helena. (Footnote: *The day of his departure he observed to Capt. Medzenger 'that the Bayou-Sarah people would be the better of having a little blood drawn,' meaning that they were rather inflamatory.)

"Suspicion was awakened, the committee found they were about to be overreached, that Governor Lassus was corresponding with Governor Folch, that Brown, after his return to St. Helena, was using every means in his power to prepossess the people against the new order of things; and at the same time was preparing for war, making pikes, building forts, &c. The committee, fully convinced of the bad faith of Lassus and Brown, and on the 21st of September collected such members of the convention as were within a short distance of St. Francisville, mouth of Bayou Sarah. Time at this moment was precious—the members of the convention who had been active in promoting the new system was denounced, and well knowing that if force would be collected to oppose the system with effect, that they must either leave their country, abandon their wives and children, and forfeit all their property, or be loaded with irons and sent to Morro Castle, at Havana. That night, the 21st of September, six members of the convention were convened at St. Francisville—this was all that could be convened at this all important crisis—let their names be recorded, they shall stand in the front rank of freemen. Firmness and independence that day marked their actions. John Rhea, John H. Johnson, Philip Hickey, John Mills, Thomas Lilley and William Barrow, were the men who gave the order to General Thomas to take the fort at Baton Rouge; and with the zeal and promptitude of a veteran, he executed the order at 3 o'clock on the morning of the 23rd of September, and had to collect his troops and march forty miles, which he did in the short space of thirteen hours.

"Some plodding mortals may say that there was a degree of hardihood in those men bordering on desperation. This I deny—they acted as honest and firm men ought always to do in a good cause.

"It is obvious that the taking of the fort, and the declaration of independence, roused the administration of the United States from their lethargy—and post haste their messenger came to give that protection which had so long been withheld. Before I close, it is proper that I should state that no disapprobation on the part of the other members of the convention was shewn, on the contrary, they most heartily concurred in the order given General Thomas.

"West-Florida is now an integral part of the U. States, The people will be good citizens ever loyal and faithful to the government who protects their rights and administers justice with a steady hand.

A BAYOU-SARAH PLANTER."

THE COUNTY OF FELICIANA

Three days before Christmas, Claiborne named the parishes of the New County of Feliciana he had established December 7, when at Saint Francisville. His proclamation read:

"Be it known, That 'for the execution of process civil and criminal' I do, by virtue of the powers in me vested, under the Ordinance of Congress, for the government of the Territory of Orleans, Ordain and Decree, that there shall be established within the county of Feliciana four parishes, whose limits shall be as follows, to-wit: all that tract of country lying below the boundary of the Mississippi Territory, and between the most eastern branch of Thompson's Creek and the River Mississippi, shall form the first Parish, and shall be called the Parish of Feliciana; all that tract of country lying between the most eastern branch of Thompson's Creek and the River Iberville, and extending from the Mississippi to the Amite, shall form the Second Parish, to be called the Parish of East Baton Rouge; all that tract of country lying below the boundary of the Mississippi Territory and between the Amite and the River Ponchitoola, which empties into the Lake Maurepas, shall form the Third Parish, to be called the Parish of St. Helena; and all that tract of country east of the Ponchitoola, including the settlements on the Chiffonta, Bogcheto and Pearl Rivers, shall form the Fourth Parish, to be called the Parish of St. Tammany; with the residue of the County of Feliciana there shall be formed such other Parishes as may hereafter be deemed expedient.

163

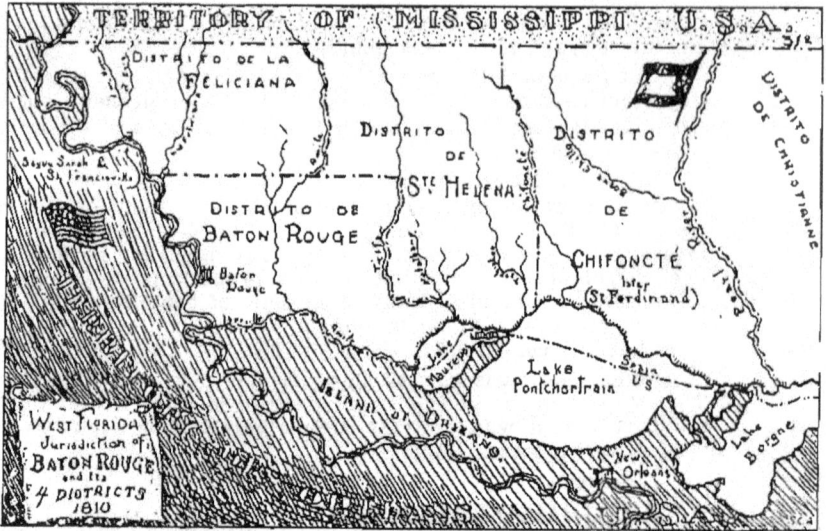

SPAIN'S WEST FLORIDA

That section of West Florida which became the theatre of stirring events in 1810, was known officially as *Florida Occidental, jurisdicción de Baton Rouge*. It consisted of four districts: *Feliciana*, which extended from the Mississippi to the Amite, being even a trifle larger than the present two parishes of the same name, (the stream that ran through its center was then called *Rio Feliciana*, but during the 16 years of British domination it was called "Thompson's Creek", before that the original French settlers knew the stream as *Bayou des Ecores*, or "Bayou of the Bluffs"); *Baton Rouge*, which extended east to the Tickfaw; *Ste. Helena*, which took in what is now that parish, Livingston, and Tangipahoa; *Chifoncté*, which lay between the Tchefuncta and Pearl rivers, had its name changed during the deliberations of the Convention and was re-christened *Saint Ferdinand*, a gesture, no doubt, of loyalty to Ferdinand VII, the Spanish king then languishing in one of Napoleon's prisons while the Little Corporal's brother sat on the throne in Madrid.

"Given under my hand and sealed at Baton Rouge on the twenty-second of December, in the year of our Lord one thousand eight hundred and ten, and of the Independence of the United States of America the thirty-fifth.

WILLIAM C. C. CLAIBORNE."

THE COUNTY OF FELICIANA

When West Florida went under the jurisdiction of the United States in December, 1810, Wm. C. C. Claiborne, governor of the Territory of Orleans, created the "County of Feliciana" which had six parishes and extended from the Mississippi river to the Perdido river, east of Mobile. The county seat was Saint Francisville and the parishes were: *Feliciana*, which constituted the area now known as West Feliciana (because of the protests of the Feliciana citizens, the governor later designated the Amite as the eastern boundary); *East Baton Rouge* was originally designated as the territory lying between Amite and Thompson's Creek, from the Iberville and the Mississippi river to the lower boundary of the Mississippi Territory; *Ste Helena* occupied the territory between the Amite and the Tangipahoa; between the Tanchipahoa and the Pearl was the parish Claiborne named *Saint Tammany*, in honor of an Indian chief; between the Pearl and the river falling into Biloxi Bay was the parish of *"Viloxi,"* as the name was then spelled; *Pascagoula*, the sixth parish, had three eastern boundary lines, first, *Bayou La Batrie*; second, *Bayou Perro* or *"Dog River"*; third, the Perdido river.

THE WHY OF "ST. TAMMANY"

In such fashion was the name Saint Tammany fastened on Louisiana. It was the name of a celebrated sachem or chief of the Delaware Indians named *Tamanend* or "Tammany" as it was afterwards spelled, meaning in the Delaware tongue "the Affable." Even before the American War of Independence there were certain Whig socities called "Sons of Liberty" and "Sons of Saint Tammany" because this Indian sachem had been adopted by these sons of liberty as their patron saint and celebrated his festival on the first of May. They worked their meetings with rituals in which Indian words were used to indicate the American character of their lodges. In 1789 an Irishman named Mooney organized the "Society of St. Tammany" or "Columbian Order," as a patriotic, benevolent, and non-political organization, with the avowed intent of counteracting the influence of what was believed to be the more aristocratic "Order of Cincinnati". This St. Tammany society

165

built its own meeting place, which it appropriately called a *wigwam*, but it was not itself the well-known New York political organization but rents its hall to the "Tammany Hall General Committee", the "Tammany Hall" of political notoriety.

Why Claiborne did not wish to continue the name of the Spanish king on the land lying between the "Ponchitoola" and the Pearl rivers is quite plain, but it is not quite so understandable why he selected the name of an Indian chief of the East when he could have selected a Southern Indian, if an Indian name he must have. The probabilities are that he was a member of the Society of Saint Tammany and did not hold membership in the more snooty Order of Cincinnati, and, as there were so many "sons of liberty" mixed up in the revolt that wrested this land from Spain, he believed that a good American, a good Whig name should replace that of Ferdinand the seventh.

It will be noted that Claiborne's proclamation reduced the area of Feliciana to the very territory occupied by the present-day parish of West Feliciana, and enlarged the parish of Baton Rouge so that it ran north to the Mississippi line. Naturally, the Feliciana folk resented this and John H. Johnson and Judge John Rhea wrote Claiborne about the sudden shrinking of their prized area. So, on the last day of January the governor promised to do something about it:

> "I have heard with sincere regret that in laying out the Parish of Feliciana, I have greatly curtailed its ancient limits and subjected many Citizens to inconvenience by placing them within the Bounds of East Baton Rouge. Will you be pleased to furnish me with your Sentiments on this subject. In prescribing the Bounds of Parishes, my sole object was to consult the convenience of the Inhabitants; and if unfortunately that end has not been attained we must endeavor to correct the wrong as soon as may be practicable."

On January fourth Claiborne had decided on the names and limits of the parishes east of the Pearl River, and he decreed: "all that tract of country which extends from the eastern bank of Pearl River to the River Veloxy and below the boundary of the Mississippi Territory, shall form the fifth parish and be called the Parish of Veloxy; and all that tract of country which extends from the eastern bank of the Veloxy River to the Bayou Batrie (including all the settlements on the Bayou Batrie and the Pascagoula) shall form the sixth parish, to be called the Parish of Pascagoula."

On the 26th of January, after a series of protests had reached him from the Gulf Coast, Claiborne issued a supplementary note in which he ordained and decreed: "that the Parish of Pascagoula, whose eastern boundary was declared to be by ordinance of Jan. 4 the Bayou Batrie,

166

shall . . . be extended to the *Rio Perro*, or Dog River, and that all the settlements east of said river shall hereafter be included in the Parish of Pascagoula."

The governor had left Baton Rouge and was at the Government House in New Orleans when he penned these ordinances. He had remained in the new County of Feliciana until the day before Christmas and won many friends and admirers by his exercise of sound judgment after taking possession of the late Republic of West Florida, and his course of conciliation did much to heal wounded feelings and broken heads. A slight insight is given of his character at this period if we read a letter he wrote President Madison just before he left Baton Rouge. "I set out for New Orleans to encounter the ensuing winter, all the intrigues and all the calumny of Clark & Co., who have at their command every newspaper in New Orleans but the *Courier*, most of the third party men, and the disappointed Office Hunters, and every Burrite in the Territory. But this coalition gives me no concern. It will be in my power, I trust, to maintain my ground against all my enemies."

In New Orleans Claiborne was forced to give serious consideration to a proper judicial system for the County of Feliciana, it was first proposed to attach it to the Pointe Coupée jurisdiction, but on April 10, 1811, the governor established the Seventh Superior Court to include the entire county of Feliciana from the River Mississippi to the Perdido, the same river that today marks the boundary between the states of Alabama and Florida, and the act provided that the court "shall be holden in and for the Seventh District, on first Mondays of March and August, at the town of Saint Francisville."

John H. Johnson was appointed by Claiborne as High Sheriff of the Feliciana County, and Dr. Andrew Steele, who had been sitting as judge of the Feliciana parish, was replaced by Judge John Rhea, president of the Convention, on January 19, 1811. When George Mather resigned as judge of East Baton Rouge Parish, Doctor Steele was named to that bench. Audley L. Osborne, who had been Claiborne's messenger when the president's proclamation was distributed, was made judge of the Ste. Helena Parish on January 14, and held sway over Saint Tammany as well until July 18, the governor appointed Thomas C. Warren to be judge of the territory between the Tanchipoa and the Pearl.

As the County of Feliciana was now officially a part of the Territory of Orleans it was only meet and proper that its citizens should have a say in the government, therefore they were given, by act of legislature and the governor's approval, the right of representation.

167

AN ACT

Providing for the Election of Representatives from the Country between the Territories of Mississippi and Orleans, and between the Rivers Mississippi and Perdido, to the general assembly of the Territory of Orleans.

Whereas possession of the said country has been recently taken by the authority and in the name of the American Government; and wherefore we are instructed that it forms a component part of this territory; and whereas all the duties as well as the rights, privileges and immunities of our citizens having been devolved on the inhabitants of that country, it is just and reasonable that they should be fully and fairly represented in the councils of the country by whose laws they are governed.

Sect. 1. *Be it enacted by the Legislative Council and House of Representatives of the Territory of Orleans in general assembly convened,* That until the population of said tract of country, now known by the name of County of Feliciana, shall be more particularly ascertained, the said county shall be entitled to five Representatives, who shall be elected from the following parishes, according to the laws and regulations in force in this Territory and at such time and places in said parishes as the Governor shall in his writs of election direct, to-wit:

Three Representatives from the parishes of Feliciana and East Baton Rouge, which comprehends all the country between the lower line of the Mississippi Territory and the Iberville and extends from the river Mississippi to the Amite.

One Representative from the Parishes of St. Helena and St. Tammany, which extends from the Amite so as to include Ponchitoula, the settlement of Chefonta, Bogchito and Pearl Rivers;

And one Representative from Biloxi and Pascagoula, which comprehends all the residue of the said district, the said parishes being limited conformable to the ordiances of the Governor.

> MAGLOIE GUICHARD,
> *Speaker of House of Representatives.*
> JEAN NOEL DESTREHAN,
> *Pres. of the Legislative Council.*

Approved February 5, 1811.

> WILLIAM C. C. CLAIBORNE,
> *Governor of the Territory of Orleans.*

To date I have found no record of such elections being held nor any names of those who might have been chosen to represent the new country.

However, on April 24, 1811, Claiborne made good his word given Sheriff John H. Johnson and Judge John Rhea and by an act of legislature enlarged the Parish of Feliciana and reduced the area of East Baton Rouge. The act provided that the "County of Feliciana" should be divided into six parishes. "The First shall be called the Parish of Feliciana, lying between the lower line of the Mississippi Territory to the mouth of Thompson's Creek, and a line running thence due East to the River Amite, and its Western boundaries shall be the Mississippi River."

East Baton Rouge was designated as the area lying between "the Parish of Feliciana and the Iberville and between the Mississippi and Amite." St. Helena was bounded by the 31o line on the north, its western and eastern boundaries being Amite and Tanchipao, and on the south by Lake Pontchartrain. Everything east of the Tanchipao to the Pearl River, constituted the Parish of St. Tammany. The act went on to state "That the fifth shall be called the Parish of Biloxi, lying South of the Mississippi Territory and extending from the Pearl River to the river falling into the Bay of Biloxi", while Pascagoula was named as "East from the river falling into the Bay of Biloxi, including all the remainder of the County of Feliciana."

And so matters remained for a twelve-month, when the state of Louisiana was formed and the territory east of the Pearl was apportioned to Mississippi and Alabama. However it cost the citizens of Feliciana something to be a part and parcel of the Territory of Orleans for the legislative council decided that the County of Feliciana should pay as a portion of the territorial tax, the sum of $6,000 per annum, and 75 cents a head for each slave a citizen owned.

THE "LONE STAR" AGAIN RISES

All went well with the new American Territory and the citizens settled down to their regular pursuits, secure in their belief that strife and trouble were buried in the past. However, in March of 1811, the inhabitants of Feliciana were once more on the verge of insurrection. Congressman Bibb of Georgia, in the national congress, was energetically backing a bill that would make the former West Florida a part of the Mississippi Territory, while Congressman Rhea of Tennessee held that the West Florida that was should be made a part of Orleans Territory. The debate waxed furious and finally, when a bill was passed admitting Orleans Territory as a state, no provision was made for West Florida! Although considered a part of Louisiana, it did not figure in that state's admission to the Union!

To suitably express their resentment the Feliciana folk on Sunday, March 17, once more raised the Lone Star flag at Saint Francisville. Governor Claiborne apprised of this act wrote Secretary Smith:

"I learn that some of the inhabitants of St. Francisville
have lately conducted themselves very improperly and that
among other acts of great indiscretion they had reared the
Florida flag. It, however, was soon taken down, without
producing any serious commotion by the orders of Gen.
Hampton, and the pavilion of the United States again displayed. The people of Feliciana are greatly dissatisfied at
the proposition made in Congress to separate them from
the territory of Orleans. It occasions many good citizens
to believe that their political destiny is yet uncertain; and
the base and designing are incessant in their efforts to
promote discontent."

A fuller account of this "revolt" was printed in the Natchez
"Chronicle", which was picked up by the "Louisiana Gazette" for Or-
leanians who were still greatly interested in everything occuring in
the territory that had so lately been the scene of momentous happenings. Said the Crescent City newsprint:

"WEST FLORIDA AGAIN!

"By a gentleman who left St. Francisville on Tuesday
last, we learn that a curious circumstance took place on
Sunday. On that morning when the inhabitants arose, they
were astonished to find the flag of Florida again waving at
the top of the flag-staff; but as there had been many mis-
chievous pranks played for several night previous, no person in town tho't any more of it than a continuance of
these pranks; under the impression, no person attempted
to take it down, and more particularly as there was no getting at it, unless by climbing the staff, which was at least
60 feet high, or by felling it. In the course of the day,
however, some gentlemen having rode into the country,
found that some uneasy sensations had been created, and a
belief was likely to become current that it was reared
in opposition to the government. In the evening, on their
return, a few persons viewing the thing more serious, resolved on cutting down the staff. The cutting down of the
staff was opposed on the ground of it being private property; this contention was likely to produce a serious riot
when very happily Gen. Hampton and Lieu. Hukill arrived in town. The general immediately called on the civil
officer, and stating that he considered the flag then flying
an insult to his government, desired that it might be ordered down. The civil officer accordingly repaired to the
flag-staff, where the right of private property was again
contended for. The Gen. observed that if the flag was
not taken down by the civil power, he would have a detachment of troops to do it the next day. The civil magistrate then ordered the staff to be cut down, which was
done instanter.

"The day following at 3 o'clock p. m., a few of those
who were at the storming of Baton Rouge, buried the flag

170

in a private lot, with great ceremony. A procession was formed, after having placed the flag in its coffin, and marched around the stump of the flag-staff, moved to the grave, where it was deposited, and three volleys of musquetry fired over it. Our informant adds that they had written an epitaph for the tomb, which was said to evince some genius, but he could not procure a copy."

TO MISSISSIPPI OR LOUISIANA?

The Feliciana folk, or at least a goodly portion of them, continued restless and impatient over the slowness of Congress to act and many movements were suggested to bring about a more prompt action upon admission and, what was more to the point, a settlement of the debts contracted by the Conventionalists by the parent government.

In September of 1811, Governor Claiborne visited the region and persuaded the citizens to remain calm and compel the impatient ones to follow suit. On the second of that month he wrote Secretary of State James Monroe from Saint Francisville:

"A news-paper here, called *The Time Piece*, has assumed a shape by no means calculated to conciliate the affections of the people toward the government. The Editor possesses Genius, but neither Judgment nor discretion. [This editor was James M. Bradford, who established the first newspaper in Saint Francisville. S. C. A.] This paper teems with abuse of Congress & their conduct toward West Florida is represented as wrongful and oppressive. That these publications have made some injurious impressions is certain, but I have reasons to believe, that the great Majority of the people, remain firm in their attachment to the Government & the Administration. It is understood that a general meeting of the Citizens is to take place on the 26th of this Month to Celebrate the Capture of the Fort of Baton Rouge by the Conventionalists, & that the occasion will be embraced by some restless Individuals, to obtain adoption of some inflamatory Resolutions; I however, rely with confidence on the patriotism & good sense of the Cultivators of the soil, & I persuade myself that the Intriguers will not be enabled to do mischief. I have seen at this place Mr. John Rhea, formerly President of the Convention, & at present Judge of the Parish of Feliciana. He is a prudent, judicious, well disposed Man, & seems to be much attached to the Government of the United States. He spoke to me of the Debts of the Convention, & expressed a great desire that the Government would direct their payment. I told him that I had already apprized the President of the Nature of their Debts, & that I sincerely hoped some provision would be made to meet them, but I was inclined to think the present an unfavorable period to press the subject, & that the persons interested, had better wait until the Government had come to some understanding with Foreign Nations relative to the possession of Florida."

171

Later Claiborne, in writing John H. Johnson, told the sheriff of the Seventh Superior Court district, something about the progress of the convention that was planning the admission of the Territory of Orleans into the Union, and expressed his personal views and desires. "A decided majority of the Convention is in favor of annexing Florida to the New State, & a strong but respectful Memorial will, I suspect, be presented on the occasion to the Congress of the United States. For myself, there is no political event I more desire than that the eighteenth State may extend from the Sabine to the Perdido, & I indulge a hope that during the present or ensuing session of Congress, an Act may pass, which will recognize such Limits."

In December another meeting of the representativs of the people was called to convene again on historic St. John's Plains. John H. Johnson had evidently apprised Claiborne of the gathering, for on the 18th of that month the governor wrote him:

"The proposed meeting of the People at St. John's Plains, will be an interesting one, & I sincerely hope that the result may prove favorable to the welfare of the County of Feliciana. In the contemplated address to Congress, I trust the Citizens will not lose sight of the good old maxim 'Gentleness in the manner, but substance in the thing.' State your wishes, your rights & your grievances with firmness but with all that respect & and Confidence due to a free, wise and virtuous government. Believe me, the government are most favorably disposed towards your District. I know the President has nothing more at heart, than the happiness of the People of West Florida and their permanent Connection with the American family, nor do I doubt but a like sentiment is cherished by a Majority of the Members of the Senate & House of Representatives of the United States. For myself, you may rest assured of my zealous co-operation in whatever concerns the prosperity of Feliciana." As a postcript he added that Congressman Magruder was planning to present a memorial to Congress praying that the tract west from the Pedido River under the Mississippi line would be permanently annexed to the Orleans Territory.

Finally, on April 12, 1812, the ninth anniversary of the day that by treaty of cession Louisiana was acquired by the United States, the Territory of Orleans became the State of Louisiana, and thereafter eighteen stars were displayed on the flag of the United States and the number of stripes reduced to the original thirteen. Four days after Congress approved the admission of this eighteenth state it passed an act to enlarge the limits of Louisiana by including that portion of West Florida from the Pearl to the Mississippi River within the new commonwealth.

In such fashion the "Florida Parishes" became a part of Louisiana, although the state's legislative assent to this inclusion bears the date of August 4, 1812, four months after the formal admission.

"THE BONNIE BLUE FLAG"

The raising of the Lone Star Flag at Saint Francisville on Sunday, March 17, 1811, was not the last time this banner blue was flung to the breeze in the Feliciana country; half a century later, at Jackson Mississippi, January 6, 1861, the State of Mississippi, in convention assembled, voted to sever her alliance with the Union. No sooner had the clerk announced the vote of the delegates, than a man rushed through the crowded convention hall holding aloft a silken banner and thrust the staff in the hands of the presiding officer, who waved it before the cheering delegates and frenzied spectators.

The flag was a solid blue banner, having in its center a single white five-pointed star! The "Lone Star" of Feliciana and the Free State of West Florida had risen from the grave!

An Irish comedian, Harry McCarthy, by name, then playing at the Jackson theatre, was one of the spectators. Animated by the dramatic scene he had witnessed, McCarthy wrote words so that they would fit an old Scottish choral and sang them from the stage that night. The words had to do with a "Bonnie Blue Flag." The next day Colonel J. L. Power printed the verses in his newspaper, the song was sent to New Orleans for printing, and in another week crowds in New Orleans were singing:

"Hurrah! Hurrah!
"For Southern Rights, Hurrah!
"Hurrah for the Bonnie Blue Flag
"That bears a Single Star!"

From that time on the Lone Star Flag of the Feliciana patriots became the best beloved of the many flags of the Confederacy.

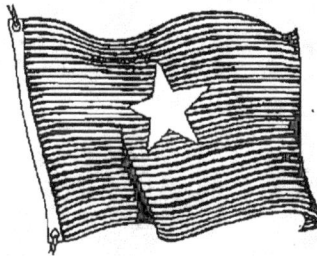

THE BONNIE BLUE FLAG

A half a century after the Feliciana patriots raised the first "Lone Star Flag" over West Florida, the same blue flag with a five-pointed white star became the best beloved banner of the Confederacy—"the Bonnie Blue Flag that bears a single star."

Here, abruptly, ends my story of the West Florida Rebellion, one of the brightest pages (if a forgotten one) in Louisiana's book of colorful history, an event crammed with romance and adventure, of bright deeds and daring, a stirring song sung to the rhythm of clattering horse hoofs, as patriotic Anglo-Saxons, forgetting nationalisms, banded together under the five points of fellowship, wrested their homes from the domination of an Old World power, and with the verve that has always animated true liberty-loving patriots, set up their own establishment. That it did not live long was not their fault.

Long may the Lone Star wave in the hearts and recollections of the descendants of those intrepid Americans, and in the hearts and memories of those now living in "The Florida Parishes."

NOTES

Proposed British Seat of Government in West Florida

(See Frontispiece)

When England secured possession of all the former French territory in North America east of the Mississippi, following the end of the seven year's war that proved so disastrous to the Bourbons, certain English officials proposed that a new and fortified town should be erected on the eastern bank of the Father of the Waters for they believed neither New Orleans nor Baton Rouge had been erected on natural defensive situations.

The several British army engineers who surveyed the river that drained the continent agreed that *Les Ecores au de Lait*, or "The Milk White Cliffs," situated between Baton Rouge and Bayou Sarah, presented an ideal site for such a fortress and city.

Soon after the British had acquired the former French strip of territory along the Gulf of Mexico, Lieutenant-Governor Montfort Browne, while serving under the first British governor, George Johnstone, took up an extensive grant on the eastern bank of the Mississippi and, strangely enough, the acreage included the "White Cliffs" which soon afterwards became known as "Browne's Cliffs." Joined by Lord Englington, owner of a grant near Natchez; Colonel William Taylor, at one time in charge of the military forces of West Florida, and General Phineas Lyman, Montfort Browne, while acting governor of the province, urged the home war office to supplant Pensacola with this new seat of government on the Mississippi River.

Captain Montressor of the army was delagated to make the necessary surveys and he drew a plan which met the approval of those most interested. This map, which is reproduced as a frontispiece to this story of the West Florida Rebellion, was sent on to London and found its way into the library of Lord George Germaine, minister of state under George III, and the man who influenced the policy of Britain during the American Revolution.

When Lord Germaine's library was sold by heirs in 1933, Captain Montressor's plan, the original measuring 17 1/2 x 27 1/2 inches, first became public. The lettering proved it: "A Plan Shewing the Situation and Construction for a Seat of Government on the Mississippi," while an inset drawing, 2 x 5 inches, was lettered: "This shews the construction on the side of each gate."

The proposed British seat of government was to be triangular in shape, having a width of about 2 1/2 miles facing the river, and the depth at the center of a little more that 1 1/2 miles. The town was to have regularly laid out streets, public squares, and three gates, one north, another south, and the third to the east. It's situation on cliffs rising 97 feet above the surface of the river would enable the guns of the fort to dominate river traffic. As the river made a sharp bend at this point, vessels sailing up or down the stream, no matter the direction of the wind, would have been forced to tack under the guns of the fort. The same situation would enable the artillery to enfilade the whole surface of the river -- a marked military advantage offered by no other site.

Another advantage claimed for this site, in addition to the dominance of the river traffic, was the fact that a highland military road could be constructed over which troops could be moved to and from the colonies on the Atlantic seaboard, without being forced to march through swamps.

Captain Montressor's map shows the lower village of Pointe Coupee' on the west bank of the river, while just above the proposed seat of government is to be seen the course of Thompson's Creek and the outlet of Alexander's Creek, now known as Alligator Bayou.

When Lieutenant-Governor Browne was transferred from West Florida to govern the Bahama Islands, the proposal appears to have lagged for in 1776 he sold the site of 17,400 acres to Daniel Hicky, father of Philip Hicky, so prominent in the West Florida Rebellion, and the place became known, in time, as "Hicky's Cliffs."

In 1779 the capture by Don Bernardo de Galvez of Baton Rouge and the other British strongholds in West Florida put an end to the scheme. But the plans were kept secret in the British War Office and when General Sir Edward M. Pakenham invaded Louisiana in 1814-15 it is supposed this was the place he was to consider as the new seat of government, after reducing and capturing New Orleans.

In 1860 this same site was known, as it is today, as Port Hudson.

The opinion of early British engineers that such a fortification would prove "a hard nut to crack" was proved correct in the War Between the States when General Frank Gardner and his Confederate forces in 1863 successfully defended Port Hudson against two determined assaults by the Union army under General Banks, not surrendering until after the fall of Vicksburg.

Page 4--The name of Louisiana's first governor should be spelled Villiantray and not "Villantary."

Pages 16-17-- The founder of Bayou Sarah was John Mills. It was his brother Gilbert Mills who married Isaac Johnson's daughter, Ann Waugh Johnson, and their son married John H. Mills. The statement that Gilbert Mill's daughter, Mary Mills, married Stephen Minor was an error -- Minor's second wife was Mary Ellis. Mary Mills was twice married -- to Thomas North and a Mr. Sholars.

Page 20--Further details of the contention between Ambrose Smith and Reuben Kemper will be found in the Louisiana Courier, March 14 to 25, 1808, following the first publication of Smith's advertisement relative to the sale of town lots in New Valentia.

Page 22--The name the French gave to Thompson's Creek was *Bayou des Ecores*.

Page 23-- Since the foregoing was printed fuller and more accurate details on Bernardo de Galves have come to light. He was not 21 when he came to Louisiana but was 30 years old. Don Bernardo de Galvez Galardo, of Madrid, was born July 23, 1746 in the town of Macharaviaya, province of Malaga, Spain. He was baptised Bernardo Vincente Polinar. He came to Louisiana in 1776 and was married Nov. 2, 1777, from a sick bed, to Dona Maria Feliciana Saint-Maxent, widow of Don Juan Honorato d'Etrehan, by whom she had one child. The children of Galvez's marriage were Don Miguel Galvez y Saint-Maxent, baptised Jan. 2, 1783. This son became a cadet of the American company of bodyguards, Knight of the Order of Calatrava, and, from 1797, the second Count of Galvez. He died before reaching manhood. The eldest daughter was named Dona Matilda Galvez. A second daughter, expected to be named Guadalupe, after the patron saint of the City of Mexico, was born eight days after her father's death. She was christened Maria de Guadalupe, Bernarda, Felipa de Jesus, Isabel, Juana Felecitas y Fernanda de Galvez. In 1784, after Galvez returned from Madrid where he was decorated for his successful campaign against the British in Louisiana, he was made governor-general of Cuba and governor of Louisiana and the two Floridas. His father, Don Matias de Galvez, died and the son was sent to Mexico to succeed him as Viceroy of New Spain. With his wife Feliciana, and three children, he arrived in Mexico City June 28, 1785, when he took the oath of office as Viceroy. His death occurred Nov. 30, 1786. The daughter of Feliciana by her first husband was named Adelaide d'Estrehan.

Page 26-- The "twin-starred" flag of the ill-fated Kemper rebellion of 1804, when the three Kemper brothers tried to wrest West Florida from Spain, is worth notice. This banner was first raised at Saint Francisville and had seven alternating stripes of blue and white, the union was red and had two white stars. Why the Kempers selected such a flag is not known nor is it ceretain what the two stars stood for. Did they mean a star for West Florida and another for East Florida? Did the seven blue and white stripes stand for the seven districts in the Spanish provinces? *Quien Sabe*?

Page 33-- Gilbert Mills was brother of John Mills. See above note.

Page 39-- The letter "by a gentleman from Pointe Coupee" was first published in the Baton Rouge Advocate.

Page 44-- Shepherd Brown, like his friend and business associate John McDonough, came to New Orleans from Baltimore, and the two formed a co-partnership and did an extensive business under the name of "John McDonough, Jr. & Co." In December of 1815 this partnership was dissolved, Shepherd Brown dying soon thereafter.

Page 46-- Although documents first examined appeared to identify John W. Leonard as the son of Gilbert Leonard, later information proves he was not the Juan Leonardo, son of the civil commandant at Baton Rouge, but that he belonged to a Tory family of New York and Massachusetts. John West Leonard came to Louisiana early in 1800 and lived first at New Orleans. In 1805 he removed to the St. Helena district and soon became intimate with the Spanish authorities and was in their confidence when the uprising began. Leonard was selected by Shepherd Brown as one who would remain loyal to the Spanish but after the first meeting of the delegates Manuel Lopez suspected he was double-dealing and so reported to Don Carlos de Lassus. Other members of the convention were playing the same game with the Spanish masters. As evidence of John W. Leonard's standing among

177

the patriots is his selection as president *pro tempore* of the first and only senate of the Tom Thumb Republic. He died in 1818 without issue.

Page 53-- For the opportunity to inspect and reproduce the original documents written by the delegates of the Convention, I am indebted to Mrs. C. A. Levert and her daughter, Miss Genevieve Levert, descendants of Philip Hicky.

Page 76-- I am indebted to Mr. Richmond Favrot for the opportunity of reproducing the 32-page pamphlet of the "Ordinances" adopted by the Convention delegates. It was found among the original documents in the "Favrot Collection" which was collected and handed down to descendants by Don Pedro Favrot who played a conspicious part in the early history of Louisiana under the French and Spanish. My acknowledgements, too, to Miss Josie Cerf, of the Louisiana State Museum, who called my attention to this pamplet -- possibly the only one in existence.

Page 101-- Fulwar Skipwith's wife, Thereze Josephine Vandenclooster, described in a notarial act as a *Belgique*, evidently divorced him and married William Herries of Montesano plantation, for she is designated as Herries' widow in an act before L. T. Caire, notary public, of Feb. 11, 1834, and Skipwith did not die until 1839. The daughter of Fulwar Skipwith and Dame Vandenclooster, Lelia Skipwith, remarried after the death of her first husband, Governor Thomas Bolling Robinson. Her second husband was Humberton Skipwith of Virginia -- by this marriage regaining her maiden name.

Page 121-- Owing to a confusion of cut lines, the "Lone Star Flag" of the West Florida Rebellion is not properly identified. The blue banner of the Feliciana patriots which replaced Spain's red and yellow ensign September 22, 1810, when the fort at Baton Rouge was taken by assault, was the first "lone star flag" in the history of the United States, thus antedating the famous flag of Texas by 26 years. It waved over the "free and independent state of West Florida" for 74 days until hauled down by Governor Claiborne of Saint Francisville, December 6, 1810. The white star represented the "five points of fellowship" under which the ringleaders of the rebellion held their secret gathereings. Masonic in character, it is the same emblem that gave the Order of the Eastern Star its title.

Page 146-- For the opportunity of reproducing the marching song of the West Floridian army I am indebted to Miss Louise Butler of "The Cottage," West Feliciana parish.

Page 159-- Charles Auguste de Hault de Lasus, son of Don Carlos, married Marie Jeanne Blanque, daughter of Jean Blanque and Delphine Macarty. Delphine Blanque was first married to Don Ramon Lopez y Angulo; Jean Blanque was her second, and her thrid husband was Dr. Louis Lalaurie. As Mme. Lalaurie she gained dubious fame in New Orleans as the mistress of the famous "Haunted House" who was said to be so cruel to her slaves. See note of page 46 regarding John W. Leonard.

Page 115-- Printed and manuscript sources are very lean regarding the Spanish forces at the Baton Fouge fort serving under Governor de Lassus at the time of the patriotic uprising. Copies of the *Papeles de Cuba, Legajo* 163, folios 4, 5, 20, 26, 67, 78, 82 243, 249 and 251, contain a great deal of information. These were examined at the Library of Congress, Washington, D.C. The commander of the forces constituting the right arm of Spain was Don Carlos de Hault de Lassus, and those under him were: Don Gilberto Leonardo, *ministro interventor, el tesorero de exercito*; Don Eulogio de Casas, *guarda almacen*; Don Frederico Dayerton, *guarda de rentas*; Don Pedro Gondeau, *cirujano*; Don Juan Perez, *cabo se sala*; Don Santiago Rault, *cirujano de Nueva Feliciana*; Domingo Olice (or Olin or Olis), *patron de falua*; Jose' Marchand, *marinero de falua*; Antonio Monget, *herrero y armero*; Captain Celestino, Captain Raphael Croker, Lieutenant Juan P. A. Metzinger, Lieutenant Francisco Morejon, Lieutenant Eulogio de Casas, Lieutenant Jose' Maria de la Pena, Subtentente Don Louis Antonio de Grand-Pre', Subteniente Don Antonio Balderas, Cadet Don Felipe de Grand-Pre', Cadet Don Estevan de Grand-Pre', Sargento Antonio Tirado, appear to be the commanding officers. The soldiers who testified at the court martial of de Lassus, Metzinger, and Croker, Pensacola, March 1811,

178

included Francisco Galvan, Jose' Mendez, Marcos Aguilera, Francisco Ximenez, Antonio Tirado, Domingo Olice, Manuel Villanueva, Joaquin Mirabal, Terodoro Inocenta, Pedro Quinto, Andres Martinez, Pablo Fallan, Miquel Ibarrola, Matias Fornieles, Domingo la Rosa, Mauricio Escobar, Manuel Guillemes, Eugenton Gony, Juan Martin, Carlos Morel, Manuel Castanos, Jose' de la Polvoar, Feliciano Sierra, Jose' Mirabel, and Pasqual Polonesa.

INDEX

AAIRS, W.: early settler, 16

d'ANVILLE, Jean Baptiste Bourguion: maps Mississippi River, 4

d'ARTAGUETTE, Diron: settles at Baton Rouge, 3, 8

ALLEN, Juan: early settler, 16

ALMONESTER, Don Andres: 9

AUDIBERT, C. M.: made navy agent, 145

AUDUBON, John James: studies bird life, 16; mentioned, 34

AUDUBON, Mrs.: 16

AVERY, Dudley L..: speaker of house, 144

BAKER: settler 14

BAKER, Col. Joshua G.: observer for Governor Holmes, 63

BALDERAS, Lt. Antonio: attends Spanish Junta, 71

BALDWIN, Captain Samuel: in charge of forces in St. Helena, 135; navy
    agent, 128, 145

BALLINGER, Captain John: organizes force at Springfield, 111; signs address,
    125; arrests King, 156

BARCLAY, Juan: early settler, 16

BARROW: settler 14

BARROW, William: selected as delegate, 39; meets at "Troy" plantation, 46;
    mentioned, 47, 53, 55: history of, 61; signs proclamation, 73; selected
    as judge, 99; committee of public safety, 139; made representative, 144

BARROW, family: 62

BATON ROUGE: named by the French, 4; becomes "New Richmond," 13;
    captured by patriots, 120

BAUDIN, Roger: writing history of Catholic Church, 19

BAYOU SARAH: original naming of stream, 3; village founded, 16

BEAUFORT, Domitille Josephe Dumont de: 30

BEDFORD, Dr. J. R.: receives Barrow's letter, 61

BELLIN, N.: French engineer maps Mississippi River, 4

BENAC, Captain de: 9

BERNARD, Felix: early settler 16

BIENVILLE, Jean Baptiste Le Moyne, Sieur de: accompanies Iberville, 5; ruled
    over Louisiana 10

BONAPARTE, Napoleon: campaign to retake Louisiana, 31; mentioned, 34,
    37, 47

BOUGARD, Claudio: early settler, 16

BRITISH DOMINATION; takes possession of West Florida, 10; plans for Seat
    of Government in Feliciana, 175

BRADFORD, James M.: editor of "Times Piece," 171

BROUTIN, Marguerite Madelaine: wife of Lieutenant de Pontalba 10

BROWDER, F. A.: backs convention, 64

BROWDER, John: backs convention, 64

BROWN, Guillermo: early settler, 15

BROWN, Shepherd: alcalde in St. Helena, 44; refuses to take oath of office,
112; recruits settlers, 133; captured and jailed, 135; attempted release,
140   (see notes)

BROWNE, Montfort: Lieutenant-Governor of West Florida. (see notes)

BUTLER, Louise: author, 3, 6

CAMPBELL: settler, 14

CARONDELET, Baron de: Governor 30

CARPENTER, Anne: daughter of Dr. Carpenter, 17

CARPENTER, Caleb: brother of Richard Carpenter, 18

CARPENTER, James: son of Dr. Carpenter, 17

CARPENTER, Louise: daughter of Dr. Carpenter 17

CARPENTER, Mary: daughter of Dr. Carpenter, 17

CARPENTER, Richard: grandfather of Dr. Carpenter, 18

CARPENTER, Dr. William Marbury: describes Bayou Sarah, 17, 18

CARSON: settler 14

CASTANOS, Lt. Manuel: attends Spanish Junta, 71

CAYNIE, Dr. M. L. T.: signs address, 125

CENIER, Etienne de Perier de: Governor of Louisiana, 9

CHAMBERS, Professor: speaks of "St. Reine's concession, 3, 12

CHARLEVOIX, Father: mentions "Ste. Reyne.", 3

CHESTER, Peter: took charge, 13

CHINN, Thomas Withers: married Elizabeth Johnson, 33, 34

CHRONICLES of the Sanhedrine: parody by Jonathan Longstreth, 141

CLARK, Daniel: mentioned, 46

CLARK, Gen. George Roger: visited by Samuel Fulton, 43

CLARK, James: early settler 16

CLAIBORNE, William Charles Cole: Governor of Territory of Orleans, 25;
goes to Washington, 36, 37; returns to Mississippi, 149; goes to Pointe
Coupee', 152; orders Lone Star Flag taken down, 153; writes President
Madison, 155; hoists U. S. flag over Baton Rouge, 157; names County
of Feliciana, 163; writes Rhea and Johnson, 166

COCHRANE & RHEA: store, 22 28

CODE: the first or tentative declararion of independence, 48

COIN, J. B. O.: early settler 16

COLLINS: settler, 14

COLLINS, B.: backs convention, 64

COLLINS, Benjamin: married Caroline Matilda Johnson, 33

CONILZ, John P.: backs convention, 64

CONVENTION: first meeting, 53; second meeting, 63

COOK, Captain David T. W.: signs address, 125; attempts to liberate de Lassus and Shepherd Brown, 140

"COON BOX": described, 16

COOPER: settler, 14

COOPER, William: selected as delegate, 46; mentioned, 53 56; warns Folch of convention, 110; refuses to sign declaration of independence, 126; ordered captured, 134; killed trying to escape, 135

COVINGTON, Colonel Leonard: commands U. S. forces, 149; takes possession of Baton Rouge fort, 158

COX: settler, 14

CROCKER, Samuel S.: clerk of convention, 53; backs convention, 64; attends Lassus' dinner, 68

CROKER, Dona: wife of Don Raphael Croker, 122

CROKER, Don Raphael: secretary to de Lassus, 32; attends Spanish Junta, 71; vanishes, 122

CURTIS, Reuben: 2nd Major, 100

CUSHING, Colonel Thomas P.: guards border, 129

DAVENPORT, John: signs petition, 41

DAWSON, Anna Ruffin: married Charles Grandpre' Johnson, 33

DECLARATION OF INDEPENDENCE of people of West Florida, 126

DERBIGNEY, Pierre: Governor of Louisiana, 31

DEVALL: settler 14

DEVALL, Richard: arrives in Louisiana, 35; mentioned, 46

DORCH, Captain John: signs address, 125

DUNCAN, Abner L.: takes Rhea's proclamation to Gov. Holmes, 125

DUNMAN, Reuben: early settler, 15

DUPASSAU, George: mentioned 43

DUPLANTIER, Armand: sold land, 20, 21; mentioned 43

DURALDY, Martin: account of indian mythology, 17

EDDINGTON, Eliza: of England, married Charles Grandpre' Johnson, 33

EGYPT PLANTATION: later "Rosalie," meeting place of first "for freedom" gathering, 36

ELDERGILL, John: early settler, 16

ELLIOTT, John: Governor, 13

ELLIS: settler, 14

ESTEVAN, Captain Tomaso: commands Bayou Sarah, 16, 32; fears revolt, 34, 35; mentioned, 71; advises of broadside, 69; evicted from Bayou Sarah, 112; escapes from Baton Rouge fort, 120
d'ESTREHAN, Jean Baptiste Honore: member of prominent family, 23
d'ETCHEPARRE, Sieur: commands Fort Rosalie, 9

FAVROT, Josephine: betrothed of Louis de Grand-Pre', 116; has prominition of his death, 129; never marries, 131
FAVROT, Don Pedro: history of, 116; writes to Marquis de Someruelos, 122; accompanies daughter to Baton Ronge, 129; writes eulogy of Louis de Grand-Pre', 130
FAVROT, Philogene: accompanies father and sister to Baton Rouge, 1219
FELICIANA: named for wife of Galvez, 22; county proclaimed, 154; description of parish, 163; map of county, 165
FERDINAND VII: prisoner of Napoleon, 36; mentioned 45, 57 68
FICKLIN, James H.: backs convention, 64
FIELD, William: backs convention, 64
FLAGS: illustrations-- Spanish banner of Castile and Leon, vi; French *fleur-de-lis flag* of Bourbons, 9; British Union Jack, 11; second Spanish flag, 24; Kemper Brothers' twin-starred flag, 26; *tricolor* of France, 52; Lone Star flag of Free State of West Florida, 121; United States flag of 15 stars and 15 stripes, 158; The Bonnie Blue flag, 173
FLANDERS, French: 30
FLORIDAS, East and West: described, 13
FLORIDA OCCIDENTAL JURISDICTION de BATON ROUGE: districts named by Spanish, 23; map of, 164
FLOWER, Henry: early settler, 16
FOLCH, Gov. Vicente: mentioned, 58, 109
FOLQUIER, M.: mentioned, 68
FOOCHTELL, Captain L. T.: signs address, 125
FORT BATON ROUGE: described, 115; captured by patriots, 120
FORT SAINTE REINE: established, 3; abandoned, 9
FOSTER, James: early settler, 16
FREELAND, George: early settler, 16
FULTON, Samuel: signs petition, 41; history of, 43; Colonel, 100

GALVEZ, Don Bernardo de: Spanish Governor of Louisiana, 14; mentioned, 68 (see notes)
GALVEZ, Don Jose' de: President of Council of the Indes, 23
GALVEZ, Don Mathias de: Viceroy of Mexico, 23
GAYARRE, history author, 3
GENTRY, James: backs convention, 64

GILLESPIE, John F.: backs convention, 64
GORDEAU, Don Pedro: attends Spanish Junta, 71
GORHAM, Aaron: married Mary Johnson, 33
GRAND-PRE', Don Carlos de: Governor of West Florida, 26
GRAND-PRE', Don Estevan de: brother of Louis, 71
GRAND-PRE': Don Felipe de: brother of Louis, 71
GRAND-PRE', Lieut. Louis Antonio de: attends Lassus' dinner, 68; attends
      Spanish Junta, 71; visits Josephine Favrot, 116; shot down defending
      fort, 120; dies from wounds, 129
GRAVIER, Father: baptizes Indian papoose, 5; describes Houmas, 8
GRAY, James: backs convention, 64
GREEN, Juan: early settler, 15
GRIFFITH, Captain Lewellyn Colville: organizes Bayou Sarah Horse, 114 ;
      leaves with troop for Baton Rouge fort, 114; signs address, 125; serves
      in expedition, 134; made representative, 144

HAWES, Edmund: signs petition, 41; mentioned, 44, 53; signs proclamation,
      73; on committee of public safety, 139
HAYNIE, Martin L.: backs convention, 64
HERE, Andres: early settler, 15
HERRIES, George: signs petition, 41,
HERRIES, William: signs petition, 41   (see notes)
HEVIA, Francisco de: assumes charge of Tiskfaw region, 70
HICKY, Daniel: mentioned, 35
HICKY, Philip: messenger for de Lassus, 35; reports to Governor, 38; signs
      petition, 41; mentioned, 44, 55, 56, 57, 66; signs proclamation, 73;
      warns delegates, 113; mentioned, 139   (see notes)
HIGGINS, John: early settler, 16
HOLLAND, Patrick: early settler, 16
HOLMES, David: Governor of Mississippi Territory, 63; receives copy of
      Declaration of Independence, 126; gets letter from John Rhea, 128;
      meets Claiborne, 153; goes to Baton Rouge, 156
HORTON, Abram: early settler, 15
HOUMAS INDIANS: first inhabitants, 4; described, 5
HUGHES, Matthew, early settler, 16

IBERVILLE, Pierre Le Moyne, Siuer d': visits Houmas Indians, 5

JOHNSON, Ann Waugh: dau. of Isaac Johnson married, 17
JOHNSON, Charles Grandpre': in charge of Baton Rouge fort, 145
JOHNSON, Eliza Collins: married Wm. Gayoso Johnson, 33
JOHNSON, family: documents handed down to, 19

JOHNSON, Isaac: settles in Natchez district, 16; marries Mary Routh, 17; his family, 33; Major of Cavalry, 99, 114, 118, 121, 134

JOHNSON, Isaac, Jr.: accompanies Gov. Holmes, 156

JOHNSON, John Hunter: leader of revolt, 33; selected as delegate, 39; meets at "Troy" plantation, 46; mentioned, 47, 53, 55; writes Gov. Holmes, 64; orders attack on Baton Rouge fort, 114; on committee of public safety, 139; mentioned, 143; reports on new constitution, 139, 140; mentioned, 143; made representative, 144; meets Gov. Claiborne, 153; appointed high sheriff of Feliciana County, 167; receives letter from Claiborne, 172

JOHNSON, Joseph Eugenius: backs convention, 64; made sheriff of New Feliciana, 99

JOHNSON, William Garret: plantation, 17; mentioned, 33

JONES, Michael: recruits settlers, 133; ordered captured, 134; "tamed" by punitive expedition, 134

JOHNSTONE, George: first British Governor of West Florida, 13

JUNTA: called by Gov. de Lassus, 71

KAVENAGH, James: early settler, 16

KEMPER BROTHERS: Nathan, Reuben and Samuel, 20, 26

KEMPER, Reuben: appointed commissioner, 139

KENNEDY: settler, 14

KIMBALL, Col.: mentioned, 135

KING, William: messenger for Gov. Claiborne, 150; arrested by Ballinger, 156

KIRKLAND, Col. William: signs address, 125; asks convention for action, 134; ordered to Mobile, 145

LANE, Martha: married Joseph Eugenius Johnson, 33

LANGRES, Father Anselm de: authorized to build a chapel, 18

LAS CASAS, Eulogio de: magazine guard, 68; attends Spanish Junta, 71

LA SALLE, Robert Cavalier, Sieur de: explores Mississippi, 5

LASSUS, Don Carlos de Hault de: Governor of West Florida, 30; accepts terms, 58; gives dinner to delegates, 68; procrastinates, 112; serves peace dinner, 112; captured by patriots, 119; lodged in *juzgada*, 123; release attempted, 140; freed by Skipwith, 159

LAW, John: company of the west, 3

LE JEUNE: settles on Big Bayou Sarah, 4

LENNAN, Francisco: priest at Bayou Sarah, 19, 33; leaves with Estevan, 36; flees Baton Rouge fort, 122

LEONARD, Adelaide Feliciana Mariana: married Don Carlos de Lassus, daughter of Gilbert Leonard, 159

LEONARDO, Don Gilberto: treasurer of West Florida, 46; attends Lassus'
     dinner, 68; attends Spanish Junta, 71; mentioned, 99; daughter
     marries de Lassus, 159
LEONARD, John W.: selected as delegate, 46; mentioned, 53; on committee of
     public safety, 55, 139; mentioned, 57, 66; signs proclamation, 73;
     president pro tem of senate, 144; signs resolution, 152   (see notes)
LILLEY, Thomas: signs petition, 41; mentioned, 44, 46, 53, 55, 56; signs
     proclamation, 73; joins Philip Hicky, 114; committee of public safety,
     139
LIMOGES, Father de: mentioned, 5
LONE STAR FLAG: made by Melissa Johnson, 114; carried by Bayou Sarah
     Horse, 114; unfurled over Baton Rouge fort, 121; hauled down at Saint
     Francisville, 154; falls at Baton Rouge, 156; rises again in Feliciana,
     169; becomes the "Bonnie Blue Flag," 173
LONGSTRETH, Jonathan: writes parody, 141
LOPEZ, Manuel: delegate to convention, 53; leaves meeting, 66; signs
     proclamation, 73
LYON, William: backs convention, 64
LYTLE, Nathan: early settler, 16

MADISON, President James: issues proclamation, 150
MARIGNY, Francois Philippe de: mentioned, 10
MAROCHE', Elizabeth: mentioned, 22
MARTIN: history, 3
MARTINEZ, Andres; wounded in attack on fort, 120
MATAMOROS, Manuel: killed in attack, 120
MATHER, Ann: wife of Philip Hicky, 35
MATHER, early settler, 14
MATHER, George, Sr.: messenger for de Lassus, 35; signs petition, 41;
     selected as recorder, 53; mentioned, 66; Jr. 1st Major, 100; appointed
     judge, 159; resigns as judge, 167
MATHER, James: emigrant 1777, 35
McCAUSLAND, Major Robert: 3rd Regt., 100; signs address, 125; commands
     Springfield, Grenadiers, 134
McCARTHY, Harry: writes "The Bonnie Blue Flag," 173
McCOY, Alexander: early settler, 16
McDERMOT, Patrick: settles Bayou Tunica, 15
McDERMOTT, Bryan: appointed, 99
McDONOUGH, John: mentioned, 45
METZINGER, Lieut. Juan: attends Lassus' dinner, 68; attends Spanish Junta,
     71; prepares to resist attack, 116; wounded in attack, 119
MEZIERS, Alhanase de: erects concession, 4

MILLS, Gilbert: son of John Mills, 17; married Ann Waugh Johnson, 33
MILLS, John: founds Bayou Sarah village, 17; partner in trading post, 17;
    selected as delegate, 39; meets at "Troy" plantation, 46, 113;
    mentioned, 47, 53, 55, 57, 61; signed proclamation, 73; navy agent,
    145   (see notes)
MILLS, Mary: married Stephen Minor, 17
MINOR, Stephen: married Mary Mills, 17
MOLLER, Don Jose': planter, 32
MOONEY: Irishman mentioned, 165
MOORE: early settler, 14
MOORE, Larry: organizes St. Helena patriots, 115; shows way into fort, 118
MOREJON, Lieut Francisco: attends Lassus' dinner, 68; attends Spaish Junta,
    71; mentioned, 115
MOREL, Pedro Luis: interpreter, 21
MORGAN, John: signs petition, 41; mentioned, 53, 56; committee of public
    safety, 139
MORPHY, Diego: Spanish Vice-Consul at Crescent City, 343
MURDOCK, John: attorney at Bayou Sarah, 21, 33; sends warning of attack,
    69

NELSON, James: makes inventory of fort, 123
NEW VALENTIA: rival village to Bayou Sarah, 20, 21
NORWOOD: early settler, 14

O'CONNOR, John/Juan: early settler, 15, 16
O'FALLON: early settler, 14
ORDINANCE OF CONVENTION:
O'REILLY, Rev. Michael: Irish priest, 19
OSBORNE, Audley L.: delivers proclamation, 150; meets Claiborne, 153;
    appointed judge of St. Helena, 167

PARKER, John M.: mentioned, 4
PAUSSET, Francisco: early settler, 15
PEISEE, H.: backs convention, 64
PENA, Don Jose' Maria de la: attends Spanish Junta, 71
PENSACOLA: made capital of West Florida, 13
PERCY: early settler, 14
PERCY, Lieut. Robert: selected as judge, 99; history, 100
PEREZ, Don Juan: attends Spanish Junta, 71
PERIER, Etienne de, de Cenier: Governor of Louisiana, 10
PUCKFORD, John M.: mentioned, 100
PIERNAS, Captain Louis: arrives at Baton Rouge, 108

PIRRIE, Eliza: wife of Robert H. Barrow, 62
PIKE, Lieut.-Col. Zebulon Montgomery: enters Baton Rouge fort, 158
PINTADO, Don Vincente Sebastian: the crown surveyor, 2; survey maps, 22
POINTE COUPEE: lower village, 11
POLLOCK, early settler, 14
POLVORA, Jose' de la: corporal gives alarm, 118
PONTALBA, Celestine de: daughter of Josephe Xavier Delfau de Pontalba, 10
PONTALBA, Jean Joseph Delfau de: commands Fort Ste. Reine, 9, 10
PONTALBA, Joseph Xavier Delfau de: mentioned, 10
POPE, Dr. Nathaniel Wells: married Martha Johnson, 33
PORT JACKSON: settlement on Thompson's creek, 28
POWER, Col. J. L.: prints words of "The Bonnie Blue Flag," 173

RAFFRAY, Juan: early settler, 16
RAINER/RAYNOR, Daniel: appointed, 99; mentioned 114
RANDOLPH: early settler, 14
RANDOLPH, Edward: writes constitution, 46, 48
RAOUL, Dr.: a French 'Emigre', 28
RAULT, Don Santiqago: surgeon, 71
RAY, John: mentioned, 47
RIVIERE DE LA PUCELLE JUIVE, la: naming by French, 2
RIVIERE DES TONICAS: name for Bayou Sarah, 3
RHEA, John: merchant at Port Jackson, 29; selected as delegate, 39; president
    of convention, 53; at "Troy" plantation, 46, 115; issues proclamation,
    73; sends letter to Governors Holmes and Claiborne, 126, 127; issues
    mmendments to ordinance, 136; writes President Madison, 137;
    mentioned, 139; made senator, 144; judge of Feliciana, 167; praised by
    Claiborne, 171
ROBERSON/ROBINSON, Thomas Bolling: Acting-Governor of Orleans
    Territory, 63; marries Skipwith's daughter, 101
ROSS, Davis: early settler, 15
ROSS, Lieutenant John: prepared military chart, 3; maps Mississippi River for
    British, 11
ROUTH, family: mentioned, 19, 33
ROUTH, Mary: wife of Isaac Johnson, 17, 33
RYAN, Jaime: early settler, 15

SAINT FRANCISVILLE: original naming, 18; capital of Independent West
    Florida, 143
SAINT MAXENT, Captain Celestino de: officer at fort, 23; attends Lassus'
    dinner, 68; attends Spanish Junta, 71
SAINT MAXENT, family: 22, 23

SAINT MAXENT, Felicite de: wife of Galvez and godmother of Feliciana, 22, 23 (see notes)

SAINT MAXENT, Francios Maxmillion de: son of Gilbert Antione de Saint Maxent, 22

SAINT MAXENT, Gilbert Antoine de: father of Felicite de Saint Maxent, 22

SAINT MAXENT, Josephine de: wife of Governor Louis de Unzaga y Amezaga, 23

SAINT MAXENT, Pupon de: married into the d'Estrehan family, 23

SAINTE-REYNE: holds concession, 3

SAINT TAMMANY PARISH: named by Gov. Claiborne, 159; origin of name, 165

SAINTS JOHN PLAINS: meeting place of first convention, 46

SCOTT, John: made representative, 144

SCRIVNER, Martha: wife of Daniel Hicky, 35

SEELEY, Cornelius: early settler, 16

SEMPLE, Moses: husband of Ann Waugh Johnson Mills, 33

SHARP, Joseph: signs petition, 41,

SKIPWITH, Fulwar: mentioned, 40; signs petition, 41; selected as judge, 99; history of, 101; rejected by de Lassus, 106; selected Governor of indepentent West Florida, 144; defies Claiborne, 152; returns to Baton Rouge, 156; releases de Lassus, 159; pen portrait by nephew, 160 (see notes)

SKIPWITH, Henry: pen portraits of pioneers, 26; describes Fulwar Skipwith, 160

SMITH, Ambrose D.: advertises lots in "New Valentia," 20, 21

SMITH, Isaac A.: backs convention, 64

SMITH, Senator John: troubles with Kemper brothers, 20, 21

SMITH, L. A.: backs convention, 64

SMITH, Robert: Secretary of State, 104

SPILLER, William: selected as delegate, 46; mentioned 53, 55, 56, 67; signed proclamation, 73; Colonel, 100

SPANISH DOMINATION: wrests West Florida from British, 14

SPEARS, Abraham: 2nd Major, 100

STARK, Roberto: early settler, 15

STEELE, Dr. Andrew: signs petition, 41; secretary of convention, 53, 57; mentioned, 99, 126; appointed judge of Feliciana, 159; judge of East Baton Rouge, 167

STEWART, Christopher Strong: sets up trading post with John Mills, 17

STIRLING, Alexander: establishes plantation, 36

STIRLING, Lewis: "Egypt" plantation first meeting place of patriots, 36; meets at "Troy" plantation, 46

STODDARD, Captain Amos: received portion of Louisiana for U. S., 31

STUART, D. B.: backs convention, 64

THOMAS, Benjamin P.: signs address, 125
THOMAS, Joseph: messenger for Brown, 45; selected as delegate, 46;
        mentioned, 53, 55, 56, 57, 67; signs proclamation, 73; 1st Major, 100
THOMAS, Philemon: signs petition, 41; commander of militia, 68; Brigadier
        General, 99; history of, 102; captures messenger, 113; gathers force
        or attack, 114; enters fort, 121; issues first order, 123; reports on
        capture of fort, 123; signs address, 124; reports on punitive expedition,
        134; prepares to attack Mobile, 145
THOMPSON: operates a ferry at lower Pointe Coupee village, 22
TONTI, Henri: first white man in Feliciana, 5
TROY PLANTATION: headquarters for revolt, 33, 46
TUNICA INDIANS: rout the Houmas, 6; meaning of name, 8
TURNBULL, Daniel: husband of Martha H. Barrow, 62

ULLIO, Don Domingo: attends Spanish Junta, 71
UNZAGA, Governor Louis de: promoted, 23

VANDENCLOOSTER, Thereze Josephine: wife of Fulwar Skipwith, 101;
        leaves husband, 160   (see notes)
VELOXY, parish named, 166
VILLANTRAY, Sauvol de: first French Governor of Louisiana, visits Indians,
        5   (see notes)
"VIVE LA": marching song of West Florida patriots, 146

WALL, Juan: early settler, 15
WARREN, Thomas C.: made judge of Tanchipahoa and Pearl, 167
WATTS, Franca Ashton: early settler, 16
WAUGH, David: early settler, 16
WEBB, Amos: backs convention, 64
WELTON, Juan: early settler, 15
WEST FLORIDA: map of Spanish area, 165
WHITAKER, Aquila: Colonel, 100
WHITE, Joseph: appointed commissioner, 139
WIKOFF, William: sells land to John Mills,15; delivers Claiborne's letter, 37;
        greets Governor at Pointe Coupee, 150
WILLIAMS, Benjamin O.: selected as delegate, 46; mentioned, 53, 56; signs
        proclamation, 73; resigns as delegate, 127; gets "cold feet," 139
WILLIAMS, Melissa Jane: married Isaac Johnson, Jr., 33
WINN, John W.: of Natchez, 76

XAVIER, Saint Francis: baptismal, 6
XIMENES, Francisco: wounded in attack on fort, 120

YOUNG, Major Robert: signs address, 125

www.ingramcontent.com/pod-product-compliance
Lightning Source LLC
Chambersburg PA
CBHW060339100426

42812CB00003B/1055